Bloom's Modern Critical Interpretations

Bloom's Modern Critical Interpretations

Ken Kesey's
One Flew Over the Cuckoo's Nest
New Edition

Edited and with an introduction by
Harold Bloom
Sterling Professor of the Humanities
Yale University

BLOOM'S
LITERARY CRITICISM
An imprint of Infobase Publishing

Editorial Consultant, Robert P. Waxler

Bloom's Modern Critical Interpretations: Ken Kesey's *One Flew Over*
the Cuckoo's Nest—**New Edition**
Copyright © 2008 by Infobase Publishing

Introduction © 2008 by Harold Bloom

Bloom's Literary Criticism
An imprint of Infobase Publishing
132 West 31st Street
New York NY 10001

Library of Congress Cataloging-in-Publication Data
Ken Kesey's *One Flew Over the Cuckoo's Nest* / edited with an introduction by Harold Bloom.
        p. cm. — (Bloom's modern critical interpretations)
Includes bibliographical references and index.
ISBN-13: 978-0-7910-9616-1 (hardcover : alk. paper)
    1. Kesey, Ken. One Flew Over the Cuckoo's Nest. 2. Psychiatric hospital patients in
literature. 3. Mentally ill in literature.—Criticism and interpretation. I. Bloom, Harold.
II. Title: One Flew Over the Cuckoo's Nest
PS3561.E667O5328 2008
813'.54—dc22   2007045157

Contents

Editor's Note

My Introduction, with benign amiability, does not allow Ken Kesey's *One Flew Over the Cuckoo's Nest* one place in my personal pantheon of Period Pieces. On rereading, it remains a comic strip. The baker's dozen of enthusiasts for it, reprinted in this volume, represent popular opinion. So be it.

Terence Martin has the temerity to invoke *Moby-Dick,* while Ruth Sullivan relies upon Freud's Oedipus Complex and James R. Huffman praises the Chief's stoic ability to live in the present moment.

The Cultural Revolution, responsible for the demise of Antioch College even as I write, is surpassed by Kesey's McMurphy as Christ, according to James F. Knapp, after which Michael M. Boardman discusses "tragic art" in *Cuckoo's Nest.*

Jack Hicks associates Kesey with Norman Mailer and Allen Ginsberg, while William C. Baurecht describes Kesey on Schizophrenia, Janet Larson studies narrative in *Cuckoo's Nest,* and Fred Madden examines Big Chief's functions in the book.

The film of *Cuckoo's Nest,* by Milos Forman, is seen by Thomas J. Slater as worthy of Kesey's novel. I myself would rather resee the movie than reread the book, unlike my usual pattern of response.

A final triad of kudos is bestowed upon *Cuckoo's Nest* by Thomas H. Fick, Robert P. Waxler, and Stephen L. Tanner. All three of these enthusiasts center upon notions of the frontier, psychic or geographical.

HAROLD BLOOM

Introduction

The "Period Piece" is necessarily an involuntary genre, and I find it always causes rage—in some—when I nominate a particular work of enormous popularity to the Period Piece Pantheon. I do not judge *One Flew Over the Cuckoo's Nest* to be worthy of that pantheon, even though I see that my paperback copy is part of printing 88. My personal treasury of period pieces includes *To Kill a Mockingbird*, *Catcher In the Rye*, *A Separate Peace*, *All Quiet on the Western Front*, several *Rabbits*, *Beloved*, *Nineteen Eighty-Four*, *Lord of the Flies*, *Tobacco Road*, *The Grapes of Wrath*, *The Jungle*, *The Old Man and the Sea*. Kesey's books palpably are not of that caliber: they sort better with *On the Road*, *The World According to Garp*, all the Harry Potter books—I forebear continuing, though Tolkien is the Emperor of inferior period pieces, perhaps never to be dethroned.

Rereading *One Flew Over the Cuckoo's Nest*, the comic strip genre begins to contaminate me, and I start to tell myself the tale from the stance of Big Nurse, the nightmare projection of the male fear of female authority. Nurse Ratched should be compared, in her function, to Vergil's Juno, not a comparison that writers far stronger than Kesey could sustain. I entertain myself with the wild notion of rewriting the *Aeneid* from Juno's perspective, but the prospect becomes phantasmagoric, and so I cease.

What is the utility of period pieces? In furniture, sometimes in costume, sometimes in songs—they can achieve, when rubbed down by time, something of an antique value. Alas, literature does not work that way, and the rubbing process leaves only rubbish, vast mounds of worn words,

1

like *The Fountainhead.* The Nineteen Sixties benefit from a general nostalgia, compounded by political correctness and the sad truth that the erstwhile Counter-culture has become Establishment-culture, visible upon every page of *The New York Times.* Dumbing-down is hardly a new phenomenon, and ideological cheerleading, before it took over the universities, had made its way through the churches, the corporations, the unions, and all our technologies. Readers of Ken Kesey or of the Harry Potter saga might risk the cure of carefully reading *Adventures of Huckleberry Finn.*

TERENCE MARTIN

One Flew Over the Cuckoo's Nest
and the High Cost of Living

When Randle Patrick McMurphy swaggers into the cuckoo's nest, brash, boisterous, with heels ringing off the floor "like horseshoes,"[1] he commands the full attention of a world held crazily together in the name of adjustment by weakness, fear, and emasculating authority. As Chief Bromden says, "he sounds big" (p. 10). When, six weeks later, he hitches up his Moby Dick shorts for the final assault on the Big Nurse and walks across the floor so that "you could hear the iron in his bare heels ring sparks out of the tile" (p. 305), he dominates a world coming apart at the seams because of strength, courage, and emerging manhood. As Chief Bromden says (repeatedly)—he has made others big.

The early McMurphy has a primitive energy, the natural expression of his individualism. And in the manner of the solitary hero his freedom and expansiveness come from being unencumbered. He has 'no wife wanting new linoleum. No relatives pulling at him with watery old eyes. No one to *care* about, which is what makes him free enough to be a good con man" (p. 89). The later McMurphy, however, is thoroughly encumbered with the shrunken men on the ward, committed to a desperate struggle for *their* manhood—even though, as the Chief sees, "the thing he was fighting, you couldn't whip it for good. All you could do was keep on whipping it, till you couldn't come out any more and somebody else had to take your place" (p. 303). That kind of

Modern Fiction Studies, Volume 19, Number 1 (Spring 1973): pp. 43–55. A critical quarterly published by the Purdue University Department of English.

struggle, necessary, sacrificial, and fierce in its dedication, is what Ken Kesey dramatizes in *One Flew over the Cuckoo's Nest* with an intensity of focus at once sanative and cleansing.

<h1 style="text-align:center">I</h1>

"We are victims of a matriarchy here" (p. 61), explains Harding to McMurphy: Doctor Spivey cannot fire the Big Nurse. The authority to hire and fire belongs to the supervisor of the hospital, a woman and an old friend of Miss Ratched's from Army days (the supervisor is anonymous, a virtual extension of the Big Nurse). It is McMurphy's first lesson in the ways of the madhouse. Women in the novel, one comes to see quickly, are powerful forces of control. They represent a sinister contemporary version of a feminist tradition in American literature that goes back, at least, to Dame Van Winkle and that percolates through the popular fiction of the nineteenth-century in the form of domestic tyranny-as Helen Waite Papashvily has shown with her chapter "The Mutilation of the Male" in *All the Happy Endings* (1956). Given the highly charged vision of *One Flew Over the Cuckoo's Nest,* female authority becomes non-domestic, hard, insistently emasculating.

Not all of the women are cast in the mould of the Big Nurse. Harding's wife, for example, is a bitch of the first order, whose visit to the hospital shows us all that Harding must overcome in himself as a prerequisite to overcoming something in her. Her remarks are guaranteed to make Harding fall back on defenses whose very existence she scorns. His laugh is to her a "mousey little squeak." His lack of cigarettes means that he "never" has "enough." And the ambiguity of that remark becomes "I meant it any way you want to take it. I meant you don't have enough of nothing *period*" (p. 173). Mrs. Harding enters flirting with a black orderly. She leaves speaking of the boys with "the limp little wrists that flip so nice" (p. 174) who come by to inquire about her husband. The Chief completes the picture: "Harding asks her if it was only him that they were dropping around to see, and she says any man that drops around to see her flips more than his damned limp wrists" (p. 174). If her visit suggests how Harding came to be in the hospital, it spells out even more clearly why he is afraid to leave.

In a different way Billy Bibbit's mother denies him the chance to become a man. A receptionist in the hospital, she is a neighbor and "dear personal friend" of the Big Nurse's; her hair "revolv[es] from blond to blue to black and back to blond again every few months" (p. 281). Billy, on a comfortable day, talks about looking for a wife and going to college. His mother tickles his ear with dandelion fluff and tells him he has "scads of time" left for such things. When Billy reminds her that he is thirty-one years old, she replies, "*Sweet*heart, do I look like the mother of a middle-aged man?" Again, the Chief has a final word: "She wrinkled her nose and opened her lips at him and made a kind of wet kissing sound in the air with her tongue and I had to admit that she didn't look like a mother of any kind" (p. 281).

Chief Bromden, too, knows of female dominance. His Indian father took his white wife's name when they married and suffered a diminishment of self ever after. The father's name signified his size and capacity as a man-Tee Ah Millatoona, the-Pine That Stands-Tallest-on-the-Mountain. But the 5'9" Mary Louise Bromden got bigger and bigger and came to be "twice his size." The father fought the Combine, which of itself would make him smaller, "till my mother made him too little to fight anymore and he gave up" (p. 208). The female reduced the male-the white reduced the Indian. The Chief has only to think of his parents to know the legacy of his people.

Only McMurphy stands outside such woman-power. His name, with its patronymic, identifies him as the son of Murphy, not of Mrs. Murphy. (At the outset, Miss Ratched attacks that identity by calling him McMurry; she would if she could deny him his father.) But even McMurphy has had to pass a test of manhood. He looks at his old home-after the fishing trip-and speaks of the precocious girl of nine who first took him to bed when he was ten. The youthful Murphy felt that they were married or that they should announce their engagement. Whereupon the young semi-pro gave him her dress and waltzed home in her pants. Under cover of night McMurphy threw the dress out the window where it caught, permanently, in a tree. She "taught me to love, bless her sweet ass" (p. 245), he remembers. From that point on he became the "dedicated lover"–rather than a man in petticoats. His latter day companions, Candy and Sandy, function both to emphasize his manhood and to measure the progress of the patients toward regaining (or finding) theirs. Drawn from the stock pattern of the fun-loving, "good" whore, Candy and Sandy evoke attitudes of freedom and openness rather than of restraint and confinement. Whereas the Big Nurse would make men little, they would make men big.

Matriarchy in *One Flew Over the Cuckoo's Nest* comes, we see, to be expressed in various forms of female tyranny. It can sink Harding into the quicksands of inadequacy or make a Lilliputian of the Chief's giant father. But its primary force and motive is to make men be little boys, to make them (want to) adjust to a role wherein lies safety. On the Disturbed Ward after the bruising fight with the orderlies (fought to protect George Sorenson—whose patronymic affords him scant protection), Chief Bromden notes the appearance of the Big Nurse: she "talks with McMurphy, soft and patient, about the irresponsible thing he did, the childish thing, throwing a tantrum like a little boy—aren't you *ashamed?*" (p. 268). If McMurphy—she calls him "Randle" at this point—will see his behavior in her terms, he will not be punished. When she finds Billy Bibbit with Candy, she shatters his new-found sense of manhood by wondering how Billy's mother will take the news. Billy wilts immediately; stuttering once again, he disavows affection and friendship, and the Big Nurse leads him into the office, "stroking his bowed head and saying "Poor little boy, poor little boy" (p. 302). After which Billy commits suicide, unable to become a man and be jerked back to boyhood all in the space of a few hours.

At Miss Ratched's disposal are the three black orderlies (hired for their hatred), the Shock Shop, and the final measure of lobotomy. With their thermometer, their giant jar of Vaseline, and their blood knowledge of rape and injustice, the orderlies make women out of men, just as the Shock Therapy machine turns men docile and lobotomy converts even the most unruly into Fully Adjusted Products. These are weapons of terror, dedicated to the proposition that the best man is a good boy. It is small wonder that the patients on the ward seek the relative safety of boyhood and allow themselves to be ruled by stern or selfish non-mothers who, like cuckoo-birds, have no instinct for building nests of their own. The Chief has his fog, but they have no other place to hide.

In such a world McMurphy, the epitome of raw, unvarnished maleness, represents all the Big Nurse needs to control. As the contours of the narrative take form, the bigger-than-life McMurphy and the bigger-than-life Miss Ratched come to be opposed in every way. He is the stud, she the "ball-cutter"; he is the brawler, she the manufacturer of docility; he is the gambler, she the representative of the house-where chance has no meaning.

II

The opposition between McMurphy and the Big Nurse goes to the very center of the novel, to the perception of Chief Bromden. Whenever the Big Nurse seems in indisputable control, the fog machine churns out its mist, scary, safe, and scary again. When McMurphy wins a skirmish, the fog disappears and the Chief sees clearly. Before the second vote on watching the World Series, the Big Nurse, in total command of the situation according to the Chief's vision, fogs up the ward "thicker than I ever see it before" (p. 127). Billy Bibbit looks "like he's a mile off" and things, including the Chief, begin to float in the eerie mist: "I never seen it this thick before, thick to where I can't get down to the floor. . . . That's why I'm so scared' (p. 128). But when McMurphy gets his majority, when he lifts the Chief "out of the fog and into the open" for the twenty-first vote, the change is dramatic. Acting collectively, the men have voted to have a say about their lives; the Big Nurse has been unable to keep them from doing so. At that point, "there's no more fog anyplace."

As part of the Chief's mode of perception, the fog machine is a metaphor for tyranny, fear, and hiding which becomes literalized in his narrative. During his army days when air fields would be "fogged" by means of a compressor for purposes of secrecy and safety, fog machines had an objective reality in Chief Bromden's life. Even then, however, the experience was subjectively ambivalent: "You were safe from the enemy, but you were awfully alone" (p. 125). An association between machinery and a paralyzing of vision, however, dates from earlier in the Chief's life. As a high school football player, he visited a cotton mill in California. "The humming and clicking and rattling of people and machinery" put him in "a kind of dream"; it reminded him of the men in his tribe "who'd left the village in the last days to do work on the gravel crusher for the dam. The frenzied pattern, the faces hypnotized by routine. . . ." As he talks to a Negro girl he notices that her face looks blurred, "like there was a mist between me and her. It was the cotton fluff sifting from the air." The scene in the mill "all stuck with me and every once in a while something on the ward calls it to mind" (p. 38).

Machinery, made by the Combine for the benefit of people who choose to live under the Combine, drove Chief Bromden's people away from nature into a world not their own. ("Joey Fish-in-a-Barrel has twenty thousand dollars and three Cadillacs since the contract. And he can't drive none of them" [p. 273].) Machinery, associated with authority, with the ward, with Miss Ratched, represents all that brings people into line. Kesey, we may note, invokes the full meanings of words to enrich Chief Bromden's vision. *Dam* can signify *mother*-and the Indians worked on "the gravel crusher for the dam" (p. 36), suggesting, at least to McMurphy-like minds, an activity as emasculating as "ball-cutting" and perhaps even more painful. (A man who "hath his stones broken." the Book of Leviticus stipulated long ago [21:20], is disqualified from entering the priesthood.) The sound of *Ratched* is virtually indistinguishable from that of *rachet*, with its associations of machinery and distaff: And *combine*, as Raymond M. Olderman points out, carries with it the idea of "a mechanism, a machine that threshes and levels."[2] The experience in the cotton mill mediates between the Chief's early days with his people and his paranoid existence on the ward; his life, cut into pieces by machinery has a frightening coherence. But McMurphy stands visibly in opposition to the fabric of the Chief's perception. Consistently unaware of the fog, McMurphy "keeps trying to drag us . . . out in the open where we'd be easy to get at" (p. 123).

The strategy of literalizing metaphors, used by authors as different as Hawthorne and Ionesco, lends force and credence to the world the Chief sees and presents to us. The Big Nurse is an expert in "time control." On a bad day she slows down time so that the minutes freeze agonizingly on the clock; on a relatively good day she accelerates time so that the men whirl through a period they might otherwise enjoy. When Harding explains to McMurphy that they are rabbits and comically singles out two patients to play the role,

"Billy the Kid and Cheswick change into hunched-over white rabbits, right my eyes" (p. 63). And the Chief, as we know, has become literally deaf and dumb to the world because the world has treated him as if he could not speak and could not hear.

The words *big* and *little* likewise take on special meaning because of the Chief's literalizing vision. When McMurphy first shakes hands with Chief Bromden "the fingers were thick and strong closing over my own, and my hand commenced to feel peculiar and went to swelling up out there on my stick of an arm, like he was transmitting his own blood into it. It rang with blood and power. It blowed up near as big as his, I remember" (p. 24). And so at the beginning—at a time when the Chief is helpless and little in a chair—we have an anticipation the end: McMurphy's vital power will flow into Chief Bromden and make him big, at a cost terribly high and terribly necessary.

III

In his essay "The Concept of Character in Fiction," William Gass remarks that "a character, first of all, is the noise of his name, and all the sounds and rhythms that proceed from him." Even in the primary sense, McMurphy is quite a character. His name not only proclaims his paternity but suggests the brawling Irishman of fiction and fact. Moreover, the *sounds* of McMurphy pervade Kesey's novel and we are all the more prepared to hear them because we have narrator like Chief Bromden. As I noted earlier, the Chief hears McMurphy before he sees him, and he "sounds big." He comes into the ward laughing-"free and loud"; it is the first laugh the Chief has heard "in years." After the first Group Meeting, McMurphy himself comments that the patients are afraid to laugh. "I haven't heard a real laugh since I came through that door. . . . Man, when you lose your laugh you lose your *footing*" (p. 68). The next morning the sound of McMurphy singing booms out of the latrine, and "everybody's thunderstruck. They haven't heard such a thing in years, not on this ward" (p. 88).

The Big Nurse's ward has its own sounds, among them those of canned music played loudly over a speaker throughout the day. Annoyed because poker bets can hardly be heard. McMurphy objects, and if we can credit his remark we can see why: "Can't you even ease down on the volume?" he asks the Big Nurse; "It ain't like the whole state of Oregon needed to hear Lawrence Welk play 'Tea for Two three times every hour, all day long" (p. 102). The consequence of his objection is that he gets another room for their game; the issue of sounds has resulted in more space for McMurphy's activities.

McMurphy's laughter and signing, his tall biographical tales, and the authentic ring of his idiom at once dominate the ward and define him to the other patients. His example, of course, evokes the choked off manhood of the men on the ward and a sense of freedom they have forgotten, or not known. When, later, McMurphy organized the fishing expedition, it is a shared adventure, exciting, fun, and noisy. During one hectic, scrambling moment on the boat, with Candy's breast bruised and bleeding and the Chief's thumb smarting red from the line, McMurphy looks on and laughs—"because he knows you have to laugh at the things that hurt you just to keep yourself in balance, just to keep the world from running you plumb crazy. He knows there's a painful side . . . ; but he won't let the pain blot out the humor no more'n he'll let the humor blot out the pain" (p. 238). Harding is laughing this time, and Scanlon, too, "at their own selves as well as at the rest of us." And Candy laughs, "and Sefelt and the doctor and all." The laughter

> started slow and pumped itself full, swelling the men bigger and bigger. I watched, part of them, laughing with them—and somehow not with them. I was off the boat, blown up off the water and skating the wind with those black birds, high above myself, and I could look down and see myself and the rest of the guys, see the boat rocking there in the middle of those diving birds, see McMurphy surrounded by his dozen people, and watch them, us, swinging a laughter that rang out on the water in ever-widening circles, farther and farther, until it crashed up on beaches all over the coast, on beaches all over all coasts, in wave after wave after wave. (p. 238).

Community laughter this, comic, aware, the signature of a deep experience, the expression of freedom—earned and shared. The fishing expedition, brilliantly handled by Kesey, accentuates the growing sense of community among the patients. It also contains the most joyous sounds in the novel. McMurphy, we know, has red hair, tattoo and hands that bear the marks of work and combat. But his capacity for laughter is fundamental to his identity as a character—along with his ability to make us laugh. "That's clean enough," he says to the orderly watching him clear the urinals, "maybe not clean enough for some people, but myself I plan to piss in 'em, not eat lunch out of 'em" (p. 151).

The McMurphy who shakes hands with all of the men and announces himself as "bull goose looney" has much to learn about his new situation beyond the fact of matriarchal authority. He is, at first, what he has always been, the con man, the gambler in search of new territory; and he has managed to get himself committed to avoid the regimen of the work farm. Characteristically, he seizes the opportunity to bet on his ability to outmaneuver the Big Nurse. Surprised and disappointed when the patients do not support his motion to watch the World Series on TV, McMurphy again bets on himself, this time with a new purpose: his failure to lift the steel and cement control panel, foredoomed, according to the Chief, is an example of courage not lost upon the others. The next day they attempt the impossible and, as we have seen, reach their majority, twenty-one, in a second vote on the Series. (Interestingly, one of McMurphy's favorite games is blackjack, or twenty-one. Another, fittingly, is stud poker.) That they sit watching a blank screen, courtesy of Miss Ratched, gives the gesture an added, self-contained, significance; the cowboy-hero turned home-run hitter is now in their midst. They are now, as even the Big Nurse knows, a different group from the one they were before the advent of McMurphy.

McMurphy goes through two other stages in the course of the novel, both the result of increasing awareness. From the lifeguard at the swimming pool he learns the difference between being *sentenced* and being *committed*. He realized for the first time that he will be released only when the Big Nurse approves a release for him. The information has an immediate effect. As they are leaving the pool a hydrocephalic patient from another ward lies helplessly on his side in the footbath, his head bobbing around in the disinfectant. Harding twice asks McMurphy to help him and Cheswick lift the boy up. "Let him lay," says McMurphy, as he walks on, "maybe he don't like deep water" (p. 163). The next morning McMurphy polishes the latrine "till it sparkled" and waxes the hall floors when asked to.

As the others recognize, McMurphy is playing the game, playing safe—"getting cagey," the way "Papa finally did." At one time the Chief's father used to poke fun at the government men, speaking to them dead-pan like a stage Indian addressing tourists—to the great amusement of his Council. Like McMurphy, Chief Bromden's father learned to play it smart. The other patients on the ward understand about McMurphy; they are not angry or even disappointed. But there is a fearful cost of McMurphy's decision to think of Number One: Cheswick, who has achieved a certain momentum toward manhood, gets caught in the drain the next time they are at the swimming pool and drowns well before McMurphy, the lifeguard, and the orderlies can bring him to the surface.

McMurphy has one staggering fact left to learn. It astonishes him into meditative silence, then catapults him into his final role of savior. He hears from Harding that only a few of the patients on the ward, indeed, in the whole hospital, are committed. The great majority are there voluntarily, because, as Billy Bibbit says sobbingly, they don't have the guts to be Outside. The news is hardly credible to McMurphy. But his reaction to it is swift and thorough. At the ensuing Group Meeting he walks "big as a house" toward the Big Nurse, the "iron in his boot heels' cracking "lightning out of the tile," and rams his hand through the window in the front of her office as he reached for his cigarettes. When a new glass is installed, he does it again. And when a third glass is put in, with a whitewashed X on it to make it clearly visible, Scanlon accidentally bounces a basketball through it before the whitewash is even dry.

Direct violations of the Big Nurse's private office, symbolic sexual assaults, are only the beginning. McMurphy, aware now of what *committed* means, aware, too, that the frightened men on the ward are there voluntarily, and aware, further, that he cannot defeat the Big Nurse and all that is behind her—even as he could not lift the control panel—begins to act for the others rather than for himself. Before McMurphy arrived, the patients were set against each other in the name of therapy and adjustment. Each man was a spy for the Big Nurse, eager to write down information about someone else in the log book near the Nurses' Station. In Group Therapy sessions they would peck at the victim of the day, currying favor by making one of their own miserable. McMurphy once says (apropos of the way in which Harding and his wife make each other impossible), "All I know is this: nobody's very big in the first place, and it looks to me like everybody spends their whole life tearing everybody else down" (p. 174). It is a central insight for the unsophisticated McMurphy—and one of the truest and most generally applicable statements in the novel.

During McMurphy's final stage things on the ward *begin* to change radically. Kesey, in masterful control of the fully activated materials in his novel, takes his madhouse men one last inevitable step, to an achieved sense of community. It is something he has consistently held dear: Ken Babbs's "great statement," Kesey remarked in an interview in the *Rolling Stone* (March 7, 1970), was—"We don't want a commune, we want a community" (p. 29). Kesey's "great statement," made eight years before, was to turn a bunch of rabbits into a community of men, "close-knit," as Joseph J. Waldmeir observes, and "functioning."[4] McMurphy organizes a ward basketball team, with Doctor Spivey (to Miss Ratched's amazement) approving, a team, with Doctor Spivey (to Miss Ratched's amazement) approving, a team fated to lose its game against the orderlies, but a team, nevertheless, composed of people playing together in a common effort. The fishing trip deepens and enlarges the sense of community; as Raymond M. Olderman points out, it likewise evokes the idea of fertility and functions as "the central incident in McMurphy's challenge to the waste land"[5] of the hospital. And the party on the ward turns the great cast of characters into a group of Merry Pranksters, contributing, one and all, to a night of spectacular celebration.

The men on the fishing trip and at the party are a far cry from the little boys who spied on each other and tattled in the Big Nurse's log book. No longer do they *tear* each other down. Before Harding signs out and is picked up by his wife, *he* deals blackjack in the tub room and tells the silent Big Nurse on her return, "Lady, I think you're full of so much bullshit" (p. 307). The language of the novel virtually insists that we see McMurphy as a kind of Christ figure (at Shock Therapy time: "Do I get a crown of thorns?" [p. 270] and earlier: "McMurphy led the twelve of us toward the ocean" [p. 227]), doling out his life so that others may live. The action of the novel dramatizes the manner in which he makes his sacrifices, amid doubts and rejoicings on the part of his followers. And the perception of Chief Bromden, now highly sensitized to the task, prepares us at times tenderly to appreciate McMurphy's legacy—manhood, friendship suffused with affection, and, finally, love. Miss Ratched's face at the time of McMurphy's last attack displays a "terror forever ruining any other look she might ever try to use again" (p. 305). She has her revenge, lobotomy, a "castration of the frontal lobes." But Chief Bromden denies the Big Nurse her trophy. "He creeps into the bed of his friend," in the words of Leslie A. Fiedler, "for what turns out to be an embrace—for only in a caricature of the act of love can he manage to kill him."[6] It is, of course, as Mr. Fiedler signifies, a true act of love, performed with a manhood McMurphy has poured into the Chief.

In the terms of the narrative, there can be no more fog or time control. Thus, the Chief, bigger than ever before, makes his escape by picking up the control panel McMurphy could not even budge, the epitome of all the machinery in the hospital, of all machinery that has victimized him and diminished his people ("I head the wires and connections tearing out of the floor"), and throws it through the window. "The glass splashed out in the moon, like bright cold water baptizing [and thus perhaps awakening] the sleeping earth" (p. 310).

IV

Despite the fact that the term Big Nurse inevitably recalls the term Big Brother and thus invokes memories of *1984* and other controlled worlds, *One Flew Over the Cuckoo's Nest* is not in its thrust and emphasis an anti-Utopian novel. The specific make-up of the combine remains vague, as indeed it must, since the word *combine* is not simply a synonym for *organization*, since it is the Chief's protean metaphor for all that mechanizes, threshes, and levels—for all that packages human beings into "products." In this sense, the idea of a Combine contributes powerfully to the dramatic coherence of the novel. The ward, the Chief says, employing the logic of the metaphor, "is a factory for the Combine. It's for fixing up mistakes made in the neighborhoods and in the schools and in the churches" (p. 38). The metaphor is not monolithic; there are other wards in the hospital. The Japanese nurse on the Disturbed Ward is pleasant—she gives gum to the Chief (a fresh stick), a cigarette to McMurphy, and she even criticizes the Big Nurse. And there is an Outside, increasingly regulated by the Combine, as is everything else, though not so rigorously as in the factory-ward.

On the trip to the ocean Chief Bromden notices "signs of what the Combine had accomplished since I was last through this country": five thousand houses "punched out identical by a machine," five thousand identically dressed kids playing on an acre of "crushed gravel," five thousand men deposited like insects by a commuter train (p. 228). It is, recognizably, the world of our suburbs and sub-divisions, standardized, mechanized, virtually anesthetized. Coming back from the ocean, however, the Chief "noticed vaguely that I was getting so's I could see some good in the life around me. McMurphy was teaching me. I was feeling better than I remembered feeling since I was a kid, when everything was good and the land was still singing kids' poetry to me" (p. 243). Again the Chief faces a world of threshed out sameness; but he brings to it now—after the fishing trip—a sense of possibility which enlarges the dimensions of his spirit. The Combine, of course, continues to adjust things. But things may be increasingly adjusted (to pick up another idea from Mr. Olderman, who got it from McMurphy) because they are increasingly adjustable-which means, we realize with a sinking feeling of responsibility, that the Combine's power to control may exist in ratio to our willingness to forfeit manhood.

One Flew Over the Cuckoo's Nest directs our attention to such a point: we have surrendered a sense of self, which, for Kesey, is involved with a sense of space—and thus possibility. "The American has a sense of something that the European doesn't have," he remarked in the *Rolling Stone* interview, "and it's a sense of space. No matter how tight things get, there's more space, there's places you can go. . . . It's the most that we have to offer the world, just to communicate that sense" (p. 30). To lose the *sense* of space is to be confined (whether it be on the Outside or on the Big Nurse's ward) to contribute to the encroaching power of the Combine.

And so Kesey gives us McMurphy, the advocate of our manhood, who brings a sense of space, freedom, and largeness onto the ward as something co-existent with his life. We hear him, we see him, and once we smell him— the outdoor odor of man working. We are even treated on occasion to the splendor of his white whale shorts. Given to him by a co-ed at Oregon State who told him he was a symbol, McMurphy's shorts have, no doubt, a sexual significance. If Melville can spell "archbishopric" with a final "k," Kesey can surely play on the name Moby-*Dick*. Beyond that, McMurphy's shorts have already become ambiguous. Joseph J. Waldmeir, in his fine essay on Joseph Heller and Kesey, comes to see McMurphy as Captain Ahab because of his shorts.[7] And that, I believe, is an error with unfortunate implications. McMurphy may represent the indomitableness of Moby-Dick himself: as Moby-Dick cannot be vanquished by the monomaniac Ahab, so the spirit of McMurphy cannot be quenched by the Combine. Much more meaningfully, however, the leaping white whales suggest *Moby-Dick,* a novel that dramatizes with a fierceness of its own the inter-dependence of man in the face of Ahab's will to stand alone Ahab curses the "inter-indebtedness" of man, that which binds one man to another; Ishmael sees it and accepts it, most notably, perhaps, when a literal line ties him to Queequeg in "The Monkey-Rope" chapter. And *Moby-Dick* validates Ishmael's vision of reality in the world.

The men on the Big Nurse's ward become stronger once they recognize their inter-dependence. McMurphy becomes heroic once he throws his lines out to them. And we come to appreciate the force of Kesey's novel once we see that *One Flew Over the Cuckoo's Nest* is an intense statement about the high cost of living-which we must be *big* enough to afford. That, I should think, is the "truth" the Chief speaks about at the outset. It will "burn" him to tell about it; it will "roar out" of him "like floodwaters." And it will remain true, for him and for all of us, "even though it didn't happen" (p. 8).

Notes

1. Ken Kesey, *One Flew Over the Cuckoo's Nest* (New York: Compass Books Edition, Viking Press, 1962), p. 10. Subsequent references to this edition will appear in the text.

2. *Beyond the Waste Land: A Study of the American Novel in the Nineteen-Sixty* (New Haven and London: Yale University Press, 1972), p. 37.

3. *Fiction and the Figures of Life* (New York: Vintage Books, 1972), p. 49.

4. "Two Novelties of the Absurd: Heller and Kesey," *Wisconsin Studies in Contemporary Literature,* 5 (1964), p. 198.

5. *Beyond the Waste Land,* p. 45.

6. *The Return of the Vanishing American* (New York: Stein and Day, 1968). p. 182.

7. "Two Novelists of the Absurd," p. 203.

RUTH SULLIVAN

Big Mama, Big Papa, and Little Sons in Ken Kesey's One Flew Over the Cuckoo's Nest

Sigmund Freud is something less than a culture hero in Ken Kesey's *One Flew Over the Cuckoo's Nest*. What else but destructive can one call a psychoanalytically-informed therapy that brands McMurphy's rebellion against the institution's ego murder as "schizophrenic reaction," his love of "poozle" and pretty girls as "Latent Homosexual with Reaction Formation" or, with emphasis, "Negative Oedipal"? [1] Kesey portrays the psychiatrists and residents as patsies of Big Nurse Ratched; portrays her as a powermaniac running a small machine within that big machine, Society (the "Combine"). Psychoanalytic therapy in this novel dehumanizes because it serves not people but technology.

Ironic then, is the fact that while the novel disparages psychoanalytic therapy, it compliments psychoanalytic theory in that Kesey structures human relationships in *Cuckoo's Nest* after his own understanding of Freud's delineation of the Oedipus complex. [2] That is, Kesey presents the typical oedipal triangle of mother, father, and sons in Nurse Ratched, Randall McMurphy, and Chief Bromden plus the other inmates of the asylum. And he dramatizes some typical oedipal conflicts: the sons witness encounters, often explicitly sexual, between the father and mother figures; and the crucial emotional issue for the sons is how to define their manliness in relation to the mother figure and with the help of and ability to identify with the father.

Modern Fiction Studies, Volume 19, Number 1 (Spring 1973): pp. 34–44.

That Kesey intends Nurse Ratched to play Big Mama not only to Chief Bromden but also to the other characters is evident by the many references to her often perverted maternal qualities. To Public Relations she is "just like a mother" (37). He believes in "that tender little mother crap" (57) as Mc-Murphy puts it, but the big Irishman and soon the other inmates see through "that smiling flour-faced old mother" (48) with her "big womanly breasts" (11). Chief Bromden observes Big Nurse draw Billy's "cheek to her starched breast, stroking his shoulder. . . ." Meanwhile, "she continued to glare at us as she spoke. It was strange to hear that voice, soft and soothing and warm as a pillow, coming out of a face hard as porcelain" (265). "'We are victims of a matriarchy here, my friend,'" (59) Harding says to McMurphy. "'Man has but one truly effective weapon against that juggernaut of modern matriarchy" (66), rape, and McMurphy is elected to do it.

Why rape? Because Kesey's Big Mama is a "ball-cutter" (57) in McMurphy's language and the men must protect themselves. Harding, too, understands about Big Nurse that one of her most effective methods of control is to render the men impotent: Dr. Spivey by subtle insinuations about his need for drugs and by depriving him of real authority; Billy Bibbit, by threatening to tell his mother about his night with the prostitute; and the young residents by making them fear her judgment on their professional performance. "'There's not a man here that isn't afraid he is losing or has already lost his whambam,'" says Harding. "'We comical little creatures can't even achieve masculinity in the rabbit world, that's how weak and inadequate we are. We are—the *rabbits*, one might say, of the rabbit world!'"(63) Harding even sees that to the Nurse, lobotomies are symbolic castrations: "'Yes; chopping away the brain. Frontal lobe castration. I guess if she can't cut below the belt she'll do it above the eyes'" (165).

Big Nurse should be keeping those in her care warm and fed and healthy; she should be loving but is instead denying, destructive, and terrifying. Big Daddy in Randall McMurphy's Big Daddyhood is only a little less obvious than Nurse Ratched's warped maternity. "Like the logger, . . . the swaggering gambler, . . . the cowboy out of the TV set . . ." (172), Randall McMurphy booms upon the scene, his heels striking fire out of the tiles, his huge seamed hand extended to lift the inmates out of fear and into freedom. He renews their almost-lost sense of manliness by denying Harding's description of them as "'rabbits sans whambam'"(63), by having them deep-sea fish, gamble, and party-it-up with pretty little whores, by encouraging the men (himself as an example) to flirt with the nurses, by spinning virility fantasies, and by introducing Billy to women. He teaches them to laugh and to revolt against Ratched's tyranny, and he often protects them while they are growing.

McMurphy plays father to all the inmates, but Chief Bromden makes explicit the Irishman's fatherly role by often comparing him to the Chief's own father. "He talks a little the way Papa used to. . . . He's as broad as Papa was tall . . . and he's hard in a different kind of way from Papa . . ." (16). "He's finally getting cagey, is all. The way Papa finally did..." (150). Chief Bromden learns from and is protected by McMurphy even as the small Indian boy learned to hunt from a father who tried to save the Columbia Indian's heritage for his tribe and son. "McMurphy was teaching me. I was feeling better than I'd remembered feeling since I was a kid . . ." (216). Chief Bromden grows big; he lifts and destroys the control panel; he frees himself from Big Nurse, the Combine, and his insanity; and he performs an act of love and mercy by killing the husk of the once-mighty McMurphy and by assuming the manhood McMurphy bestowed upon him. The big Irishman seems to pump life and blood into the Indian:

> I remember the fingers were thick and strong closing over mine, and my hand commenced to feel peculiar and went to swelling up there on my stick of an arm, like he was transmitting his own blood into it. It rang with blood and power. It blowed up near as big as his, I remember . . . (27).

In fact, McMurphy encourages the Chief to surpass his model. Christ-like, the father sacrifices himself so that his sons may live free men.

Kesey sketches in the oedipal triangle, then, in dramatizing an intense emotional relationship among father, mother, and son figures and by having the father teach the sons what it means to be a man. He teaches them about self-assertion, aggression, fun, and sex — the latter sometimes in relationship to Big Nurse. After all, the inmates expect McMurphy to make Ratched into a woman by performing some sexual act with her and McMurphy eventually does that. Meanwhile, he acts sexually toward her by making teasing remarks about her big breasts.

But Kesey gives the reader his own unique version of the oedipal struggle. What the sons witness in the interaction between Big Nurse and Randall McMurphy is pseudo-sex. The most urgent emotional issue between them is really power. McMurphy will strip Big Nurse, but he will do so in vengeful destruction of her power. When he teases her about her womanly body suppressed by the starched uniform, his motive is to humiliate her. When he takes up the inmates' challenge to best Big Nurse he says, "I've never seen a woman I thought was more than me. I don't care whether I can get it up for her or not . . ." (68–69). "So I'm saying five bucks to each of you that wants it I can't put a betsy bug up that nurse's butt within a week. . . . "Just that. A bee in her butt, a burr in her bloomers. Get her goat'" (69).

The imagery here is not genital but anal. He wants to be free of her control, wants to be in control himself; and wants the inmates to gain self-control and control over Big Nurse. So, the central symbolic act in the novel is the unseating and destruction of the control panel. Big Nurse herself is a caricature of the anal personality, a typical obsessive-compulsive creature with those typical needs for order, cleanliness, and power, with the tendency to treat people like objects, the inability to relax and to relate to others with tolerance for their frailties. Chief Bromden associates her with machinery, whiteness, frost, starch, cleanliness, rules, time, manipulation, and the Combine. She does try to castrate her sons, but it is in the interest of power. She denies them warmth, autonomy, and manhood in order to keep her own world intact. Her biggest fear, and the sign of her defeat, is loss of control.

It seems, then, that in Kesey's version of the oedipal struggle, the sons learn that mature women are dangerous because they want to emasculate (i.e., to control so as to incapacitate) their men. Almost every woman who stands in an explicitly sexual relationship to men in the novel poses a threat to her man's virility. Billy Bibbit's mother as well as the wife of Ruckly ("Ffffff*fuck* da wife!'" [21]) and of Harding are most blatant examples, the latter because she makes cutting comments about Harding's effeminate mannerisms and flitty friends during a visit to the asylum in which she wears blood-red nail polish on sharp fingernails, high heels that make her as tall as her husband, and a blouse so low that when she provocatively bends over, Chief Bromden can see down it from across the room. "I am a woman," she says in effect, "but I am more of a man than you are."

Even for McMurphy, set forth as an almost-legendary lover, women are often aggressive bitches without tenderness or generosity. When McMurphy recalls the occasion on which he lost his virginity he seems not delighted but sad. That nine-year-old "little whore" (217) callously presented her ten-year-old lover with her dress as a memento of an act that McMurphy had wished to sanctify. She was the "'first girl ever drug me to bed,'" (217) he says, and "'from that day to this it seemed I might as well live up to my name — dedicated lover . . .'" (218). McMurphy does not embrace the role as eagerly as his boasts on other occasions seem to indicate, for in telling his tale, his expression is "woebegone" (218) and in the dark, when he thinks no one can see him, his face "is dreadfully tired and strained and *frantic*" (218). The event seems disillusioning partly because, boy-like, he believed that sex and commitment were complements (he proposed to the girl) but discovered that for his girl they were not; and partly, perhaps, because she rather than he was the aggressor. McMurphy jokes about this, about the underaged and over sexed girl who got him arrested for statutory rape, for instance, but the pattern in the novel seems nevertheless constant: aggressive women hurt their men.

The women in Chief Bromden's past were also almost always ball-cutting bitches too, beginning with that female responsible for cheating the Columbian Indians of their land. She was "an old white-haired woman in an outfit so stiff and heavy it must be armor plate" (179). She plotted to have the offer to buy made "by mistake" to Mrs. Bromden, for she knew instinctively that women, and not men, wore the trousers there. She was right. Mrs. Bromden made Chief Tee Ah Millatoona little: "'Oh, the Combine's big—big. He fought it a long time till my mother made him too little to fight any more and he gave up'" (187). By overmanagement, Mrs. Bromden ruined her husband and her son, too. So the sons in *Cuckoo's Nest* learn that the only women who are fun and harmless are not mature women but girls, sisterly girls who are easily controlled and undemanding. The feminine ideals in this novel are Candy and Sandy because they bring joy and warmth into the asylum. But they do not need to be taken seriously: they are whores, they can scarcely be distinguished from one another, and they are like children. Kesey makes them sentimental portraits, whores-with-hearts-of-gold whose younger-sister role is made explicit by Chief Bromden when he describes McMurphy and one of the "girls" at the end of the night: "I could see McMurphy and the girl snuggled into each other's shoulders, getting comfortable, more like two tired little kids than a grown man and a grown woman in bed together to make love" (258–259). In fact, Candy and Sandy are most closely associated with the little-kid's-fun of the party, where the liquor is as much sticky-sweet cough syrup as vodka and the principal delight lies in fooling the grown-ups, Big Nurse and her night supervisors, who think that the children are asleep when really they are playing through the night. Even Billy's sexual initiation by Candy is more infantile than adult. The scene in which Big Nurse intrudes upon Billy's love nest is rather like a parent's discovery of children engaged in forbidden games (Ratched threatens to tell Billy's mother), a discovery followed by the child's extreme guilt-ridden response, first in denying all responsibility and tattling on his friends, then in committing suicide as self-punishment.

Kesey's oedipal triangle, then, is not casebook pure. It bears the stamp of the preceding emotional phase, the anal, in which the crucial issues are control over one's own body and the environment, rebellion and submission, autonomy and shame. Such a pattern works itself out in the novel thus: the oedipal elements revolve around the wish of the sons to love and be loved by adult women and by the women originally closest to them, mother and Big Nurse. They turn to the father, McMurphy, as role model; he teaches them by anecdote and example how to be men. The anal elements color this pattern because the sons are frustrated in their desires toward a woman so threatening as Big Nurse. They want to be men but she wants them to be automatons; they want to love but she wants to control. Because Big Nurse manages every aspect of their lives—their bodies, activities, shelter—she deprives them of autonomy. Oedipal elements mixed with anal reappear when McMurphy both "feminizes" Big Nurse in his symbolic rape that exposes her breasts; and also dethrones her, breaks her control.

Further, the novel displays emotional conflicts even more primitive than these, for if the men fear woman because she can emasculate her man (a phallic issue) or because she can control him (an anal issue), they also fear her because she withholds emotional warmth and physical care (oral issues). A deep disappointment that the novel expresses concerning women is not only their failure to be equal and generous partners of men or even their unwillingness to submit to men in a battle of the sexes, but their failure to play a warmly maternal role or, when actually assuming that role, their failure to play it effectively,

Though Nurse Ratched is an obvious example of this, almost all other women in the novel are, too. The birthmarked nurse, for example, cannot take adequate care of the men because she fears and hates them, holds them responsible for her "dirtiness," as she conceives of her birthmark.

> In the morning she sees how she's stained again and somehow she figures it's not really from inside her—how could it be? A good Catholic girl like her?—and she figures it's on account of working evenings among a whole wardful of people like me [Chief Bromden]. It's all our fault, and she's going to get us for it if it's the last thing she does (143–144).

Even the Japanese nurse, who has more sensitivity than any other woman in that institution, who understands why everyone hates Ratched, and who wants to help McMurphy and Chief Bromden after their fight with Washington—even she is ineffectual. Chief Bromden describes her as "about as big as the small end of nothing whittled to a fine point . . ." She has "little bird bones in her face" and her hands are little, "full of pink birthday candles" (233). She is maternal but not powerful enough to ensure her men's safety.

One motherly person is appreciatively portrayed in the novel, Chief Bromden's grandmother, who, "dust in her wrinkles" (239), sat beside the small boy at the salmon falls and counted on his fingers: "Tingle, tingle, tremble toes, she's a good fisherman, catches hens, puts 'em inna pens . . . wire blier, limber lock, three geese inna flock . . . one flew east, one flew west, one flew over the cuckoo's nest . . ." (239). "I like the game and I like Grandma," (239) the Chief says, for she is a loving woman associated with all that is healthy in the Chief's background—his Indian heritage, the natural order, and the warm bond his people felt for one another. But like the Japanese nurse who cannot for long protect her men, this old woman could not save her men from moral and mental disintegration. Her son, the Chief, becomes a drunken derelict and her grandson falls insane. "Next time I saw her she was stone cold dead . . ." (239). She in effect abandons them when they are most needy and the nursery rime she chants is in certain ways a sinister prefiguration of what will happen to the Chief and his son. The rime is about a *woman* who catches things and puts them in pens (like Big Nurse, who pens up "Chief Broom"); about a dispersing flock of geese (like, perhaps, the dispersal of the Columbia Indian tribe and of their salmon) one of whom flies over the cuckoo's nest, over the mental institution that for the chief is both an escape from the world (a nest) and a prison. So the loving grandmother is shown abandoning her sons and indirectly predicting their defeat. Women who should be able to help and protect, or at least take care of their men are often disappointing in *Cuckoo's Nest.*

Then there is Harding's wife, who more than castrates him and beats him in a power struggle. She also actually denies him the emotional support and tenderness he needs, a failure symbolized for her as for Nurse Ratched by her outsized breasts: "'one hell of a set of chabobs . . . Big as Old Lady Ratched's'" (159), McMurphy says. Now Mrs. Harding's breasts signal for Harding her especially active sexuality and sexual appeal but unconsciously such breasts likely stir remembrances of motherly giving, a quality in which Mrs. Harding is deficient.

So is Nurse Ratched, the most formidable woman in the novel and possessor of the most formidable bosom. All the men are impressed, but Chief Bromden seems to express for all of them the deep yearning that Big Nurse's actions should answer the promise of her anatomy, the promise of softness and abundant giving one can associate with a mother's breasts. Instead, she seems to the Chief to resent her body and to work hard to suppress it in her starched, clean white uniform. He is deeply troubled by this as by the porcelain-and-plastic quality of her face, the burning cold or burning heat of her lipstick and nailpolish, in fact by many aspects of her body. He fixes upon it almost obsessively and upon her emotional states, to which he is attuned as closely as an anxious child is attuned to his mother. His fixation upon her body is discriminating, though. He is captured by the quality of the whole body in its stiff uniform, then by her breasts, face, mouth, eyes, and hands; not the hips, say, or the belly or shoulders but all those portions of anatomy that a child fastens on in relating to his mother. And when he observes these body parts, it is with anxious eagerness to know her mood (it is almost always dangerous). "Her painted smile twists, stretches to an open snarl" (11). "Gradually the lips gather together again under the little white nose, run together, like the red-hot wire had got hot enough to melt, shimmer a second, then click solid as the molten metal sets, growing cold and strangely dull. Her lips part, and her tongue comes between them a chunk of slag. Her eyes open again, and they have that strange dull and cold and flat look the lips have . . ." (90). "She darted the eyes out with every word, stabbing at the men's faces . . ." (262). "Her more than ever white hand skittered on the pad like one of those arcade gypsies that scratch out fortunes for a penny" (268).

Chief Bromden's dramatized need for a warm mother is appropriate to his condition as schizophrenic, a man whose emotional regression is often so severe that he withdraws from reality completely (retreats into the fog), refuses to speak or acknowledge that he can hear, and cannot control body functions. The emotional pattern Kesey draws for Chief Bromden is severe withdrawal alternating with periods of intense, if often negative, fixation on a mother figure, then apparent growth to attachment to a father and finally to growth beyond an infantile need for a family.

How much of Kesey's delineation of the oedipus complex is deliberate, how much is inevitable revelation of his own complexes is impossible to know accurately. Clearly, he does label his Big Mama, Big Daddy, and little sons; but when he involves them in a power struggle and in a search for a generous, caretaking mother, likely his emotional constellations are no longer consciously created. But our subject is not biography; it is interpretation of one work of art. Hence we might ask how Kesey's oral, anal, and oedipal patterns, deliberate and not, influence a reader's emotional response and interpretation of themes.

For instance, one might wonder what psychological events make the novel so especially appealing to the young (and others). Big Mama is indeed defeated and Chief Bromden as well as several inmates do escape, but the victory is pyrrhic. Cheswick, Billy Bibbit, and most crucially, Randall McMurphy are all sacrificed to achieve that end. Furthermore, the novel promises, that there will be more Big Nurses in the future:

> They talk for a while about whether she's the root of all the trouble here or not, and Harding says she's the root of most of it. Most of the other guys think so too, but McMurphy isn't so sure any more. He says he thought so at one time but now he don't know. He says he don't think getting her out of the way would really make much difference; he says there's something bigger making all this mess and goes on to try to say what he thinks it is (165).

Chief Bromden knows what it is:

> McMurphy doesn't know it, but he's onto what I realized a long time back, that it's not just the Big Nurse by herself, but it's the whole Combine, the nation-wide Combine that's the really big force, and the nurse is just a high ranking official for them (165).

In oedipal terms, the novel promises that the matriarchy cannot he defeated. To do battle with it means the castration of both the father and most of the sons: indeed, all of the sons, for the rehabilitation of Chief Bromden is fairy tale, not reality. He has been on the ward nearly twenty years; he has had over two-hundred shock treatments; and he is, by the revelations of his own speech, a paranoid schizophrenic. A man so deeply scarred is unlikely to recover so completely in a few months no matter how brilliant his model and nurturer is.

This anxiety-filled fantasy of mechanical, destructive motherhood cannot account for the enthusiasm of Kesey's readers any more than can the genius of the style or plotting. The latter two are significant, of course, but for reasons beyond the aesthetic or intellectual pleasures they afford. The novel must somehow also create other, but satisfying fantasies and also such an effective defense against its nuclear fantasy that a reader, especially a young one, feels not only reassured but triumphant.

One of the appeals of the novel is the opportunity it affords its readers to feel unjustly persecuted and to revel in self-pity. "Poor little me. See how helpless and good I am: yet They hurt me." Because persecution of those undeserving sets the tone for *One Flew Over the Cuckoo's Nest*, a reader can scarcely escape the novel's stimulation of these unconscious feelings in himself. Everyone has in his early life experienced the apparent omnipotence and omniscience of adults who, on occasion, must frustrate the demands of their infants and must therefore seem unjust, even cruel. But such experiences usually are painful. Why should their arousal in *Cuckoo's Nest* prove delightful? Because, first, the novel is convincing about the power of the Combine and its agent, Nurse Ratched. Americans particularly have reason to feel oppressed by Big Government, Big Business, and Big Industry and to be convinced that the individual alone can do little to influence them to his benefit or to prevent their harming him. Chief Bromden is paranoic, but not everything in his vision is false: "You think the guy telling this is ranting and raving my *God*; you think this is too horrible to have really happened, this is too awful to be the truth! . . . But it's the truth even if it didn't happen" (13). The novel offers its readers a sympathetic forum, a justification for feeling oppressed, even congratulations for being so sensitive as to have those feelings. Kesey's novel says in effect that someone understands.

A second reason for the pleasure-in-persecution feelings evoked in the reader's unconscious by *Cuckoo's Nest* is this: "Poor little me" fantasies are pleasurable if one knows that one's audience is kindly and even effective against the alleged or actual abuse. The anti-establishment, anti-tyranny tone of the novel answers these needs; so does the person of McMurphy because he functions the way a powerful father figure might against a cruel mother. The plaint of injustice is largely carried by the helpless inmates; their target is Big Nurse and the Combine; their forum and protection is McMurphy. Finally, one might speculate that forum and protection is McMurphy. Finally, one might speculate that being unjustly persecuted is pleasant if it arouses one's masochism and if it provides a sense of moral superiority. "You may be bigger than I am but I am superior to you in other, especially moral, ways." *Cuckoo's Nest* dramatically demonstrates the righteousness and goodness of the inmates over Big Nurse, her cohorts, and the Combine. And of course she is overthrown. Injustice may live, but in *Cuckoo's Nest* it does not thrive.

The novel also richly gratifies latent or conscious hostile impulses against authority. Obviously the novel delights in jibes and pain inflicted upon Nurse Ratched (an audience applauds whenever Big Nurse is bested in the play; it even hisses and boos when the actress who plays her takes her bow). But the book allows expression of hostile impulses toward loved authorities as well, for the inmates not only care about McMurphy, they also resent him. Big Nurse succeeds in turning most of them against him for a while when she hints that he exploits them. Billy Bibbit turns against him when caught in his sexual misdemeanor. They all use him to fight their battles, egg him on to engage Big Nurse when they, but not McMurphy, know that he can be punished in the "Brain Murdering" room. Most significantly, they kill him. They are responsible for his lobotomy "We couldn't stop him [from attacking Big Nurse] because we were the ones making him do it. It wasn't the Nurse that was forcing him, it was our need that was making him push himself slowly up . . ." (267).

Chief Bromden performs the actual killing. Manifestly, the deed is euthanasia; symbolically, it is an enacted crucifixion; thematically, it is evidence that the son has grown up and surpassed his father even while loving him; and latently, the killing expresses the ancient hostility of the son to even a loving father.

To permission for indulgence in self-pity and in attacks on loved and hated authority figures, the novel adds permission to gratify dependency wishes. A theme of *One Flew Over the Cuckoo's Nest* concerns the nature of individual freedom political, social, and psychological. It asserts that in the psychological realm, certain kinds of dependence are healthy: the dependence of a child upon good parents; of a patient upon effective nurses and doctors; and of weak adults upon nurturing strong ones. But this dependent condition is healthy only if it fosters eventual independence. Big Nurse destroys because she must control; hence she blocks the autonomy of her patients, whereas McMurphy nurtures because while he protects, he also encourages the inmates to use their own resources in order to meet the world. This theme, readily apparent to a reader's intelligence, disguises the abundant latent gratification the novel offers one's often unacknowledged pleasure in dependency upon an omnipotent figure. Throughout the novel, with a few exceptional times, McMurphy acts on behalf of the patients, acts so magnificently that a reader laughs. "'We ain't ordinary nuts; we're every bloody one of us hot off the criminal-insane ward, on our way to San Quentin where they got better facilities to handle us'" (199–200). So McMurphy informs the gas station attendants who would bully the inmates. Here the weak overpower the strong the way children overpower giants in fairy tales. The inmates overpower Big Nurse when McMurphy, a sort of kindly helper figure also common in fairy tales, shows them how; and they overpower her in part gayly, jokingly, in part grimly. The child-like fun of the novel, the use of ridicule as a weapon against oppression, and the demonstration on the part of McMurphy that he is a bigger, better person than Big Bad Nurse all contribute to a reader's readiness to accept the novel's tacit invitation: allow yourself to depend upon the good, omnipotent father; he will help you conquer the wretched stepmother.

Cuckoo's Nest is gratifying especially to the young, then, because while on the one hand it creates an anxiety-ridden fantasy about a destructive mother (and social order), it allays it by creating a powerful caring father. It also grants indulgence in certain unconscious needs and wishes to be dependent, to feel unjustly treated (masochistic and moral-righteousness pleasures), and to attack and defeat ambivalently-held authority figures (even McMurphy is killed).

To unearth unconscious fantasies as a way of understanding why *One Flew Over the Cuckoo's Nest* is emotionally satisfying is not to dismiss the power or validity of themes one understands intellectually. Indeed, unconscious fantasies isolated from theme in a piece of fiction sound grotesque, perhaps meaningless. In *Cuckoo's Nest* as in all fiction, theme not only gives meaning to unconscious fantasy but also functions as a kind of defense.[3] For instance, *Cuckoo's Nest* is usually read as an indictment of our technological society, which, by standardization and forced conformity, murders human brains even as the shock shop murders the inmates' minds. Psychotherapy is dangerous because this novel alleges that it has become mechanized, a tool for social control wielded by the Combine. But the novel also affirms that man's drive for independence is so strong that no matter how overwhelming the obstacles, he will break free. Too, perhaps nature will once more nurture man where technology now destroys him.

Kesey's anti-technology, pro-nature theme is fittingly supported by his deliberate use of an oedipal triangle marked by a man-woman power struggle, a triangle in which mother acts like a machine against rather than for her children and father tries valiantly to restore them to their own natures and to freedom. The unconscious needs the novel stimulates in its readers also reenforces the theme. For instance, though men yearn to be free, they also fear it and wish to he dependent. Chief Bromden sits in the cuckoo's nest because he has not the courage to face the world. No more do those voluntarily committed — Billy Bibbit and Harding, say, who admit their fear of leaving the institution.

Now *Cuckoo's Nest* has another theme that seems to counterpoint its blatant Darwinian survival-of-the-fittest message. The strong do indeed aggress against the weak; and though a few escape the trap, most are caught and destroyed. But the Combine is only the ostensible enemy; the real one lurks in men's own minds. Just as in a paranoid fantasy the external persecutors are projections of the sufferer's self-hatred, so is the Combine a projection of the destructive power-drive in men — especially in weak, ineffectual men. While *Cuckoo's Next* does show how the strong oppress the weak, it also shows how the weak can destroy the strong. Chief Bromden understands this at the end of the novel, for he knows that McMurphy attacks Nurse Ratched because the inmates compel him to. Harding understood this earlier. In explaining why be must he institutionalized he at first blames society:

> "It wasn't the practices, I don't think, it was the feeling that the great, deadly, pointing forefinger of society was pointing at me — and the great voice of millions chanting, 'Shame. Shame. Shame.' It's society's way of dealing with someone different" (257).

But McMurphy counters that he, too, is different, yet he was not seriously affected. Harding answers:

> "I wasn't giving my reason as the sole reason. Though I used to think at one time, a few years ago . . . that society's chastising was the sole force that drove one along the road to crazy [sic] . . . you've caused me to re-appraise my theory. There's something else that drives people, strong people like you, my friend, down that road . . . It is us." He swept his hand about him in a soft white circle and repeated, "Us" (257–258)

The theme of *Cuckoo's Nest* is not merely the assertion that society will get you. It also realistically affirms that if society gets you, it is because you have complied in both your own and others' destruction. The weak are tyrants, too, subtle and dangerous because they can wake in the strong a sympathetic identification and perhaps guilt: "Why should I have so much when they have so little? Then, maybe I am in some way responsible for their fate." Like the inmates of the asylum, the weak can unintentionally exploit and cannibalize their benefactors, driving them to ruin.

This more subtle theme functions as defense in the novel because without it *Cuckoo's Nest* would offer a sentimental, over-simple diagnosis of an individual's ills rather than dramatizing without moralizing a complex relationship between man and his society. The novel is idealistic, but not at the expense of clearsightedness. It abundantly gratifies the id hut it also recognizes the needs of an ego that must bring the psyche into harmony with the real world, and the demands of a superego that will not condone flagrant abuses of morality: the guilty are punished, Witness the fate of Nurse Ratched — and of Randall McMurphy for mauling her.[4]

Unlike, say, Tolstoi's *Kreutzer Sonata*, whose condemnation of social conventions is transparently paranoic, hence clearly not to be taken as seriously as the protagonist's psychology, *Cuckoo's Nest* almost from the beginning tempers its anti-technology theme with realism. Everywhere in the novel the ego has control over a potentially too-rapacious superego and a demanding id. For instance, Chief Bromden is the narrator; he is a paranoid schizophrenic, hence the world he describes is his world, not everyone's. Then, as the Chief comes more and more often out of the fog, his perceptions grow more accurate. For a long time he sees McMurphy as "a giant come out of the sky to save us from the Combine that was networking the land with copper wire and crystal" (224); later he understands the man's weaknesses: that is, his humanity. He at first believed that McMurphy might save them; he later sees that the men are using him and that they must eventually save themselves. Finally, while the novel does permit Chief Bromden to fly like a goose northward, home, it tempers the promise that Chief Bromden's freedom is hazard-free. For Kesey implicitly compares the Chief's escape scene with another in which the latter sees clearly for the first time where he is, in an asylum deep in the country. A lively, revelling dog investigates the countryside while "the moon glistened around him in the wet grass . . ." (143). Then the Chief listens attentively to Canada honkers flying above, "a black, weaving necklace, drawn into a V by that lead goose . . . a black cross opening and closing . . ." (143). Finally, he runs off

> in the direction they [the geese] had gone, toward the highway . . .
> Then I could hear a ear speed up out of a turn. The headlights loomed
> over the rise and peered ahead down the highway. I watched the dog
> and the car making for the same spot of pavement (143).

The Chief has identified with the geese, flying free after a lead goose even as the Chief and the others do when led by that "Bull Goose Loony" McMurphy, later to crucify himself (" 'Do I get a crown of thorns?'" [237]) for them. He identifies with the dog, too, young and free and curious about his environment but also heading for potential death on the highway. Once more, natural things are threatened by machines. Will the Chief, too, be crushed?

> I ran across the grounds in the direction I remembered seeing
> the dog go, toward the highway. . . . I caught a ride with a guy, a
> Mexican guy, going north in a truck full of sheep . . . (272).

Kesey does not mislead his readers. For those who choose to hear he says that while the social order is indeed a mighty, complex organism difficult to understand, more difficult to influence and change, nevertheless men are responsible for their own fates. One must be strong to survive, even stronger to prevail, but if such a man is inspirited with that most valued of American qualities, the drive for independence and freedom, he can make it.

Kesey's novel is a kind of phenomenon, though, for the skillful way in which he manages to be hard-headedly realistic (hence to appeal to the ego) as well as indulgent of so many and such powerful unconscious, even infantile drives (the novel richly gratifies the id) and respectful of certain ethical considerations: the evil are punished, but so are those who inflict punishment: crime does not pay (the superego is appeased). The fact that the theme can be doubly-perceived as that technology is responsible for man's destruction and that men are responsible for their own — this both stimulates and manages the anxiety-ridden nuclear fantasy because on the one hand a reader can fully respond to his own regressive fantasies and on the other, he is encouraged to put out of them and cope with external reality. Kesey's use of the oedipal constellation to pattern human relationships in *Cuckoo's Nest* functions in much the same way, for by content the novel damns psychoanalytically-informed psychotherapy in such a way as to cater to fantasies of persecution and helplessness; while by artistic design the book uses psychoanalytic theory so as to reassure the reader (as all skillful handling of artistic form and style do) that nevertheless everything is safe. "I, the artist, can handle this material, dangerous though it may be. See, I make it part of the solid structure of this novel. You need not be afraid while I am in control." Mama may be dangerous, but Big Daddy is here to protect his children.

NOTES

1. Ken Kesey. *One Flew Over the Cuckoo's Nest* (New York Signet, 1962): p. 135. Hence forth, all quotations from the novel will come from this edition. Page numbers will be noted in my text.

2. Ken Kesey worked in a mental institution while writing *Cuckoo's Nest* and he knew of Freudian psychology through Vic Lovell, to whom the novel is dedicated ("To Vik [sic] Lovell, who told me dragons did not exist, then led me to their lairs") and about whom Tom Wolfe says: he was "like a young Viennese analyst, or at least a California graduate school version of one. . . . He introduced Kesey to Freudian psychology. Kesey had never run into a system of thought like this before." (Tom Wolfe, *The Electric Kool-Aid Acid Test* [New York: Bantam, 1969], p. 36.)

3. For this theory and for most of the psychoanalytic literary methodology in my essay I am indebted to Norman N. Holland's works, especially to *The Dynamics of Literary Response* (New York: Oxford University Press, 1968).

4. For further elucidation of how fiction satisfies all parts of the psyche, see Simon O. Lesser, *Fiction and the Unconscious* (Boston: Beacon Press, 1957), *passim*.

JAMES R. HUFFMAN

The Cuckoo Clocks in Kesey's Nest

Now that several critics have flown over Kesey's nest, readers have a number of perspectives from which to view what Kesey is hitching. Some critics have deposited their own eggs in the nest, of course. As John Clark Pratt discovered in compiling an anthology of criticism on *One Flew Over the Cuckoo's Nest*, the novel "often plays upon the preconceptions of its readers . . . Teased by shapes that elude him, one critic after another goes wading through the fog and finds that it is full of allusions. Not one of them comes back with a satisfactory discussion of the novel as a whole, but all have interesting points to make."[1] When I first read Kesey, I was deeply involved in a study of the sense of time in novels, so my own preconceptions focused on the nature of time in his work. *Sometimes a Great Notion*, with its "dissolving of chronological time so that past and future events swim into each other" and its attempt "to achieve the illusion of temporal and spatial simultaneity," reveals that Kesey too has an ongoing interest in time and the novel.[2] So perhaps my perspective on Kesey's first work is not far from its center. A number of Critics have noticed the use of time in *Cuckoo's Nest*, but no one discusses it fully.[3] If I may strain my opening metaphor further, I think that particularly the metaphorical uses of time in Kesey's novel nestle in the center of its theme and structure. Certainly, at any rate, I have been sitting on this conception long enough. If my interpretation

---

Modern Language Studies, Volume 7, Number 1 (Spring 1977): pp 62–73.

does not provide a satisfactory overall view, perhaps it does no worse than lay another egg in Kesey's nest.

Among the eggs in the nest, biographical criticism may have left the least legitimate. Like Kerouac, Kesey tempts the reader into easy identifications of characters with authorial viewpoint. But the chauvinistic Randle P. McMurphy is not Ken Kesey, any more than the obviously psychotic Chief Bromden can stand in for him. Neither McMurphy nor Bromden fully understands the situation in the ward, so extracting Kesey's views must be a matter of careful inference. The reverse procedure, importing Kesey's views to explain the novel, is valid only if those views are demonstrably present. Far too much has been made of Kesey's experimentation with LSD as a key to the novel. According to the theory that psychedelic stimulation created the work, *Cuckoo's Nest* supposedly preaches a "retreat to private 'irrational' satisfactions," "the unrestricted sensorial life," and a "radical dedication to the ecstasy of the present moment."[4] However, while the present and the senses are important elements in leading Chief Bromden toward sanity, the novel does not contain the drug-oriented message Kesey later preached and followed. In *Cuckoo's Nest* drugs are shunned, not sought, and many patients avoid taking even necessary medication. Sefelt brings on epileptic seizures by failing to take his pills, McMurphy refuses Seconal before shock treatments, and the Chief avoids all drugs as tools of the Combine. Given this attitude toward drug-induced alterations of consciousness, it is difficult to conceive the LSD trip as "the underlying superstructure" growing organically through the work, or that all Kesey's novels are "literally metaphors for psychedelic experiences."[5]

Placing primary emphasis on other external concerns creates similar distortions. Leslie Fiedler traces images of blacks and Indians very interestingly through recent literature, but his preoccupations exactly reverse the emphasis of the novel. Fiedler sees here "the archetype of the love that binds the lonely white man to his Indian comrade—to his *mad* Indian comrade, perhaps even to the *madness* of his Indian comrade, as Kesey amends the old tale."[6] But this view ignores the fact that Chief Bromden is only one of many men that McMurphy sacrifices himself for; that McMurphy is debatably mad even in attacking Big Nurse; and that the opposite relationship—Bromden's attachment to McMurphy—is more central to the work's movement and meaning.

Similarly, Charles Witke's comparison of Kesey's novels to pastoral conventions in Vergil is more suggestive than definitive. His conclusion that the pastoral ideal is no longer viable in Kesey is well supported by *Sometimes a Great Notion*. To say simply that "*Cuckoo's Nest* was a kind of purely fantastic pastoral retreat in an insane asylum," however, does not relate the pastoral ideal fully enough to the ethic of the novel.[7] Olga Victory's comparison of the ward to Dante's *Inferno* is fertile, but again just reinforces intrinsic interpretations of the work.[8]

Standing outside the novel with a feminist viewpoint is not much more helpful. Marcia Flak charges Kesey with "blatant sexism" and racism, and condemns "the psychic disease out of which the book's vision was born."[9] McMurphy is obviously a male chauvinist, but his chauvinism is not the "solution" to the ward's problems. Men like Harding and Billy Bibbit cannot cope with such an image, nor is it presented as ideal. McMurphy's sense of identity, not his male chauvinism, is the model. Furthermore, Miss Ratched and the black aides are not so much stereotypes as metaphorical figures. As Joseph Waldmeir points out, "It is neither accident nor racism that Kesey makes them Negroes or that one of them, a dwarf, is the result of his mother's rape by a white man."[10] The aides represent what oppression can do to blacks in American society. Even McMurphy realizes that the Big Nurse is not what he is fighting. "Ball-cutters" can be "old and young, men and women."[11] And McMurphy is not sure that getting the Big Nurse "out of the way would really make much difference; he says that there's something bigger making all this mess" (181). McMurphy is never certain what is behind the problem, showing again that he is no straight spokesman for the author. But he perceives that the Big Nurse is more a metaphorical than a literal villain, more asexual than matriarchal. Kesey may have trouble pinpointing the enemy with the Big Nurse and the Chiefs metaphors of the "Combine," but the focusing problem is not the result of simple racism and sexism.[12]

Robert Boyers judges the novel from a psychological perspective. Charging that McMurphy's methods would not reclaim the ward's victims, Boyers does not present a strong criticism either, for the novel does not claim that the ward is cured. Curable Acutes just start on the way to recovery by asserting their own wills and worth for a change. Boyers also wrongly claims that Kesey uses a "*reductio ad absurdum* of familiar Freudian propositions," so that repressed sexuality "lies behind every psychosis" and causes the acquiescence of all men in the confining conventions of Western society."[13] Certainly Kesey uses basic Freudian ideas. But to the extent that the novel contains a *reductio ad absurdum* of Freud, Kesey is revealing the absurdity of using psychoanalytic ideas to explain all human behavior. The oversophisticated intern with a pipe, Mr. Gideon, is clearly satirized in the staff meeting when he infallibly pronounces McMurphy a "*Negative Oedipal*" (148). Like the Biblical Gideon, he is trying to bluff the enemy with false weapons. The anecdote on the nine-year-old girl who starts McMurphy's career is perhaps comically Freudian (244–245). McMurphy himself, however, thinks the Freudian view is too simple: "'But if it was no more'n you say, just this old nurse and her sex worries, then the solution to all your problems would be to just throw her down and solve her worries, wouldn't it?'" (181). McMurphy's actual attack on the Big Nurse is a parody of this Freudian "Solution," a metaphor of the deeper struggle. Similarly, Chief Bromden correctly rejects a Freudian cause, homosexuality, as the explanation of his attachment to McMurphy (210). Even the psychoanalytic Harding ultimately revises to accept Freudian principles as definitive: "'Oh, I could give you Freudian reasons with fancy talk, and that would be right as far as it went. But what you want are the reasons for the reasons, and I'm not able to give you those'" (294). Surely Boyers is wrong in assuming that sex is not used as metaphor in the novel, but as a literal solution. If sex cures, why does Billy Bibbit commit suicide after his first treatment? Why does Chief Bromden improve without any sexual treatments at all? And why doesn't McMurphy hold a therapeutic "gang bang" on the boat, as the heckling manors suggest? As in the aides' buggering of the patients (34), representing "the shaft" wielded by the Combine, sex is metaphorical in the novel.

Not only sex and race, but virtually every other major element in the novel should be taken metaphorically. One of the advantages of using a psychotic narrator who "talks crazy" yet makes good sense is that the themes of the book can be couched in metaphors. The "cuckoo's nest," or mental hospital, is itself a "metaphor for modern America."[14] As Irving Malin so correctly sees, Kesey is more poet than philosopher, and "the images *are* the real meaning of the novel."[15] Consequently the most accurate analyses of *Cuckoo's Nest* rely on his thinly veiled names as keys to symbolic figures, on his allusions to the Bible and popular media, and on his images and metaphors.[16] This essay adds to these intrinsic studies and places them further in perspective by analyzing the use of time in *Cuckoo's Nest*, particularly as time becomes an index to the themes of the novel.

The connection of the word "cuckoo" with insanity, making the "cuckoo's nest" an insane asylum, is well known. The word is also readily associated with clocks, and Kesey makes more of the association than is generally recognized. Each Acute neurotic is metaphorically a cuckoo clock which Miss Ratched must readjust to a proper schedule. Successfully rehabilitated patients are clocks that "run down after a pre-set number of years" (38). Even the doctor is like a clock, a very "uptight" one; he "stops winding his watch on account of it's tight enough, another twist is going to spray it all over the place" at a tense staff meeting (145). The Big Nurse allegedly carries a watchmaker's pliers in her purse, presumably to help her adjust the inmates (4). She always wears a wristwatch, using it to control the one o'clock therapy sessions, and puts it on McMurphy's folder as a sign of her control over him (140–45). The whole ward runs on a strict hourly schedule. From the nurse's station with its glass observation window on the ward, Miss Ratched dreams of a world of precision efficiency and tidiness like a pocket watch with a glass back" (27). (Kesey may be playing here with the meaning of "watch" as a term denoting surveillance as well as timepieces.) In the ward time is always explicitly on her side (70–71, 109, 150).

Apparently readers have not noticed how far Kesey carries these images. Although Miss Ratched's "precise, automatic gesture" and "smooth, calculated, and precision-made face" is first compared to a baby doll's (5), she becomes more and more a living clock. Sometimes in group meetings she will sit twenty minutes in silence, "quiet as an electric alarm about to go off" (48). Confronting McMurphy, she has a "calm whir coming from her eyes, but down inside of her she's tense as steel," like the mainspring of a clock (26). Her schedule is "delicately balanced" (114). Late in the novel her face starts to "warp and flow" like Einsteinian time (141), and to move with a "ticking noise" (188). Like a ratchet, a common ticking device in many clocks, the Big Nurse allows movement in only one direction—hers. One of her favorite sayings is "everything in its own good time" (24). She always tears a sheet off the calendar each day (31). She taps her watch with a thermometer, indicating that both instruments may be diagnostic and therapeutic. Through the telltale logbook, she uses "past history" to power-grip the present and mold the future (48). When her conflict with McMurphy nears the climax, with her "enamel and plastic face" as "hard as porcelain" and with "her back to the wall" (301–302), Miss Ratched resembles the ward clock that McMurphy had pelted with butter. The Big Nurse is the asexual institutional clock face of the Combine.

Furthermore, the black aides, in becoming her "hands" on the ward, take on the images of clock hands. The hour hand is "a twisted sinewy dwarf the color of cold asphalt," whose "eyelids hang loose and thin from his brow like he's got a bat perched on the bridge of his nose" (28). Like this slow moving hand of time, the dwarf learns to apply steady pressure to the inmates. His two fellows, faster moving and taller, look remarkably like pointed clock hands too. As the minute and second hands, "both looking so much alike I think she had a replica made of the one who came first," the other two aides "are tall and sharp and bony and their faces are chipped into expressions that never change, like flint arrowheads. Their eyes come to points." All three are "black as telephones," and "they never make any noise when they move" (28–29). In ward basketball games, they score baskets "with mechanical accuracy," like clockwork (195). When they move, the clock moves (101). To the patients, each aide seems to float against the wall, his black face contrasting sharply with the institutional white. Before long the aides are even in electrical "contact on a high-voltage wave length of hate" with the Big Nurse, and "are out there performing her bidding before she even thinks it." They are indeed her hands: "So After the nurse gets her staff, efficiency locks the ward like a watchman's clock" (29).

A few patients challenge the routine of the clock and Miss Ratched's control. Pete Bancini, living on memories or working thirty years for the railroad, has not been adjusted to society because he was born with too little intelligence to act unnaturally. His complaint. "I'm tired," sounds "real and true" in the artificial atmosphere. Pete has to work hard to read a watch that measures artificial time (130) When he hits Williams, significantly he breaks the aide's watch (53), and the other two clock hands freeze, "the big one and his tiny image, in exactly the same position" (51). Pete is a cuckoo clock that cannot be fixed; he is "like an old clock that won't tell time but won't stop neither, with the hands bent out of shape and the face bare of numbers and the alarm bell rusted silent, an old, worthless clock that just keeps ticking and cuckooing without meaning nothing" (53). As in McCullers' *Clock Without Hands*, published the year before *Cuckoo's Nest*, mechanical time cannot measure progress in human psychology.

Randle McMurphy is of course the major challenger of sterile life by the clock. His first statement to the ward after a routine greeting shows his connection with more natural measures of time, the seasons: "'Mighty nice fall day'" (11). The clock in the mess hall is a literal and metaphorical target for McMurphy to attack. He refuses just to watch the clock, and although he misses the face with his first pat of butter, he still beats the clock by betting on when the butter will melt to the floor (100). As he says in betting that he can beat the Big Nurse, "she may have the element of time, but I got a pretty long winning streak goin' myself" (71). McMurphy talks the patients into disrupting the schedule, as in stopping the work hour to watch the World Series on a blank television screen. He causes them to ask subversive questions, such as "'What's so wrong with changing time?'" (133). Twice he breaks the glass that represents her ability to "watch" the ward, influencing Scanlon to break it the third time (190–196). From Miss Ratched's viewpoint. McMurphy causes the group meeting to lose time. From McMurphy's viewpoint, he is helping the patients escape from a time-ridden, sterile world.

But McMurphy knows that time is working against him, as it works against all men moving toward death. His face begins to look "dreadfully tired and strange and *frantic*, like there wasn't enough time left for something he had to do" (245). He takes the patients back to his own childhood, replacing their devastating pasts with his own exploits. McMurphy "doled out his life" for the others to "dream" into (245).

He is right to worry. After fighting for Sefelt, he is sent up to Disturbed, where "time is measured out by the di-*dock*, di-*dock*, of a Ping-pong table" (263). McMurphy has full power to disrupt mechanical time at first; "the Ping-pong clock died down in a rapid ticking on the floor after he entered. But after a few shock treatments, McMurphy acts as though he has been connected electronically to the Big Nurse's time, and sits "following the ping-pong ball with his eyes like he was wired to it" (277). When he enters the Shock Shop, "a hand takes off his wristwatch . . . drops it near the panel, it springs open, cogs and wheels and the long dribbling, spiral of spring jumping against the side of the panel and sticking fast" (270). Big Nurse is fixing his clock for good. She destroys him, but not before he shows the curable Acutes the way toward sanity, and reveals that she is more than just another porcelain face.

The use of time in the novel is not confined to images of the Combine, to Big Nurse's control of the ward, and to McMurphy's fight against depersonalizing influences. Time is even mere central to the work. Through the narrator, Chief Bromden, time is intimately connected to sanity and insanity, and to the meaning and purpose of the work. The Chief's conceptions and experiences of time are a clear index to his state of mind throughout the novel. When his psychological clock is "cuckoo," so is he. As a result, considering the relation of time to the narrator in *Cuckoo's Nest* provides a reliable point of reference for putting interpretations of the novel in proper perspective.

This viewpoint strongly supports interpretations of the novel which center on Bromden's fight toward sanity.[17] The importance of curing individuals is clear in Kesey's thought, perhaps the result of his working in a mental hospital. As he argues in an interview, "What this country needs is sanity. Individual sanity, and all the rest will come true. . . . You can't do it any other way. You work from the heart out, you don't work from the issue down."[18] With McMurphy to show him the way, Chief Bromden is ultimately the main one who flies over the cuckoo's nest, not yet fully sane but well on his way.

Bromden tells the story in the historical present, and the very telling of it is part of his therapy, an essential attempt to grasp the significance of his past. Surely his narration, even when it reveals his still faulty conception, "represents a breakthrough rather than a breakdown."[19] Carrying Fiedler's argument on the Indian as a symbol of madness to an extreme, Terry Sherwood suggests that perhaps *all* events in the book are hallucinations.[20] But Chief Bromden's "talking crazy" makes clear sense, as McMurphy realizes (210). And the very fact that he is narrating the book reveals that he is well out of the protective fog and attempting to communicate with others. He realizes how hard it is to keep a clear mind in thinking about the ward. Statements such as "It's the truth even if it didn't happen" (8), however, are not meant to discredit the reliability of the narrator so much as to indicate that his truths are psychological ones. As in Malamud's *The Tenants*, the reader can always preceive what is happening in the outside world and what takes place only in the main character's mind. The Chief gradually learns to differentiate fantasy from external reality too. But he does not deny the internal reality of fantasy. As Bromden argues of his visions of the Combine, "If they don't exist, how can a man see them?" (87). They do exist—as psychological truths even if they did not happen.

The novel uses the Chief's gradual adjustment to time as an index of his improving sanity. At first his perception is obviously faulty. In his paranoia, he thinks the Big Nurse controls the pace of clock-time. As a result, time becomes totally existential or psychological for the Chief in John Henry Releigh's sense of these terms;[21] he controls its pace subconsciously, sometimes suspending time entirely or slowing it to a crawl, sometimes accelerating events almost to slapstick speed (73–75). But this psychological control or lack of control of the pace of time fails, for the Chief feels frustrated, insecure, and disoriented without some stable routine and measurement of time. He risks irreversible psychosis when he hides in the fog, hoping not to perceive the present nor to recall the past by blotting out all particular consciousness, but he always returns to the relative security of Miss Ratched's schedule.

Early in the work he uses the past like the fog, as a place to hide from the threatening present: "But like always when I try to place my thoughts in the past and hide there, the fear close at hand seeps in through the memory" (6). Pretending to be hunting with his father does not always work partly because much of the past Chief Bromden has to escape into is not happy. In fact, he generally tries to avoid remembering the past, since it is even more painful than the present he has built for himself.

As a result, the Chief's memory is very faulty early in the novel. He remembers getting hysterical about being shaved one particular morning, and then being locked in Seclusion. But he cannot remember whether he got breakfast or not. He "can call to mind some mornings" when the aides stole his breakfast, but this morning he just does not remember (8). His memory is understandably selective, to protect him from the unpleasant. He drifts in the fog as a way to escape past and present. In it "time doesn't mean anything. It's lost in the fog, like everything else" (75). Interestingly enough, Bromden thinks the fog must affect memory, since none of the others seem to notice it. He does not yet apply these supposed memory losses to himself. However, even in these faulty memories, he can reason. He figures out that he probably did not have breakfast on the morning in question, and cannot remember because he was drugged. When he awakens, he reckons that it must be after eight o'clock because the ward door has been opened. Clearly some signs of improvement between his earlier state and his perspective as narrator are already showing.

Shock treatments and other remedies on the ward are no help at all, though. He has had over two hundred of these, resulting in "disorientation for days" and the inability to recall things (67). As Pratt's selections on psychotherapy show, shock treatments and lobotomies cause patients to be confused about the time of day and not to think about the past or future. Kesey may well have known that "the feeling of somehow going on in time—the feeling of being essentially the same individual as one was yesterday and will be tomorrow, but recognizing that one has changed since childhood and may go on changing"—that this feeling would be lacking in such patients as the

Chief.[22] In any case Kesey's description of the Chief's disorientation in time is strikingly similar to clinical descriptions, and the cure he presents is precisely the regaining of that sense of self which is so dependent on a perception of continuity and change through time.

Bromden's true therapy begins when McMurphy arrives. The Irishman is a positive influence on his memory from the beginning. When McMurphy first enters, Bromden can "remember all this part real clear," including even his handshake. For a time McMurphy is all that keeps the Chief from drifting forever in the fog (39). Soon the Chief's memory steadily improves. He places events in clear sequences: "I remember it was a Friday again, three weeks after we voted on TV" (177). He learns to *try* to remember: "You forget—if you don't sit down and make the effort to think back" (122). He also learns the important psychological truth in the old German proverb, "Happy is he who forgets what cannot be changed." Instead of losing himself or becoming terrified in flashbacks, he learns how to recognize and deal with them: "That's not even happening now. You see? There's nothing you can do about a happening out of the past like that" (132). He is finally able to put his boyhood together: "It was the first time in what seemed to me centuries that I'd been able to remember much about my childhood" (203). Since he recognizes the difference between actual time passage and seeming in this passage, he is clearly gaining control over psychological time.

Being able to perceive the past is part of a simultaneous ability to live in the present. One night for the first time in years he is "even able to see out the windows" and experience the present fully. He walks to the screen and feels the cold wire mesh against his cheeks, with his eyes closed, only the mesh and "that cold linoleum was real right then, only that moment" (154–155.). After a time, without drugs, "all was sharp and clear and solid" as he "forgot it could be" (186).

Chief Bromden's differentiation of past and present parallels his recognition of acts of his own will instead of his paranoid presumption that others always control him. He admits that he lifted his hand himself to vote with McMurphy (136), and is able to cut through his lies to himself about why he would like to touch McMurphy (210).

His developing sense of time is not merely an adjustment to the tick-tock time of Miss Ratched, however. Like the early McMurphy, he now lives on natural time. As he smells burning leaves, he realizes fall is coming, "just like that was the strangest thing ever happened. Fall. Right outside here it was spring a while back, then it was summer, and now it's fall—that's sure a curious idea" (155). Time is marked by the sun, moon, and seasons, not by clock's (cf. 281). That moon, almost stereotypical Indian measure of time, puts past and present together for Chief Bromden as it dwarfs the stars; it makes him recall how he had noticed the same thing when he was hunting with his father years before (155). As if to emphasize the health of Bromden's sense of past and present now, Kesey lets him listen to Canadian geese fly across that moon until all he can hear is his "memory of the sound" (156).

On the fishing trip he is able to relate past and present, continuity and change even more extensively. He is alert to all that has developed in twenty years. As a result of his confinement, he has a better sense of change than those who have lived through it (226–227). The trip also renews the joy he had felt as a child (243).

Once back on the ward, the Chief does not lose this improved sense of time and sense of renewal even when he is threatened with memory-killing shock treatments. He may not remember the nurse on Disturbed who had treated him while he was most deeply psychotic (265), but even on the way to the Schock Shop he remembers later details such as the digger squirrel holes which he had seen a dog explore in the moonlight (269). True, he cannot control his involuntary fear of shock (271). But his flashbacks under the influence of electricity are comparatively coherent memories of his childhood. His sense of time remains sound, as he can "remember hot, still electric-storm afternoons" and perceive "it's cold because the sun is late afternoon." Kesey makes these images of natural time explicit in the shock dream, and Chief Bromden emphasizes what he and "the *moon*" have going for them (273–274). Bromden is able to question how McMurphy made him big again, and realizes that the shock made him think the recovery room "was a dice" (275). He chooses never again to slip off into the fog to hide. Although he cannot regain his whole memory at once, he works at it for the first time, and knows he has won now. Formerly he spent weeks recovering. This time he is aware of "fighting out of it in less than a day, less time than ever" (276).

By now McMurphy and Bromden have reversed positions, as Fiedler notices but also interprets in reverse. The Chief tries to convince McMurphy to play along for protection just as he had, but McMurphy refuses. Randle is losing his clear consciousness and, perhaps significantly, must squint up at "the dim clock" to read it. This time the clock beats him, for he does not wake up in time to escape. After the lobotomy his eyes just "stared into the full light of the moon," that "cold moon at the window" which looks in on the ending of his natural life (308).

Bromden knows that McMurphy's message must live on through him. A big fisherman like Peter, he tries on McMurphy's hat, then is ashamed of trying to wear it (310). For McMurphy's message is individualism, not discipleship. Now the Chief sides with the moon against the mechanical control panel which runs on artificial time. Moonlight "glinted off the chrome and glass gauges," so cold that Bromden "could almost hear the click of it striking" (320). In smashing out with the control panel, the Chief combines the image of a comic-strip hero with Christian imagery and natural metaphors of time, as the "glass splashed out in the moon, like a bright cold water baptizing the sleeping earth" (310).

Marcus Klein feels that the plot breaks down at this point, "where Chief Bromden, become ambulatory, will just manage to escape back to the mythic free life of his Indian forbears, which is an item of faith."[23] But Bromden is not going back to his tribe for good, nor will he be happily-ever-aftering. He wants to look at the Columbia "just to bring, some of it clear in my mind again" (311). Then he may go to Canada. But as Colonel Matterson, another mad oracle in the novel, has explained in his homemade language, "Canada" is "the cal-en-dar" (129). Chief Bromden is entering a long period of righting himself with the world so he can play some role in righting that world; he has not found any panacea. Like E. E. Cummings, the Chief has had to learn how to make his body put on space and his mind take off mechanical time. He has learned that in a mad world, fleeing through space is a way to gain time to adjust, and that fleeing from all sense of time leads only to madness.[24] In that time-weighted final sentence of the novel, he realizes the simple truth that the past always converges with the future at the present: "I been away a long time." He will remain in the present, the only place a sane man can stand and fight.

Notes

1. Ken Kesey, *One Flew Over the Cuckoo's Nest*, ed. John Clark Pratt (New York: Viking Press, 1973), p. xii. Hereafter Pratt.

2. Tony Tanner, *City of Words: American Fiction 1950–1970* (New York: Harper and Row, 1971), p. 379.

3. Cf. Tony Tanner, p. 382; Pratt, pp. viii and xii on "multivalent synchronicity," and p. 341 quoting Kesey himself; James O. Hoge, "Psychedelic Stimulation and the Creative Imagination: The Case of Ken Kesey," *Southern Humanities Review*, 6 (1971), pp. 382–383; Joseph J. Waldmeir, "Two Novelists of the Absurd: Heller and Kesey," *Wisconsin Studies in Contemporary Literature*, 5 (1964), pp. 192–204 passim; Nicolaus Mills, "Ken Kesey and the Politics of Laughter," *Centennial Review*, 16 (1972), pp. 83, 90; and Janet Sutherland, "A Defense of Ken Kesey's *One Flew Over the Cuckoo's Nest*," *English Journal*, 61 (January 1972), p. 29.

4. Hoge, pp. 381–382.

5. W. D. Sherman, "The Novels of Ken Kesey," *Journal of American Studies*, 5 (1971), pp. 185, 188.

6. Leslie Al Fiedler, *The Return of the Vanishing American* (New York: Stein and Day, 1968), p. 185. See also his article "The New Mutants, "*Partisan Review*, 32 (Fall 1965), p. 524.

7. Charles Witke, "Pastoral Convention in Vergil and Kesey," *Pacific Coast Philology*, 1 (1966), p. 24.

8. Olga W. Vickery, "The Inferno of the Moderns," in Melvin J. Friedman and John B. Vickery, ed., *The Shaken Realist: Essays in Modern Literature in Honor of Frederick J. Hoffman* (Baton Rouge: Louisiana State University Press, 1970), pp. 159–163.

9. Marcia L. Falk, letter to the editor of the *New York Times* (1971), as reprinted in Pratt, pp. 450–453. Compare Terence Martin, *"One Flew Over the Cuckoo's Nest* and the High Cost of Living," *Modern Fiction Studies*, 19 (Spring 1973), pp. 44–46.

10. Waldmeir, p. 199.

11. Ken Kesey, *One Flew Over the Cuckoo's Nest* (New York: The Viking Press. 1964), p. 58. All numbers in parentheses refer to this readily available Compass Books edition, which has the same pagination as the first edition.

12. Terry Sherwood presents an interesting criticism of Kesey's wavering symbols in *"One Flew Over the Cuckoo's Nest* and the Comic Strip," *Critique: Studies in Modern Fiction*, 13 (1971), p. 106. Pratt, p. 349, also records Kesey's similarly metaphorical statement that media wires all lead to the Bank of America, reprinted from "An Impolite Interview with Ken Kesey," *The Realist*, 90 (May–June 1971).

13. Robert Boyers, "Attitudes Toward Sex in American 'High Culture'," *The Annals of the American Academy of Political and Social Sciences*, 376 (March 1968), pp. 36–52, as reprinted in Pratt, especially pp. 436–437.

14. Richard Blessing, "The Moving Target: Ken Kesey's Evolving Hero," *Journal of Popular Culture*, 4 (Winter 1971), p. 615.

15. Irving Malin, "Ken Kesey" *One Flew Over the Cuckoo's Nest*," *Critique*, V (1962), 81–84, as reprinted in Pratt, especially pp. 432–433. Stephen L. Tanner, in "Salvation Through Laughter: Ken Kesey & the Cuckoo's Nest," *Southwest Review*, 58 (Spring 1973), pp. 125–137, traces several of these "meaningfully consistent patterns of imagery" very well, centering on images of Nature and the Machine, but he neglects time images. Cf. Martin, p. 48, on the "strategy of literalizing metaphors."

16. See Blessing, Malin, Mills, Sherwood, and Waldmeir; John A. Barsness, "Ken Kesey: The Hero in Modern Dress," *Bulletin of the Rocky Mountain Modern Language Association*, 23 (March 1969), pp. 27–33, reprinted in Pratt; Richard B. Hauck, "The Comic Christ and the Modern Reader," *College English*, 31 (February 1970), pp. 498–506; and Bruce E. Wallis, "Christ in the Cuckoo's Nest: Or, the Gospel According to Ken Kesey," *Cithara*, 12 (May 1972), pp. 52–58. (Wallis's interpretation is hurt by a doctrinal bias, but has a sound foundation.) Perhaps fortunately, name hunters who have identified Randle P. McMurphy as a mover (RPM), Miss Ratched as a part of the machine (ratchet-but also "wretched" or worse), and the stuttering Billy Bibbit as another Billy Budd, have not tackled the aides (Williams, Warren, and Washington-dominated by political allusions and "w"), Mr. Gideon (and the institutional Gideon's Bible), Doctor Spivey, nor Tee Ah Millatoona (Take A Miltown?). And the hunters of allusions to Christianity have not yet mentioned the rosary bead sparrows on the electrical wires (270), the parallel to Christ's last words in the question "Is it finished?" (309), nor the Pontius Pilate in Disturbed who keeps saying, "I wash my hands of the whole deal" (264–266).

17. Cf. Stephen Tanner, pp. 128–136; Mills, p. 82; Harold Clurman, reviewing the theatrical version in *The Nation*, 212 (April 5, 1971), pp. 442–443, as reprinted in Pratt, 443; Ronald G. Billingsley, "The Artistry of Ken Kesey," Diss, Oregon 1971, as abstracted in *DAI* 32: pp. 3293a–94a; Carol S. P. Havemann, "The Fool as Mentor in Modern American Parables of Entrapment: Ken Kesey's *One Flew Over the Cuckoo's Nest*, Joseph Heller's *Catch-22* and Ralph Ellison's *Invisible Man*," Diss, Rice 1971, as abstracted in *DAI* 32: pp. 2091A–92A; Richard B. Hauck, "The Comic Christ and the Modern Reader," *College English*, 31 (February 1970), p. 501; and William Schopf, "Blindfolded and Backwards: Promethean and

Bemushroomed Heroism in *One Flew Over the Cuckoo's Nest* and *Catch-22*," *BRM-MLA*, 26 (Fall 1972), pp. 89–97. Several studies have espoused briefly this basic view of the novel or implied it, but none has worked it out fully with the support of the use of time.

18. Quoted in Pratt, p. 360.

19. Mills, p. 83. Cf. Vickery, p. 163, and Tom Wolfe, *The Electric Kool-Aid Acid Test*, as quoted in Pratt, p. 331.

20. Sherwood, p. 109, n. 8.

21. John Henry Raleigh, "The English Novel and the Three Kinds of Time," *Time, Place and Idea: Essays on the Novel*, Carbondale: Southern Illinois University Press, 1968, pp. 43–55.

22. Mary Frances Robinson and Walter Freeman, *Psychology and the Self* (New York: Grune and Stratton, Inc., 1954), as quoted in Pratt, p. 496. Cf. Sherman. p. 185, defining the Chief's madness.

23. Marcus Klein, ed., *The American Novel Since World War II* (Greenwich, Conn.: Fawcett, 1969), "Introduction," pp. 20–21.

24. Cf. Martin, p. 54, on the "sense of space" in Kesey.

JAMES F. KNAPP

Tangled in the Language of the Past: Ken Kesey and Cultural Revolution

Literary Critics have always found ways to contradict each other. But sometimes their disagreements can help us to get beyond the niceties of literary interpretation to see deeper contradictions, not only in the particular work under scrutiny, but in the very culture which includes both the writer and his critics. Consider two statements concerning Ken Kesey's *One Flew Over the Cuckoo's Nest:* according to Terrence Martin, "The men on the Big Nurse's ward become stronger once they recognize their interdependence. McMurphy becomes heroic once he throws his lines out to them." but W. D. Sherman says that "The kind of affirmation which arises from Kesey's novels is an anarchic 'yes' to life, which, despite its joyousness, leaves a man prey to unbearable isolation." Both observations ring true, and yet surely Kesey cannot be affirming a vital individualism, whose price is personal isolation, at the same time that he offers a vision of the necessity of inter-dependence and mutual brotherhood.

This apparent contradiction exists at the level of "meaning": which is the true interpretation of Kesey's novel? But Eliot M. Zashin, a political scientist, discussing Kesey's rise and fall as an active leader of the sixties' counterculture, has identified a similar contradiction at the level of practical action: "Being part of the group-mind implied going with the flow of the collective psyche, while the theorist wanted to shape the elements of his vision. If Ke-

The Midwest Quarterly, Volume 19, Number 4 (Summer 1978): pp. 398–412.

sey directed the Pranksters, their activity could not really be an expression of the group-mind." Thus the ambiguous titles for Kesey (e.g., "non-navigator") which Tom Wolfe describes in *The Electric Kool-Aid Acid Test*. Self-assertive leader imposing his vision on the group? Or member of an inter-dependent collective of equals? He apparently sought the magic to be both.

So we could attempt to decide whether Kesey's writings preach independence or inter-dependence, just as, presumably, he struggled to reconcile those two poles in his own mind. His books, however, as well as that part of his life which was made a public fiction, became part of a popular movement whose importance, for a time at least, was far more than artistic. The counter-culture of the sixties promised (threatened) to change the nature of America, and then, as suddenly as it had come, it collapsed into the quietism of a more conservative decade. Like other movements of history, this one had innumerable causes—political, economic, psychological, even scientific—but my own concern in this essay is with just one part of that process. The structure of a society—its range of acceptable roles and behaviors, its values, its ideals—is reflected in that symbolic network of stories, pictures, and metaphors which we might call its body of popular myth. We generally assume that such an agency functions to "socialize" the young, and that its effect is more often than not a conservative one, preserving traditional attitudes as it passes them on to a new generation. By the nineteen-sixties, of course, such a sociological notion was commonplace, and it could easily be inverted and used consciously by those who were eager to change the nature of their society. If traditional images socialize traditionally, then *new* images might be found which would have the power to shape minds in *new* directions. Social change could be brought about through the simple, non-violent agency of "creative mythology": initiate a cultural revolution, and the rest will follow,

The reality appears to be more complicated. Ken Kesey certainly began with many of the assumptions of the "cultural revolutionaries." He became a public figure by writing *One Flew Over the Cuckoo's Nest*, a novel which depends heavily on the sort of critique of society which was being made throughout the serious media during the nineteen-fifties. America has become a lonely crowd of organization men, offering its affluence only to those who are willing to pay the price of strict conformity. Increasingly hierarchical, technological, and efficient, society has become that dehumanizing machine which Chief Bromden calls the Combine, producing "things like five thousand houses punched out identical by a machine and strung across the hills outside of town, so fresh from the factory they're still linked together like sausages." Complete with identical commuter husbands and identical children in the back yards, those houses represent society's primary demand: adjustment.

By choosing a mental hospital for his setting, Kesey was able to picture society's pressure to adjust at its most coldly, and explicitly, coercive. Identifying social evil with institutional constraints which hinder individuality, he proceeded to set a microcosmic revolution in motion by introducing a powerfully individual character. Randle McMurphy succeeds in destroying the order of the ward, and in liberating some of its patients, not through any kind of direct attack on the system, but simply by refusing to speak the language which sustains it. His most telling weapons are jokes, games, obscenity, make-believe, verbal disrespect. The patients have seen physical violence before, and been left unchanged by it. But when McMurphy violates that language which had marked out, invisibly, the social space of the ward, they begin to be freed of its power, begin to see that other patterns of relationship, other values might be possible. McMurphy's singing in the shower is disturbing and exciting precisely because it challenges that web of indirect, symbolic control through which the *voluntarily* committed patients have been made to choose their own oppression. Like a bawdy William Blake, McMurphy is a cultural revolutionary whose function it is to smash the "mind-forg'd manacles" of his time.

When Kesey moved away from fiction to create the real-life games of his Merry Pranksters, he adopted the same strategies he had created on paper. Tom Wolfe's account opens with his being driven through the streets of San Francisco by several Pranksters in a pick-up truck, and a crucial distinction is made at the outset. Driving through a city which is largely the alien territory of those straight citizens whose surest emblem is their "black shiny FBI shoes," the Pranksters are set apart by bizarre costumes certain to startle and disturb the expectations of anyone trapped in the grey conformity of "well-adjusted" America: "Here comes a beautiful one, attache case and all, the day-is-done resentful look and the . . . shoes—how they shine!—and what the hell are these beatnik ninnies—and Lois plugs him in the old marshallow and he goes streaming and bouncing down the hill" (*Kool-Aid*, 2). As Kesey and his group gradually refine their intentions in preparing for a trip across America, they begin to see the possibility for initiating radical changes through the simple expedient of offering people the sight of a multi-media bus full of Day-Glo crazies. Like drugs, or kicking a jammed soda machine, this approach is based on the assumption that violent, temporary alteration of a too-rigid system can be liberating. Since the system at question is the uniform, unimaginative, overly conditioned mentality of corporate America, the mental games of the Pranksters seemed an obvious way to begin the process of change.

In his second novel, *Sometimes A Great Notion*, Kesey had defined a similar set of oppositions. Setting a hero whose unpredictable independence passes all bounds of reason against a loggers' union whose members are plodding fools at best, Kesey affirms his opposition to institutional conformity—among workers no less than owners. His hero, Hank Stamper, sets out to undermine the strikers' position by supplying their mill with logs almost singlehandedly, because he will not bow to group pressure—justified or not.

In a gesture which becomes the central image for his defiance, he runs his father's severed arm up a flagpole, all its fingers but the middle one tied down. That act, which, paradoxically, destroys the dignity and authority of the union leader in the eyes of his men, is essentially an audacious, macabre *prank*. The point I would stress, however, is that in each of these cases, we are asked to identify with characters who set themselves in opposition to a world of stultifying, institutional conformity—whether Combine and hospital, or company suburb, or manipulative union. It was institutions such as these which came to be grouped together, during the sixties, under the label Establishment. From this point of view, Kesey is a decidedly "anti-Establishment" figure whose works, in life as well as in art, encouraged social change.

Why did so little change occur? Marvin Harris, the anthropologist, has argued that the counter-culture itself was in fact a powerful force acting *against* change, that it "has all the classic symptoms of a lifestyle dreamwork whose social function is to dissolve and fragment the energies of dissent. This should have been clear from the great importance given to 'doing your own thing.' You can't make a revolution if everybody does his own thing. To make a revolution, everybody must do the same thing" (*Riddles*, 257). The Pranksters were certainly among those whom Harris describes as seriously believing that they could "kiss away the corporate state as if it were an 'evil enchantment.'" Addressing a Vietnam War protest, Kesey simply played his harmonica and advised the crowd to "just look at, look at the war, and turn your backs and say . . . Fuck it . . ." (*Kool-Aid*, 199). That is to say, the Pranksters confronted the Vietnam War as they did the plastic suburbs—as cultural revolutionaries. To say that such a revolution of the mind only supports the status quo by mystifying those who might bring about genuine change is certainly to validate the feelings of those anti-war organizers who felt the unity and resolve of their crowd melt away under the spell of Kesey's harmonica. But it does not deal with the fact that for many millions of people the hippies seemed as tangible and terrible a sign of radical change as ever appeared in the fiery cloud of a mystic's vision.

At this point, we might frame an argument something like this: though the counter-culture offered a fearsome appearance of change, it was in fact powerless, because a society cannot be changed simply by the symbolic magic of altering its myths. That is to say, cultural revolution is bunk. Before dismissing the endeavor of the Pranksters as doomed from the start, however, it might be well to look more carefully at just how their elaborate showmanship did attempt to invoke, and change, traditional American myths. Structural linguists make a distinction between *langue* and *parole*—between the underlying rules which constitute the grammar of a language, and the endless variety of particular utterances which may be patterned by those rules. If there is rapid change, even fashion, at the level of individual sentences, change is very rare and very gradual at the deeper levels of grammar. In attempting to understand cultural change, we must make a similar distinction. "Lifestyle" may tell us much about the nature of a society, but novelty in these endlessly interchangeable "words" of a culture—its fashions, its pop heroes, its slang—does not necessarily represent change at the deeper levels of cultural patterning. A luminescent soap bubble appears to be very different from a bubble of hot mud, but at the level of structure, they are the same. If there is such a thing as myth, it surely exists in fundamental, potential patterns of social relationship, and not in the particular manifestations of those patterns. Adam ruling Eve defines a pattern which can then be brought to flesh by any male chauvinist at all.

As Kesey's Pranksters presented themselves to the world, they seemed to offer mixed signals. In their Day-Glo strangeness they sought to create an impact of unheard-of novelty. And yet Kesey himself was adept at drawing on the most traditional of images: "Somehow the Perry Lane set got the idea that his family were Okies, coming out of the Dust Bowl during the Depression, and then up to Oregon, wild, sodden Oregon, where they had fought the land and shot bears and the rivers were swift and the salmon leaped silver in the spring big two-hearted rivers" (*Kool-Aid*, 32). In his buckskin shirt and cowboy boots, Kesey played a role whose implications he fully understood. When he created a hero to break up the order of Big Nurse's ward, he made him in the mold of a thousand dime novels: "he's got iron on his heels and he rings it on the floor like horseshoes. He shows up in the door and stops and hitches his thumbs in his pockets, boots wide apart, and stands there with the guys looking at him" (*Cuckoo's Nest*, 16). Nor is Hank Stamper, muscles rippling like steel cables, any exception to Kesey's image of the proper Western hero.

As Kesey conceived it, these frontier heroes must engage in acts which reveal their gritty, solitary fortitude. McMurphy strides to his deadly showdown with the corrupt enforcer of bad laws. Or Kesey, explaining his decision to go beyond acid, pictures himself as a Daniel Boone of psychic exploration: "'Don't say stop plunging into the forest,' Kesey says. 'Don't say stop being a pioneer and come back here and help these people through the door. If Leary wants to do that, that's good, it's a good thing and somebody should do it. But somebody has to be the pioneer and leave the marks for others to follow'" (*Kool-Aid*, 27). Uninterested in the administrative drudgery of organizing a wagon train, Kesey views his role strictly as that of pathfinder. And since America had long since reached the shores of the Pacific, his trailblazing would have to turn to a psychic wilderness. Nevertheless, the legend on the front of his bus is "Further" and his destination is "Edge City."

By adopting traditional metaphors such as these, Kesey invests his new experiments with the authority of a national history full of exploring. He can be traditional and revolutionary at the same time. In embracing the image of the pioneer, however, he invokes a body of tradition which has helped to sustain a deep continuity within the American experience. Although there has never been a single dominant version of the "myth of America," one thread of the tradition does lead directly to Kesey and his Pranksters. Robert Bird's 1837 novel, *Nick of the Woods*, was an extremely popular tale of the frontier, and it offers a particularly clear use of that ultimate text for American myth—the Fall of Adam and Eve from Eden. Bird begins his book by quoting a few lines from *Paradise Lost*, choosing the point at which the fallen pair leave Paradise and enter the world for the first time. Rather than emphasizing their sin or the sadness of their loss, Bird uses his allusion to point out the enormous possibility that lay before them. It was just such a possibility which confronted the pioneers who settle Kentucky—"the first region of great ultra-montane Wilderness penetrated by the Saggenah, or Englishman,—the first torn from its aboriginal possessors, and converted from a desert hunting-ground into the home of civilized men" (*Nick*, 27). So perceived, the myth of the Fall could sanction, as it did for Bird, the movement of European civilization into the new continent. Perceiving nature as fallen, and yet available for salvation through human toil, he saw the proper course as clear: gain mastery over that alien world and so transform it that it might assume the altered shape of a New Jerusalem.

If Kesey plunged into the forest as a pioneer of the avant-garde, he did so in pursuit of a very old vision: "Sandy could see that Kesey wasn't primarily an outdoorsman. He wasn't that crazy about unspoiled Nature. It was more like he had a vision of the forest as a fantastic stage setting . . . in which every day would be a happening, an art form" (*Kool-Aid*, 51). The Pranksters painted the redwoods with Day-Glo, and wired them up with multiple speakers for jazz and rock music, and filled them with junk art. For Kesey, nature was an alien presence that must be transformed by the arts of civilization before it could serve a human purpose. His aim was not to build the mines and mills and cities of the earlier dreamers, but his starting point, like theirs, was the assumption that nature must be mastered by human technology. One consequence of such an attitude has been the enormous physical transformation of the continent, but the full implications of the myth must be understood. When a part of the world was marked as alien territory, that label sanctioned the mastery of everything beyond the frontier—including the people.

One of the interests of the Merry Pranksters was the attempt to achieve an intimate sense of psychic unity among themselves—to be "in synch." And yet their empathy was strongly narrow. Like much of the counter-culture in general, the Pranksters combined an intense desire for openness and emotional sharing with a habit of perception which entirely excluded most people from their sympathy. The formula was explicit and categorical: "'There are going to be times,' says Kesey, 'when we can't wait for somebody. Now, you're either on the bus or off the bus. If you're on the bus, and you get left behind, then you'll find it again. If you're off the bus in the first place—then it won't make a damn' "(*Kool-Aid*, 74). Like a pioneer contemplating the benighted savages who lurk in the forest before him, Kesey was willing to accept any converts to the true faith, but those who chose to remain beyond the pale were not worth further consideration. Tom Wolfe's book is full of incidents in which Prankster behavior depends on the perception of a clear line between "us" and "them." Stark Naked goes insane in Houston, and the bus moves on, leaving her to be picked up, eventually, by the cops. A girl freaks out at an Acid Test, and her hysteria is piped into the sound system to become part of the atmosphere. At a Beatles concert, Kesey watches with fascination as the crowd becomes a jellyfish before its rock heroes, and at another Acid Test he experiences that kind of mastery himself as he controls the crowd by manipulating the electronic media which determine its mood. Stoned at La Honda he indulges the ultimate fantasy of separation as he imagines himself to be God, the whole world subordinate to his power.

The Pranksters move through a world of non-people, projecting their own movie onto faces which remain unrecognized, and presumed to be blank. Kesey's fiction was no different. In *Cuckoo's Nest,* for instance, the service station attendant only exists to be badgered into submission, the charter boat captain to be outwitted, the psychiatrist to be used, Big Nurse to be defeated by any means possible. Nor are we allowed to feel any real sympathy for the self-pitying, blustering, diarhetic, athlete's-foot-ridden union men of *Sometimes A Great Notion.* Against such backgrounds, the Kesey hero (himself or his fictions) stands out all the more clearly as dynamic entrepreneur. He imposes his will on the unenlightened like any Calvinist preacher armed with Bible and gun, and the effect seems to be to affirm a powerful individualism. There is a strong case, then, that for all the "anti-Establishment" cast of its surface appearance, Kesey's work actually conveys the most traditional of messages: it is the right and the destiny of strong individuals to shape the world to their wills. Even within the circle of friends and family there can be only one "bull-goose looney," one top stud logger, one chief of the psychedelic avant-garde.

But this essay began with the paradox that Kesey has been seen to affirm both independence and inter-dependence, and I am not quite ready to resolve that contradiction on the side of unqualified individualism. Nor would I conclude that Kesey was simply a deceptively reactionary part of a social movement mis-named as "counter-culture." There is a clear concern in each of these books for the problems of forging some kind of community in the face of a cold, alienating world. The Merry Pranksters shared their adventure as fully as we might imagine, while Randle McMurphy establishes a new kind of human solidarity among his fellow patients. Kesey does indeed adopt the role of intrepid, self-reliant pioneer, and I have argued that that role is richly precedented in the American past. If salvation after the fall depends on our right use of a natural world which is equally available to good or evil, then it would seem that we must set off into the heathen darkness, and build our holy city with ax and gun—or strobe light. But that is only part of the myth. Salvation cannot in fact be complete until Christ, as Second Adam, makes his sacrifice and offers a new pattern for human life.

Kesey and his heroes are obviously cast in the mold of the frontiersman, but there is an equally strong suggestion of self-sacrifice in the adventures they seek. These are not the invincible white-hats of old movies, emerging spotless from one brawl after another. In Wolfe's book, Kesey gives up the easy leadership of a pop cult he helped to create, becoming instead the ragged, persecuted, misunderstood fugitive. Justifying himself to a puzzled would-be follower, he emphasizes his suffering in the cause of others: "'If you don't realize that I've been helping you with every fiber in my body . . . if you don't realize that everything I've done, everything I've gone through. . . .' "And he pictures himself as willing martyr to a hard age: "'We're in a period now like St. Paul and the early Christians,'" Kesey says. 'St. Paul said, if they shit on you in one city, move on to another city, and if they shit on you in that city, move on to another city—'" (Kool-Aid, 26). In Cuckoo's Nest he creates a character who quite simply learns to be Christ. As McMurphy begins to feel a bond of sympathy for his fellow patients he comes to their aid at increasing cost to himself. Publicly failing to lift a heavy control panel he seems to say: I am mortal like you, but I am not afraid to commit myself. Smashing Big Nurse's window, he cuts himself badly, but restores the spirit of the ward. And when he forgoes his self-interested good behavior to defend another man, and so faces the punishment of shock treatment, he consciously identifies himself with Christ: "They put the graphite salve on his temples. 'What is it?' he says. 'Conductant,' the technician says. 'Anointest my head with conductant. Do I get a crown of thorns?'" (p. 237). Ultimately, McMurphy sacrifices his mind and then his life so that his brothers may be reborn out of the living death in which he had found them.

In attempting to understand particular works in terms of mythic patterns such as these, however, it is essential to realize that no myth has a simple, unvarying meaning which is automatically conveyed to the reader as soon as the familiar allusions are made. When Robert Bird chose to invoke the story of the fall, he offered a version which was entirely compatible with the need of his own time to justify the final stage in the conquest of the American continent. If myth is an active force in shaping values and attitudes, it is also conditioned by the particular historical demands of each new age. Anyone who has glanced through a history of religious painting knows, for example, that the image of Christ has undergone great change. Early pictures of the Good Shepherd are nearly indistinguishable from classical representations of Orpheus, but that portrayal gives way to the Christ enthroned of Byzantine art, to be followed still later by a Renaissance emphasis on the physical suffering of a very mortal body. When Kesey associates his character with Christ he does not choose the pink-cheeked Jesus of modern calendar art. McMurphy goes to his crucifixion with winks and wisecracks, a tough guy trying to buck up his fellow victims. If there is a precedent for such a Christ it must surely be that Anglo-Saxon warrior who strides to the cross in "The Dream of the Rood":

> Then the young warrior. God our Saviour,
> Valiantly stripped before the battle; with courage and resolve
> Beheld by many He climbed upon the Cross to redeem Mankind.
>
> (*Old English Poems*, 129)

When Christianity came to the Germanic peoples of northern Europe, it quickly took a shape acceptable and understandable to their society of warlike lord and thane.

And so with Kesey, Christ becomes a pattern for heroic, assertive action. He is a frontiersman whose bold sacrifice opens the way for everyone else able to follow his example. But like his Anglo-Saxon predecessor, such a Christ can only be the leader of a small band of brothers. His stance toward the evils which would kill him demands that he be set over against a hostile world. No respecter of theology, this version of the myth has little sympathy for the unstoned and no forgiveness at all for Big Nurse. Setting himself against the cold impersonality of modern society, Kesey would create a new community based on self-sacrifice and mutual dependency. And yet his community would include only the elect, and, set in opposition to a world of outsiders he regards as unenlightened or downright evil, it would offer no vision of the larger, inclusive society. There was a kind of siege mentality about much of the counter-culture, and perhaps that had something to do with Kesey's attraction to this beleaguered warrior-Christ. But whatever the cause, he seems to embrace aggressive individualism one moment and self-sacrificing brotherhood the next, and the contradiction cannot be resolved because it is rooted in the only words he knew. Society's myths are always open to the movement of history, responding to change, or causing it, or mediating it in such a way that new patterns may be spoken in the reassuring categories of an older language. But to consciously master so complex a process, to understand all the social messages being transmitted by any body of tradition, and to try to bend them to your own ambition—is to fly awfully close to the sun. Ken Kesey was a cultural revolutionary, all right, but the beast he sought to control had a mind subtler, and more willful, than he ever guessed.

WORKS CITED

Bird, Robert. *Nick of the Woods*. New Haven: College and University Press, 1967.

Crossley-Holland, Keven, and Bruce Mitchell, eds. *The Battle of Maldon and Other Old English Poems*. New York: St. Martin's Press, 1967.

Harris, Marvin. *Cows, Pigs, Wars, and Witches: The Riddles of Culture*. New York: Random House, 1974.

Kesey, Ken. *One Flew Over the Cuckoo's Nest*. New York: Signet, 1962.

———. *Sometimes A Great Notion*. New York: Bantam, 1969.

Martin, Terrence. "*One Flew Over the Cuckoo's Nest* and the High Cost of Living," *Modern Fiction Studies*, 19 (Spring, 1973).

Sherman, W. D. "The Novel of Ken Kesey," *Journal of American Studies*, 5 (1971).

Wolfe, Tom. *The Electric Kool-Aid Acid Test*. New York: Bantam, 1969.

Zashin, Elliot M. "Political Theorist and Deniurge: The Rise and Fall of Ken Kesey," *Centennial Review*, 17 (Spring, 1973).

MICHAEL M. BOARDMAN

One Flew Over the Cuckoo's Nest:
Rhetoric and Vision

Ken Kesey's *One Flew Over the Cuckoo's Nest* illustrates well the difficulties of writing a successful tragic action in the modern world. In large part,
the problem stems from what David Daiches long ago termed "the breakdown of the implicit agreement between author and readers about what
was significant in human experience," a collapse lamented by Virginia
Woolf, among others. "Only believe," she wistfully wrote, "and all the
rest will come of itself." But what if many readers find belief difficult or
impossible? Any novelist who sets out to free himself from "the cramp
and confinement of personality," who attempts to represent as moving and
important a sequence of imagined life, depends heavily, today more than
ever, on creating through "rhetoric," the way he tells his story, a community of values that may not exist in the real world. If an author's donnée
is the spectacle of a character passing from happiness to misery—always a
difficult subject to represent successfully—and that author wishes to avoid
the "disagreeable spectacle" David Hume saw as attendant on "the mere
suffering of plaintive virtue, under the triumphant tyranny and oppression
of vice," problems peculiar to tragedy arise to complicate matters. Tragedy,
that "higher form of art" than even the epic, can fail to move or convince
if the plea to "believe" falls on ears assaulted daily with conflicting claims
for credence.[1]

The Journal of Narrative Technique, Volume 9, Number 3 (Fall 1979): pp. 171–183.

Among those conflicting claims are the critical formulae that have been used to explain Kesey's first novel. Why should one see *One Flew Over* as a tragic action, rather than as comic allegory or melodramatic fable? After all, Bromden, whom many regard as the central character, not only does not die, but experiences a kind of liberation. The book also seems to contain far too much humor to be beaten with the stick of tragedy. One justification for seeing the book as tragic is that tragedy, as a formal model, explains better than other conceptions the reasons for the book's specific and general features, its teleology. If, like Sheldon Sacks and Robert Wess, who have both suggested that *One Flew Over* fits that pattern of the tragic action, we consider, even as a mere possibility, that tragedy may be a form, rather than a special vision or philosophy, capable of appearing in a variety of guises, then the "designedness" of the book, the way seemingly comic elements serve purposes other than the comic becomes clear.[2] The tragic model also enables us to explain the source of several complaints about the technique and rhetoric, or "philosophy," if one prefers, and why they may be misguided, given the hypothesis of tragic form. Finally, moving past the purely formal, we can begin to recognize the difficulties, by no means solved with complete success, that Kesey encountered when he sought to give form and significance to a basic tragic conception. This more general question involves nothing less than the possibility for tragedy in the modern age.

I

We gain some insight into the magnitude of Kesey's task by sketching out what kind of story this was to be. Take a character who, though basically good, is far from "elevated" in the classic sense, show him subjected to a situation of coercion in which he acts, sacrificially, to help others at the risk of his own destruction, and try to represent the pattern as moving and significant. How can Kesey feel that his notions of the value of human sacrifice will be shared by his readers? If the human condition for many readers— and perhaps more critics—entails necessarily seeing the individual as puny and ineffectual in the face of the void, "doom" becomes not an arresting aberration but a shared condition of existence, as quotidian and unremarkable as eating and drinking. The tragic action entails on the modern author an additional, related burden. To avoid the maudlin or, worse, the simply horrible, the hero must in a real sense choose his doom, with that "noble courageous despair" that raises human misery above the merely dolorous.[3] If many readers doubt the meaningfulness of individual choice, a sense of its importance, at least in the self-contained world of the work, must be conveyed by fictional rhetoric. When we have witnessed the last twilight of all the idols and seen the future dim to a *nada y pues nada,* lending significance to a single act of rebellion becomes a crucial problem of the novelist's art.

A number of modern authors seem so aware of the difficulty that they have eschewed attempting to portray tragic declines and turned instead to delineating static states of futile existence. If there is anything tragic about the characters of Beckett or Vonnegut, or of that contemporary chronicler of the execrable, Jerzy Kozinski, it is that they are condemned to be human. At the same time, other modern authors, such as Fitzgerald, Faulkner, Hemingway, and, I am suggesting, Kesey, have sought ways to build into their tragic actions sufficiently strong systems of positive belief so that the "fall" approaches, at least, tragic proportions. Often such beliefs are, as it were, the instruments of the telling and not necessarily identical with the author's view of the world; they can by, in Wayne Booth's terms, the "rhetoric" of the "implied author" rather than the reasoned philosophy of the novelist, a distinction virtually identical to Henry James' calling some things of the "essence" and some of the "treatment." *One Flew Over* clearly depends on a number of artistic decisions designed to produce at least a temporary community of value so that McMurphy's destruction can be experienced as both plausible and significant. Other, much more general, ethical elements are part of the basic conception, Kesey's "tragic vision," and he must assume full responsibility for their validity. In the criticism of the book, rhetoric and conception have not always been carefully distinguished, perhaps because some modern criticism tends to assume that any element of thought not obviously repudiated in a novel must be part of its author's intended meaning.

The most serious charge against Kesey has been sexism: a "concealed sexist bias" that makes the book "a bit dangerous." Peter G. Beidler summarizes and extends the charges: the book has "obvious flaws as a novel—its *merely* heroic hero, its once-latent (now blatant) anti-feminism, its too carefully contrived plot, setting and characters."[4] Even when critics attempt to defend the novel's basic conception an uncomfortable awareness of the current difficulty in generalizing about questions of value intrudes: "*One Flew Over the Cuckoo's Nest* was written from the point of view that man's problems are caused by woman who refuses to allow him to play the domineering role which nature intended him to play."[5] In 1962, when Kesey's book appeared, such a "defense" might have ruffled few feathers. But, as Leslie Horst put it, in an essay provocatively titled "Bitches, Twitches, and Eunuchs: Sex-Role Failure and Caricature," a "liberation" that "exhilarated" one "more than a decade ago" now seems "derogation of women . . . attractively packaged."[6] Values, that is, have changed and the newly discovered difficulty many readers have with the novel points to a need to understand which ideas really represent Kesey's articles of faith and which are rather elements in his rhetoric of significant fabulation. My contention is that most of what readers have found objectionable is "local" rhetoric designed to allow the reader to experience McMurphy's tragedy as moving and significant. The basic conception left after the rhetoric of "telling" has been distinguished is universal: the significance of sacrifice characteristic of one variant of the tragic experience.

II

When McMurphy enters the hateful world of the Big Nurse, he reminds the narrator, Chief Bromden, "of a car salesman or a stock auctioneer," hardly a candidate for martyrdom.[7] No one can "tell if he's really this friendly or if he's got some gambler's reason for trying to get acquainted with guys so far gone a lot of them don't even know their names" (p. 21). Against this long-developed instinct for survival wars a common human concern his independence has not extirpated: will he act to help the men or to help himself? At first, he bets he can "bug" the "Big Nurse," a sexually repressed and supremely efficient force for conformity who has learned to "smell not" the fear of her patients and "put it to use" (p. 17). In numerous important scenes, we learn the extent of her power to prevent noisome independence: she can, in addition to all the little arts of prodding the guilty recesses of her "patients'" consciences, order electric shock, even lobotomize the recalcitrant or merely disruptive patient. The connection between Mac's behaving himself, playing it "cagey," and staying in one piece becomes clear to us and to him when, after promising to "bug" the nurse "till she comes apart at those neat little seams" (p. 72), he learns that he can be institutionalized as long as the nurse sees fit. He immediately becomes cagey, satisfying, temporarily at least, the Chief's earlier question about his motivation: Mac is for Mac. He has had "no one to *care* about, which is what makes him free enough to be a good con man" (p. 89), and the first duty of a con artist is survival. The terms of the action are set. If he acts to defy the nurse, he risks destruction, past reminders of which, the "Vegetables," are conveniently and conspicuously placed around the ward. If he plays it cagey, as all his past experience has taught him to do, not only will he be safe but eventually free.

Kesey's problem with this pattern should be apparent. How could he show McMurphy acting, in a manner entirely out of character, to insure his own destruction? In addition, even if Kesey could find a plausible way to motivate McMurphy's sacrifice, how, given the power of the combine and Nurse Ratched, could the horror of senseless waste be avoided?

Whether Kesey knew it or not, many novelists have sought solutions to similar problems. One of Hardy's greatest difficulties, one he did not always solve satisfactorily, was to give us a sense of the *importance* of the fall of characters who, "objectively," are mere toys of the "President of the Immortals." Conrad, facing a similar problem with Kurtz and, especially, Jim, invented a sympathetic narrator who was personally involved with the tragic figure, invested him with authority, and allowed the intrinsic advantages of a first-person narrator—we tend to trust the "I" unless given reasons not to—to establish the importance of what he has witnessed. Marlow and Fitzgerald's Nick Carraway are just two in a long line of I-narrators designed primarily as rhetorical devices to assist the realization of tragic potential out of seemingly untragic materials. They are not *mere* devices, of course, since the skilled novelist makes pleasurable virtues of artistic necessities.

But Kesey's problem was more than just persuasion. Not only was Mc-Murphy to give his life away; he was to do so in conflict against a microcosmic representation of a brutal and unforgiving society that valued his independence not at all. The potential for horror was great. Kesey's solution was to create not only a first-person narrator, but one whose entire well being depended on the sacrifice toward which McMurphy gradually moved. The Chief's "fog" is the sign that McMurphy is playing it cagey; for the reader, it is the signal to regret Mac's caution and desire his continued resistance to the Big Nurse, even though we may care greatly for him and fear his peril. When everything seems "hopeless and dead," when the Chief feels "McMurphy can't help. . . . Nobody can help," that is when "the fog rolls in" (p 110). Kesey carefully handles the relationship between Mac's attitude toward the hospital and the nurse, and the Chief's mental health. Very quickly, one implies the other with almost syllogistic force.

As Mac inches toward destruction—it is never really in doubt, once we have seen the past and present power of the Big Nurse—a corresponding auction in the Chief's psychosis takes place. The other inmates are part of the immanent and powerful pattern, showing clear signs of independence, sexual and otherwise. It is as if the entire cast of characters supporting Mac and the Big Nurse has been invented to convert an implausible and horrifying tale into one that is inevitable and transcending. There should he no confusion over just who this story is "about." For all of the Chief's importance and vividness as a narrator, he is still part of the "telling" and not the "essence." Aside from being one of the strangest "reliable" narrators in fiction, the Chief provides the compelling need that, coupled with that of the other men, drives Mac on. On the other hand, replace Mac with another *kind* of character, and the entire donnée of the novel changes drastically.

The Chief's desires, and those of the other men, would not be enough to establish the instability that leads, in a series of gradually more direct acts of rebellion, to Mac's lobotomy and death. Even with "every one of those faces" on the Disturbed Ward "turned toward him" and "waiting" for him to act, something in Mac's personality must make the confrontation inevitable. Here is where Kesey had perhaps his trickiest problem. If the battle were simply between the Nurse's absolute desire for control and Mac's con man independence, we have melodrama. What Kesey does instead is to represent, largely from the outside, through the perceptions of the Chief, a change in Mac. The tragic fate he endures—distinct from the lobotomy and death that are its effects—is to lose his personality in the other men. The McMurphy who leads his twelve disciples down to the sea to fish for salmon has relinquished his role as dynamic and independent rabblerouser. On the trip back, with seas high, he takes a life-jacket, even though they were three short. The old Mac would have played the tough leader, disdaining the whipping waves. But now, "McMurphy hadn't insisted that he be one of the heroes; all during the fuss he'd stood with his back against the cabin . . . and watched the guys without saying a word" (p. 240), a reticence equally unusual for Mac. Harding, near the end, sees the change clearly. It hasn't been the nurse "bugging" Mac "about one thing or another." "That's not what drove you crazy," Harding says. It was "us," the men who turned the independence of Mac into the only kind of weakness that could have destroyed him: the ability to care about others (pp. 294–295).

Kesey risked creating a mere comic book hero in Mac, a caricature of real heroism. We do not see the psychological process that turns Mac from egocentric sinner to sacrificial saint; it is portrayed through signs: Mac's uneasiness, noted by the Chief, his "dreadfully tired and strained and *frantic*" (p. 245) look as he realizes, we surmise, what he must do. For four reasons I can think of, three probably essential and one at least highly desirable, the change *must* be represented indirectly. For the sake of plausibility, such a drastic change is better shown from the outside. Then too, if we were to see Mac's internal state of confusion, what he *feels* could become more important that than what he does—and his actions form the tragedy, not his state of mind, Thirdly, dwelling on the ruminations of a man who quite clearly is going to act in a manner that will insure his own destruction risks creating that sense of horror at the "triumphant tyranny of vice over virtue" David Hume contended was counter to the tragic. We could become *too* close to Mac, and our concern for his safety overpower our desire to see him resist. Finally, the dramatic tension—the suspense—is heightened by our uncertainty in conflict with our desire.

That there existed a potential in Mac's "flaw" for melodrama is apparent, Some readers find the comparisons of Mac to Christ not only heavy-handed but inappropriate. But this too is a rhetorical problem: to elevate Mac's actions to tragic proportions, not only must a great deal be at stake (the other men) but his struggle must seem larger than it objectively is. Kesey may intend a "statement" about the "Combine," the American society with its passion for homogenization; but that "lesson" is present only indirectly as a function of Kesey's need to raise the confrontation above the level of local melodrama. At points such as this, it does seem that the "rhetoric" of tragedy has shaded perceptibly over into conception. Perhaps, once the problem of shared values becomes so crucial, rhetoric designed to create necessary belief actually becomes a part of the author's vision, even if, analytically, the two are always separable.

Many other elements of the novel function as rhetoric to establish the importance of McMurphy's fall, including the sense that it is not merely idiosyncratic, but somehow "true," universal in its implications and importance. Here is where Kesey has run into the most trouble with critics and general readers. Some of the objections seem merely matters of misreading, but others strike to the heart of what Kesey was trying to do. The Big Nurse, for example, has been seen as evidence of Kesey's "demeaning" attitude toward women, a charge that could be brought against Shakespeare because he created Lady Macbeth. For the dramatic requirements of the story, Nurse Ratched had to be very nearly an incarnation of evil, unthinking or otherwise. For Mac's struggle to seem important, the forces opposing him must not only seem nearly omnipotent, but must not be too "understandable," and never sympathetic. Here is one place, among many, where Milos Forman, and laudatory critics of the movie version, seem to me to have gone completely astray. The last thing Kesey needed was a "humanized portrait of Big Nurse," one that would make "viewers wish to know more about the character."[8] We have totally confused the exigencies of representation with life when we argue that given "the opportunity to run that ward in her own right, instead of having to manipulate the rabbity doctor, perhaps Miss Ratched might have run it more humanely."[9] To criticize Kesey for not showing how the Big Nurse got to be a "bitch" is to forget that she is not a real person but a character subordinated to the realization of a tragic plot. A little understanding, where villains are concerned, often courts artistic disaster; with the Big Nurse, as with Iago, the moral terms of the struggle need to be clear in order to prevent confusion.

There is little doubt, however, that Kesey's decision to incarnate the forces of oppression in Nurse Ratched led, under conditions that have become widespread since he wrote the novel, to the current view of the book is "sexist." Kesey needs a sharp confrontation; but why did he not, I have often been asked, make the director of the hospital a man, and the head nurse his instrument of control, herself in effect another victim? For the sake of immediacy and even plausibility, the threat to the men needs to be visible and present. But that is a weak consideration, since Kesey could have found a way around the problem. We may, finally, be forced to concede that Kesey saw something in the male-female conflict that was "to him the fatal Cleopatra for which he lost the world, and was content to lose it." Before so doing, however, it would be well to examine to what extent, in the text, we are given the impression that Nurse Ratched is the *cause* of all the men's problems. Surprisingly, we find that Kesey was careful to signal that she too is just a local manifestation of the pernicious desire to manipulate the lives of those too weak to resist. McMurphy's indictment of her occurs early in the novel; critics often quote it, but seldom quote enough.

> No, that nurse ain't some kinda monster chicken, buddy, what she is is a ball-cutter. I've seen a thousand of 'em, old and young, men and women. Seen 'em all over the country and in the homes— people who try to make you weak so that they can get you to toe the line, to follow their rules, to live like they want you to. . . .If you're up against a guy who wants to win by making you weaker instead of making himself stronger then watch for his knee, he's gonna go for your vitals. And that's what that old buzzard is doing. . . . [p. 58]

The words are important: "men and women . . . people . . . guy." Mac here speaks of what the Chief calls "the Combine": "It worked" on his father "for years."

> He was big enough to fight it for awhile. It wanted us to live in inspected houses. It wanted to take the falls. It was even in the tribe, and they worked on him. . . . Oh, the Combine's big—big. He fought it a long time till my mother made him too little to fight any more and he gave up. [p. 208]

His mother, a white woman, reflected the much wider forces that would destroy anyone; but she too was a pawn, and not by virtue of her sex. The Big Nurse, with all the other emasculating women in the book, is to be seen as the Chief sees her: a cog in a big grinding machine. It may be, as Addison C. Bross contends, that Kesey's is a "weary ideology."[10] But it clearly is not so much antifeminist as antiskinnerian.

The sexual problems of the men become, in this view, symptoms of weakness rather than causes. As Harding says, "There's not a man here that isn't afraid he is losing . . . his whambam. We. . . . can't even achieve masculinity in the rabbit world, that's how weak and inadequate we are" (p. 65). The causal relationship is clear: "weak" *therefore* impotent. All of the patients, except McMurphy, suffer from "flaws born in, or flaws beat in" (p. 14), like Pete Bancini, who has "been a Chronic all his life" because the doctor at his birth "pinched his skull" (p. 49). Nurse Ratched is just the efficiency expert in this "factory for the Combine" (p. 38); her cruel effectiveness, and the way she represents an entire society, make her, for Kesey's dramatic purposes, a perfect adversary for Mac. She is no more like a 'real" nurse than Iago is like a real soldier. That sort of critical naiveté should have disappeared with Thomas Rymer. Even so, there is nothing terribly implausible about her. She plays a part. Harding's ability to look her in the eye and tell her she is "full of so much bull shit" signals the independence that will enable him to leave the hospital. This is the goal on which the tragic impulse of the book depends. To have made the Big Nurse anything "less" than she is—more "human," more understandable—would have been to attenuate the force of the final victory, as deadly as it must be for Mac.

McMurphy's fate is indeed to become the kind of "savior" he scorns being treated as earlier in the novel (p. 182). All of the rhetoric of the book is designed to make plausible his final attack on the nurse, an act he cannot avoid, that will destroy him, and yet one that is out of character for the "cagey" Mac. Like most tragic figures, Mac's physical destruction is not identical to his doom. His tragic fate is to become fatally dependent on the men, to act in a way that makes clear that he is under the control of their needs and desires. What removes the "conversion" of Mac from the merely melodramatic is that he loses himself largely without recognizing—at least, so that *we* can see it—what is happening. Harding, usually a perceptive witness, errs for once when he argues, after the fishing trip, that "everything he's done was done with reason" (p. 254). We have seen no process of ratiocination indicating a calculated intention. In fact, at crucial points in the book, when Mac must take another rebellious step closer to lobotomy, what we see is a man who would avoid the confrontation if he could. In the shower room scene, Mac finally makes himself fight only when it is clear that Washington will not leave the men alone, will insist on soaping down the frantic and helpless George. McMurphy reacts, with "helpless, cornered despair" in his voice (p. 261). By keeping the thoughts of McMurphy hidden, by indicating his state of mind through signs the Chief interprets, Kesey manages simultaneously to achieve two difficult ends: we do not question the plausibility of Mac's actions, and we desire more and more that he continue them. Our fears for him are not allowed enough strength to conquer our stronger desires that he act to help the men. It is as if Kesey had discovered that a powerful tragic action could be constructed around the spectacle of a man who is destroyed because he is forced to become better than he was. All the authorial rhetoric at Kesey's command, including the hiding of certain things, had to be employed to prevent such a character from seeming merely pitiful or his destruction evidence of the multifarious horror of existence.

If we grant this description of the formal exigencies of the book, many complaints cease to have objective basis. Some have already been discussed: portrayal of the Nurse Ratched, the necessity for a somewhat oblique point of view, the alleged sexism. As a further test case, we might ask two simple questions to test the power of the hypothesis: why are the attendants black and why is there a sympathetic female nurse on the Disturbed ward?

The formal requirements I have sketched dictate that the lives of the of Chief and the other men must be made as miserable as possible, under the guise of "therapy," so that our desire for McMurphy to act will be strong. They must be watched, pushed around, even sexually abused, since depriving a person of sexual integrity is especially demeaning. Many of these activities the nurse could not plausibly engage in. The attendants, furthermore, must have sufficient motivation to commit such acts against men who are not only pitiful but largely helpless. Without spending the time to construct case histories for all the attendants, to make their hate *individually* plausible, Kesey hit upon the device of making them black and sketching in a kind of collective past for them. The first one watched as "his mother was raped in Georgia while his papa stood by tied to the hot iron stove with plow traces, blood streaming into his shoes . . . and he never grew an inch after" (p. 28). The choice of black attendants is a kind of shorthand; but Kesey was careful to include signals that *he* does not think of blacks as inherently cruel. Nurse Ratched had already rejected "thousands" because they did not "hate enough" (p. 27). The attendants are themselves victims, an important point to convey if one wants this confrontation to be not only unique and vivid but universal.

Like the nurse, their individual motives must not claim our interest. They must become independent of her influence, but act, rather, as her surrogates, vessels into which she has poured her own hate, which is never explained either.

Although she plays no real part in the action, the gentle nurse on the Disturbed ward serves a few of the same rhetorical purposes; she is primarily a device of disclosure. She tells Mac and the Chief that things are not everywhere as bad—though "a lot of it is"—as they are on Nurse Ratched's floor, but she also reminds them (and us) that the Big Nurse "has seniority" and can therefore do what she will. We learn of the possibilities for hope, are assured that the conflict in front of us is an important and general one, and then brought back immediately to the specific horrors of this situation. Although we may not think of this as we read, we are reassured that Kesey himself knows not all women are "bitches" and "ball cutters."

What remains when we have isolated the elements of Kesey's rhetoric? It is tempting to accept Kesey's own appraisal of his subject, to concur with his often quoted statement that "It's the Indian's story—not McMurphy's or Jack Nicholson's." But Kesey goes on, immediately, to suggest what I think is the real conception underlying the novel: "The emphasis should . . . be . . . on the battle going on in the Indian's mind between this man and the Combine that is loose in America."[11] The Chief, that is, controls our responses to the conflict by himself responding in ways that compel us to wish for McMurphy to act. Several critics have seen the similarities between Bromden, Nick Carraway, and even Melville's Ishmael; but they have not seen that the function of such narrators, no matter how extensive a role they play in the story (or sometimes by virtue of that role), is largely rhetorical: to control judgment and emotional response. The typical conclusion drawn from the example of these novels is that they are "'about' many things" and that the question, "whose *is* the story." cannot be answered.'[12] I have tried to demonstrate that when we ask, of Bromden's role as narrator, "for the sake of what," the answer is clearly to tell McMurphy's story as powerfully as possible. At any point in the novel, our fear or happiness for the Chief results almost entirely from how he views McMurphy.

The tragic conception, then, rests on McMurphy. Kesey is correct, in addition, to suggest that the conflict is between Mac and the Combine. The Big Nurse is a representative. But what gives the book its tragic power, what assimilates it to the great tragedies of all ages, is that the conflict is never merely *between* figures but leads to an internal struggle, mirrored at every point by the Chief's responses. Despite the vast dissimilarities between Kesey's novel and many of Shakespeare's tragedies, there are yet these two important similarities. The struggle with Nurse Ratched and the Combine becomes, inside McMurphy, a fight between two opposed principles of his being. Like Hamlet, McMurphy must become something other than what he was for the disaster—and the victory that accompanies high tragedy—to take place; and like many of Shakespeare's tragic heroes, McMurphy finds himself in a situation in which the ethically "correct" choice— although it will doom him—is one for which none of his previous experience has prepared him. When faced with the chance to escape at the end of the novel, he calmly turns the opportunity down: "I've took their best punch." Harding realizes that Mac does not "fully comprehend" what can happen to him (p. 298). But the Chief has already told us that "it was bound to be and would have happened in one way or another . . . there wasn't any way of him breaking his contract" (p. 296). The "bull goose loony" has become loony indeed; he can no longer care only for his own survival.

That such an "old fashioned" conception, based on convictions of human worth and the value of sacrifice, has provoked some jeers is not surprising. John Barsness summarized the problem:

> . . . it has become increasingly difficult to maintain that rugged frontiersman as hero, particularly since at midcentury the society approaches an overwhelming urbanization, and contemporary literature seems totally preoccupied with non-heroes whose landscapes are concrete and steel and whose primary characteristics are fixed upon failure. In such surroundings, faced with such assumptions, the hero is an anachronism, out of scale and out of kilter with contemporary *standards of truth.*[13]

That elements in any author's repertoire of rhetoric might seem outdated in time is not unusual. As Wayne Booth noted, "At one time the invention of the turtle, heading southwest across the highway in *The Grapes of Wrath* . . .

paralleling in his direction, his helplessness, his determination, and his pace the loads' hopeless, dogged lives, may seem brilliant. . . . But after twenty years, that turtle seems decidedly outmoded and obtrusive."[14] The task would seem to be to choose no element of rhetoric that will succumb to time. But realistic fiction demands some reflection of the way lives are lived at any time, and what seems enduring truth in one decade, or one century—say, the universality of the "battle of the sexes"—can evoke indignant protest in the next. In an age, like ours, of value confusion and increased social sensitivity, it may be that authors can please widely only by pleasing blandly, or will have to resort to that last refuge of value timidity, ambiguity.

Tragedy, in whatever medium, is neither bland nor timid. The spectacle of a human being experiencing his or her doom can be one of the most moving and powerful in art. But it cannot occur without the prior existence, or creation, of values shared between author and reader. The "institution" Croce pronounces to be at the bottom of the artistic transaction involves, in the tragic action, belief in the significance of human choice and human sacrifice.[13] Much that we have valued in the past, and still do, despite our critical theories of indeterminacy and plurisignificance, would be lost if we actually stopped lending credence, even if only for the nonce, to the systems of belief, often very different from our own, that inform, must inform, tragic works. This is not to say that we should credit any philosophy merely in order to gain a powerful artistic experience. But we must carefully distinguish between what is basic to the tragedian's conception and what beliefs he uses, as instruments, to make the experience possible. To hold artists responsible for every value that appears in their works may seem the height of enlightened social responsibility; but a failure to discriminate among intentions can destroy unnecessarily the noble treasure that is tragic art.

Notes

1. David Daiches, "What Was the Modern Novel?" *Critical Inquiry* I (1975): p. 813; Daiches first made the point in 1939, in his seminal study, *The Novel and the Modern World*; Virginia Woolf, "How It Strikes a Contemporary," *The Common Reader* (New York: Harcourt, Brace & World, 1953): pp. 243–244; David Hume, "Of Tragedy," *Four Dissertations* (New York: Garland, 1970): p. 199; Aristotle, *Poetics*, 26.

2. Sheldon Sacks, "Clarissa and the Tragic Traditions," *Studies in Eighteenth-Century Culture*, vol. 2, *Irrationalism in the Eighteenth Century*, ed. Harold E. Pagliaro (Cleveland & London: Case Western Reserve University Press, 1972): pp. 209–210; Robert V. Wess, "Modes of Fictional Structure in Henry Fielding and Jane Austen" (University of Chicago dissertation, 1970), Appendix i.

3. Hume, p, 199.

4. Elizabeth E. McMahan, "The Big Nurse as Ratchet: Sexism in Kesey's *Cuckoo's Nest*," *CEA Critic*, 37 (1975): p. 26; Leslie Horst, "Bitches, Twitches, and Eunuchs: Sex-Role

Failure and Caricature," *Lex et Scientia*, 13 (1977): p. 17; Peter G. Beidler, "From Rabbits to Men: Self Reliance in the Cuckoo's Nest," *Lex et Scientia*, 13 (1977): p. 56.

5. Robert Forrey, "Ken Kesey's Psychopathic Savior: A Rejoinder," *Modern Fiction Studies*, 21 (1975): p. 224. Not only is Forrey's judgment, suspect, he cannot get the chronology of the novel straight.

6. Horst, pp. 14, 17.

7. Ken Kesey, *One Flew Over the Cuckoo's Nest* (New York: Viking, 1964), p. 12. Subsequent references are in the text.

8. Marsha McCreadie, *"One Flew Over the Cuckoo's Nest:* Some Reasons for One Happy Adaptation," *Literature/Film Quarterly*, 5 (1977); p. 130.

9. McMahan, p. 27.

10. Addison C. Bross, "Art and Ideology: Kesey's Approach to Fiction," *Lex et Scientia*, 13 (1977): p. 61.

11. Ken Kesey, in Beverly Grunwald, "Kesey: A Sane View from 'Cuckoo's Nest,'" *Women's Wear Daily*, 18 December 1975, p. 1.

12. John W. Hunt, "Flying the Cuckoo's Nest: Kesey's Narrator as Norm," *Lex et Scientia*, 13 (1977): p. 27.

13. John Barsness, "Ken Kesey: The Hero in Modern Dress," *Bulletin of the Rocky Mountain Modern Language Association*, 23 (1969): pp. 27–33; reprinted in John C. Pratt, ed. *"One Flew Over the Cuckoo's Nest": Text and Criticism* (New York: Viking, 1973), p. 420 (my emphasis).

14. Wayne C. Booth, *The Rhetoric of Fiction* (Chicago: University of Chicago Press, 1961), p. 197.

15. Benedetto Croce, *Guide to Aesthetics*, translated by Patrick Romanell (Indianapolis & New York: Bobbs-Merrill, 1965), esp. pp. 3–27.

JACK HICKS

The Truth Even If It Didn't Happen:
One Flew Over the Cuckoo's Nest

I been silent so long now it's gonna roar out of me like floodwaters and you think the guy telling this is ranting and raving my *God;* you think this is too horrible to have really happened, this is too awful to be the truth! But, please. It's still hard for me to have a clear mind thinking on it. But it's the truth even if it didn't happen.

—Ken Kesey

Along with Norman Mailer and Allen Ginsberg, Ken Kesey represents the familiar unsettling artistic type.[1] For all three of these men, the once comforting borders separating the artist's work from his life are thoroughly dissolved. Mailer's prominence as a public figure, as the personal existential eye of the American hurricane, has dominated our attentions and his as well, and his work has surely suffered for it. But Ginsberg and Kesey are younger breeds and knottier figures: each has sought to transcend the category of poet or novelist by making his life a larger poem or fiction. Both Ginsberg and Kesey have become powerful cultural figures over the last decade, exemplars and proponents of a countercultural life-style, modes of being attractive to millions of young Americans. In the case of Kesey, especially, biographical concerns have overshadowed the writing, a fact demonstrated by the mere existence of Tom Wolfe's pop biography, *The Electric Kool-Aid Acid Test.*

Jack Hicks, *In the Singer's Temple: Prose Fiction of Barthelme, Gaines, Brautigan, Piercy, Kesey, and Kosinski* (Chapel Hill: University of North Carolina, 1981): pp. 161–176.

Wolfe's fascination with Kesey is natural. The man has lived at the heart of America, and his path has traced a chain of separations and returns. Born in 1935 in Colorado, Kesey migrated westward with his parents, several generations beyond the desperate vitality of the Okies. As Wolfe recalls, the elder Keseys were less unwilling adventurers than "entrepreneurs, who looked to the West Coast as a land of business opportunity."[2]

Kesey attended the University of Oregon and graduated in 1958. During his years in Eugene, he was a minor campus celebrity, an athlete, and an accomplished actor. In that time span, Kesey also came under the influence of the first of a series of prominent writer-teachers, James B. Hall. By 1958, when he entered Stanford University as a writing student. Kesey had completed a decent body of writing: short stories, one-act plays, poetry, and an unpublished novel about college athletics, *End of Autumn.* The years following (1959–1960) were a natural watershed for Kesey. He was fully engaged at Stanford, where he studied writing with Wallace Stegner, Frank O'Connor, and Malcolm Cowley; he lived and worked on Perry Lane, a quasi-bohemian Palo Alto artist's colony that provided a yeasty medium for his energies.[3]

Another unpublished novel, *Zoo* (1960), about San Francisco's North Beach, grew from Stanford's writing seminars, but an unlikely extracurricular experience as a medical volunteer was of far greater import to Kesey's life and writing. By this time Kesey had married and fathered a child and, like the classic graduate student, found his debts exceeding his income. Heeding a friend's tip that a government medical experiment paid human guinea pigs at the rate of seventy-five dollars a day, Kesey presented himself at Menlo Park Veterans Hospital, volunteering for experiments with "psychomimetic" drugs. Between spring of 1960 and spring of 1961, fully two years prior to psychologists Timothy Leary and Richard Alpert and their infamous experiments at Harvard, Kesey ingested a wide variety of psychedelic (mind-altering) drugs: LSD-25, psilocybin, mescaline, peyote, morning glory seeds, IT-290 (a meta-amphetamine)—the list swells to a small pharmacopoeia. Kesey extended the experiments beyond the hospital. Although the singular effects of his drug experiences would have been quite powerful enough, Kesey took a job as night attendant on a psychiatric ward at Menlo Park Hospital to supplement his income. As he recounts vividly in *One Flew Over the Cuckoo's Nest* and later in *Kesey's Garage Sale,* he was fascinated and disgusted by life on the ward; and he often raised his perceptions to a higher power with on-the-job doses of peyote.[4] Out of this experience grew his first and most successful novel, *One Flew Over the Cuckoo's Nest* (1962), and an entire life-style, neither of which the American public will soon forget.

In the years following. Ken Kesey's literary achievements have not matched the power of his first published novel. His second novel, *Sometimes a Great Notion* (1964), is longer and more ambitious but for great stretches nearly impenetrable.[5] Stage versions of *One Flew Over the Cuckoo's Nest* have continued for ten years: one starring Kirk Douglas in New York (1963) ran briefly and with little success; a revised version was well received in New York and San Francisco, where it ran very successfully until 1977. Between 1964 and 1973, Kesey published only letters and occasional fragments, which were riddled frequently by a kind of careless obscurantism, as if he were content to address only himself and a coterie of friends who already knew the language. Cynics have suggested that he may well have lost great sections of his mind to heavy drug use, like many young Americans of the time. More accurately, we can say that Kesey became bored with the possibilities of fiction after *Sometimes a Great Notion;* perhaps he came to believe that the novel was an inadequate form for recording his complex human experience. In the early 1970s, he worked mainly in the visual arts (films and drawings) and made recordings, and also co-edited (with Paul Krassner) *The Last Supplement* to the highly popular *Whole Earth Catalogue.*[6]

Deeply into the drug culture by 1964, Kesey invested much of his royalties in a remarkable coast-to-coast bus trip, documented in lurid detail by Wolfe. In the attendant deluge of legal harassments that followed, he was arrested several times for possession of marijuana and related offenses. Finally, in mid-1966, Kesey melodramatically faked a suicide and fled to Mexico, to avoid prosecution by the FBI. In October of that year, he "surrendered" to the authorities and soon thereafter served two concurrent three-month jail sentences in San Mateo, California. Many of Kesey's experiences are recounted in *Kesey's Garage Sale,* an uneven ragbag of memoirs, letters, interviews, and articles woven together by his own illustrations. As the title page very modestly suggests, aesthetic considerations are at least matched by a need for money, the book stemming from "The Ancient Search for AND Subsequent Discovery, Application, Loss and Reappearance of $$$."[7]

Following the acid hijinks that very nearly destroyed him as an artist, Kesey retired to a family dairy farm near Pleasant Hill Oregon—a move "up to the country" undertaken by a whole generation of young agrarian zealots and in many ways the precursor of the current evolution of interest in ecology and self-supporting communities. Unlike many others, Kesey was successful in building a family and a vocation, often from a blend of intense desire and a willing ignorance.

In 1975 he began writing seriously again and published "Abdul and Ebenezer" in *Esquire,* an essay on his early life among the cows, the first substantial writing in many years. Since that time, Kesey has been hard at work with a small circle of friends, and his renovated literary interest has led to the publishing of a "family" little magazine, *Spit in the Ocean (SITO). SITO* has been a vehicle for his most recent fiction, *Seven Prayers by Grandma Whittier,* a markedly biographical sequence of seven dense interior monologues by a loving grandmother among the crazies. It marks a daring shift in Kesey's art and, as John Clark Pratt notes, "Keseyphiles ... who appreciate him only for *Cuckoo's Nest* will be at least startled if not openly distressed."[8]

Ken Kesey's overriding passion in the last eighteen years, both personally and artistically, has been the qualities and possibilities of human consciousness and particularly the modes of literary rendering of every sort of mental state. This passion has been a constant element, from the fragments of the unpublished *Zoo* to those in the current *Seven Prayers by Grandma Whittier*. Frankly, one can learn as much in the turnings and tracings of his life as in his fiction, for we can read in the scattered lees of his past a cultural history of underground America in the 1960s. But my main interest here is in the particular artistic uses of those experiences in his single major fiction to date, *One Flew Over the Cuckoo's Nest*. More exactly, I wish to consider the novel as one of the few successful literary treatments of the alteration or expansion of human consciousness.

That the novel was warmly greeted seems indisputable. Critic Malcolm Cowley, teaching at Stanford during Kesey's stay, saw the promise in a rough, semifinished manuscript. He advised Kesey in a letter that the book contained "some of the most brilliant scenes I have ever read" and "passion like I've not seen in you young writers before." Thirteen years later, Cowley seemed to have renewed his estimate by including *One Flew Over the Cuckoo's Nest* in his Viking Critical Library series. Cowley's early appraisals strike me as correct: the novel is vividly and powerfully realized and, though Kesey remembers long scenes as coming "more easily to my hand than anything before or since," it was doggedly written and revised.[9]

His account of the novel's origin is an apocryphal variant among modern underground novelists. Much of Malcolm Lowry's *Under the Volcano* issued from the author's alcoholic deliriums; William Burroughs attributes the surreal qualities of *Naked Lunch* to his use of marijuana; his friend Jack Kerouac wrote much of his fiction—*On the Road* and *Dr. Sax*, for example—with the aid of benzedrine. Kesey's version differs only in detail, the drug of his choice being peyote, "because it was after choking down eight of the little cactus plants that I wrote the first three pages."[10] Actually, before his experiences with peyote, Kesey had been fumbling through the book, mainly because of problems with point of view. With the aid of Wallace Stegner at Stanford, he worked toward a resolution. A letter to Kesey's friend Ken Babbs recalls: "I am beginning to agree with Stegner, that it is truely [sic] the most important problem in writing. The book I have been doing on the lane is a third person work, but something was lacking. I was not free to impose my perception and bizarre eye on the god-author who is supposed to be viewing the scene. ... I am swinging around to an idea that

I objected strongly to at first; that the novelist to be at last true and free must be a diarist."[11]

So, at Stegner's suggestion, he shifted to a first-person narrative and, under the unsubtle pressures of peyote, the first three pages emerged as follows:

I think it way time to let somebody in on it, if they can stand it I can. I think I can. You must read about it in those advances those sheets you get every morning which have what they desire you to know. You got that same part that makes them a dime a sheet. Nothing else. I think it way time one of us tried to tell you and let you see what truely happened.

The basic story is this: one of us is dead, and it don't make much difference which one because you won't even remember and you just read it this morning at the bottom of the last page of that sheet you get. One dead. He dead. A man dead. Died in hospital. Died of Pneumonia. Exhasstion. Recent, once long ago, sometime way back, A Colonel in Europe. Oh yes.

That you get in you sheet and go right on with you business, running a tunge around a coffee cup edge. That much you can digest and puke not back up. But I think it way time somebody, me, told you. I have decided I can stand it if you can.

Let's go back to when he came in.

Let's go back to before he came in, the morning, so you can look around. It's all part of the filthy machinery and combine, anyway.

They out there. Black boys in white suits, up before I am to commit sex acts in the hall and get if moped up before I can get up to catch them. They are mopping when I come out of the dorm and they all look up at me, eyes out of a vacuum tube. They stick a mop at me and motion which way they figure me to go today, and I go. Behind me I can hear them humming hate and other death; they always hum it out loud around me, not because they hate me special, but because I don't talk and can't tell about it.

The big ward door is a funnel's bottom. We keep it locked so all the backlog won't come pouring in on us and suffocate us like ants in the bottom of an hour glass. When the big nurse comes through she close it quick behind her because they're out their pinching at her ass. She locks it with a sigh and swings a load of clanking bottles off her shoulder; she always keep them their in a fresh laundried pillow case and is inclined and grab one out at the tiniest provocation and administer to you right where you stand. For that reason I try to be on the good side of her and let the mop push me back to the wall as she goes by. "Home at last," I hear her say as she drags past and losses her pillowcase into a corner where it crashes, mixing everything. "What a night, what a night." She wipes her face and eyes like she dipping her hands in cold water. "What a relief to get back home," is what she say near me, because I don't talk.

Then she sight the colored boys. Wheoo, that's something different! She goes into a croach and advances on them where they huddled at the end of the corridor. My god, she gonna tear them black limb from limb! She swole till her back splitting out the white uniform, she let her arms get long enough to wrap around them five six times, like hairy tentacles. I hide behind the mop and think My god, this time they're gonna tear each other clean apart and leave us alone. But just she starts mashing them and they start ripping at her belly with mop handles all the patients come pouring out of the dorms to check on the hullabaloo and the colored boys fall in line behind the nurse, and smiling, they herd the patients down to shave. I hide in the mop closet and listen to the shriek and grind of shaver as it tears the hide off one then another; I hide there, but after a while one colored boy just opens out his nostrils like the big black ends of two funnells and snuffs me right into his belly. There he hold me wrapped in black guts while two other black bastards in white in white go at my face with one of the murder combines. I scream when they touch my temples. I can control the screaming until they get to the temples and start screwing the electrodes in, then I always scream and the last thing I hear that morning is the big nurse whooping a laughing and scuttling up the hall while she crash patients out of her way with the pillowcase of broken glass and pills. They hold me down while she jams pillowcase and all into my mouth and shoves it down with a mophandle.[12]

Self-disordered states of consciousness may be initially helpful for a writer, but some sort of refining and revision is always necessary. In this case, revisions brought the style and structure of the novel into focus. Comparing the early and final manuscripts, we can note several changes. Primarily, the difference is one of telling and showing. Note that Kesey places emphasis in the original on Chief Bromden's *narration* of events, on the oral qualities of his tale. Kesey is more concerned here with capturing the semiliterate qualities of Bromden's speech, with creating an idiolect replete with intentionally awkward and agrammatical constructions, phonetic spellings, and dropped verbs. His speech is clanging and oddly awkward to the ear, but it is also more metaphorical than the final version ("The big ward door is a funnel's bottom" [334];

this is yet another narrative detail placing the narrator squarely between events and the reader. The early manuscript is generally unfocused: it lacks the detail allowing us to see characters, observe action, overhear dialogue.

By contrast, the final manuscript is more sharply focused and more thoroughly dramatized. Emphasis is properly placed on establishing vividly differentiated characters in a concrete situation. Although the black attendants are phantasms in the pervasive fog of Bromden's tale in the early version, revision focuses them on the stage of the narrator's consciousness. They are described more trenchantly, their actions made specific, they are given idiomatic dialogue: "Here's the Chief, the *soo*-pah Chief, fellas. Ol' Chief Broom. . . . Haw, you look at 'im shag it? Big enough to eat apples off my head an' he mine me like a baby" (3). Because the drama of Bromden's consciousness is Kesey's main interest, he reshapes his narrator into a less obviously mediating character. Much dialect is dropped and metaphor diminished in favor of a more fully dramatized narrative. The final focus early in the novel is on Chief Bromden's acutely heightened but passive *state of consciousness;* his narrative is a distorted, detailed film on which a menacing world leaves its grain and shadow. "They're out there" is buried in the second page of Kesey's first draft. This phrase opens the completed novel, establishing the major emphasis on Bromden as pure receiver: mute for twenty years, he can only receive the world and have if impinge upon his consciousness, and his only weapons are scrambling devices. Hallucinations, nightmares, and fantasies heighten characters and scenes that press on his mind, and his last retreat is into the fog that descends regularly to seal him deeper in his own insanity.

The state of Chief Bromden's consciousness is clinically termed paranoid schizophrenia. He is insane. He can perceive the world only in fragments that happen to him, fragments that assume menacing cartoon shapes from which unconsciousness is the only refuge. Terry G. Sherwood accurately reads *One Flew Over the Cuckoo's Nest* as a kind of comic strip, the aesthetic of which is "that of the caricaturist, the cartoonist, the folk artist, the allegorist. Characterization and delineation of incident are inked in bold, simple, exaggerated patterns."[13] But this is a recurring mode of perception limited to Bromden's early consciousness. Things are unreal for him, "like a cartoon world, where the figures are flat and outlined in black, jerking through some kind of goofy story that might be really funny if it weren't for the cartoon figures being real guys" (31). Thus the world of the asylum, rendered through Bromden's schizoid mind, is a black and white world, one in which people are dehumanized, represent or embody qualities, or exist as static states. The Chief's hallucinations and nightmares further define the specific threat of each character. Our first glimpse of Big Nurse, for example, occurs when she enters the ward to find the black attendants loafing:

I can see she's clean out of control She's going to tear the black bastards limb from limb, she's so furious. She's swelling up, swells till her back's splitting out the white uniform and she's let her arms section out long enough to wrap around the three of them five, six times. . . . So she really lets herself go and her painted smile twists, stretches to an open snarl, and she blows up bigger and bigger, big as a tractor, so big I can smell the machinery inside the way you smell a motor carrying too big a load. I hold my breath and figure, My God this time they're gonna do it! This time they gonna let the hate build up too high and overloaded and they're gonna tear one another to pieces before they realize what they're doing!

But just as she starts crooking those sectioned arms around the black boys and they go ripping at her underside with the mop handles, all the patients start coming out of the dorms to check on what's the hullabaloo, and she has to change back before she's caught, in the shape of her hideous real self. [4–5]

Bromden's nightmares caricature truth even more. On the evening of the "vegetable" Blastic's death, he has a terrible premonitory vision. As he enters sleep, he has a vision of the entire ward being lowered into a deep, hellish chamber: "a whole wall slides up, reveals a huge room of endless machines stretching clear out of sight, swarming with sweating, shirtless men running up and down catwalks, faces blank and dreamy in firelight thrown from a hundred blast furnaces. . . . Huge brass tubes disappear upward in the dark. Wires run to transformers out of sight. Grease and cinders catch on everything, straining the couplings and motors and dynamos red and coal black" (83–84). Out of this inferno, a gigantic worker swings a hook toward Blastic, the man's face:

so handsome and brutal and waxy like a mask, wanting nothing. I've seen a million faces like it.

He goes to the bed and with one hand grabs the old Vegetable Blastic by the heel and lifts him straight up like Blastic don't weigh more'n a few pounds; with the other hand the worker drives the hook through the tendon back of the heel, and the old guy's hanging there upside down, his moldy face blown up big, scared, the eyes scummed with mute fear. He keeps flapping both arms and the free leg till his pajama top falls around his head. . . . The worker takes the scapel and slices up the front of Old Blastic with a clean swing and the old man stops thrashing around. I expect to be sick, but there's no blood or innards falling out like I was looking to see—just a shower of rust and ashes, and now and again a piece of wire or glass. [85]

Chief Bromden's aberrations are a form of peculiarly heightened truth. He *does* foresee Blastic's death accurately. His paranoid vision of Big Nurse, recurringly depicted as a mechanical, domineering figure entombed in ice or glass, is likewise accurate in its symbolism. She oversees this world from a raised glass booth, a doubly threatening figure who is obviously in control and thoroughly shut off from the human consequences of her power: "What she dreams of there in the center of those wires is a world of precision efficiency and tidiness like a pocket watch with a glass back" (27).

When the knowledge of what goes on around him is too intense for his consciousness to transfigure by distortion, the fog descends. The device is effective under Kesey's hand and works in several ways. Because Bromden is both paranoid and passive, he imagines that Big Nurse regularly turns on the fog machine to hide her machinations. And it is here that she is caught up in the web of institutions impinging upon and blinding Bromden's consciousness. The army, Department of Interior, his Anglo mother, Big Nurse—all are aspects of "The Combine," "a huge organization that aims to adjust the Outside as well as she has the Inside" (26). The fog is a paranoid metaphor, a concrete figure of fear and secrecy, of the threat that "they" are systematically deceiving you. But the fog is also a grotesque comfort representing unconsciousness for Bromden. As he recalls his army days, "You had a choice: you could either strain and took at things that appeared in front of you in the fog, painful as it might be, or you could relax and lose yourself" (125).

Briefly then, this is the state of the Chief's consciousness before Randall McMurphy arrives on the ward. Bromden, who was born a half-blooded Columbian Indian of immense stature, has been worn down by life. Evidently, he has been deaf and dumb fur the last twenty years, consigned to sweep the floors of this microcosmic ward and unable to perceive people humanly or to leave his imprint on the world. But inmate McMurphy's appearance alters much of this.

Bromden's first impression of Randall McMurphy is that of a vital, protean figure. He strikes the diminished narrator as being like his lost, disgraced father, a full-blooded Columbian Indian chief. But, more than a surrogate father, McMurphy is a cartooned, holy con man: "The way he talks, his wink, his loud talk, his swagger all remind me of a car salesman or a stock auctioneer—or one of those pitchmen you see on a sideshow stage, out there in front of his flapping banners, standing there in a striped shirt with yellow buttons, drawing the faces off the sawdust like a magnet" (12–13) Like the best American con men, McMurphy finally sells himself. He does not offer a product but evokes and embodies a way of life to ponder and desire.

His effect on the patients is electric. They are collectively dominated by Big Nurse and her staff, but he very quickly sets off human responses in them; his impulse runs precisely counter to Big Nurse's. He runs toward vitality, spontaneity, friendship, and warmth—the accumulated detritus that makes a human life and a person. By the midpoint of *One Flew Over the Cuckoo's Nest*, he has propelled his fellow patients into a major act of resistance. Randall Patrick McMurphy (Revolutions Per Minute) is exuberant; through his efforts near the end of a group therapy session, the fog parts for Bromden, and he recognizes that his fellows are also fogged in: "Maybe Billy's hid himself in the fog too. Maybe all the guys finally and forever crowded back into the fog" (128). Billy Bibbit and Colonel Matterson, Old Pete and his own wrecked alcoholic father, their "faces blow past in the fog like confetti" (131).

Bromden has a sudden, insightful hallucination of "that big red hand of McMurphy's . . . reaching out into the fog and dropping down and dragging the men up by their hands, dragging them blinking into the open. First one, then another, then the next. Right on down the line of Acutes, dragging them out of the fog till there they stand, all twenty of them, raising not just for watching TV, but against the Big Nurse, against her trying to send McMurphy to Disturbed, against the way she's talked and acted and beat them down for years" (134). In those hands and faces, Bromden sees a fused image of all that has systematically driven him into the fog. For the first time in twenty years, he can act. With Bromden casting the deciding vote, the ward rebels and turns on the television to watch the World Series (one of the stranger acts of rebellion for our time). They see, appropriately, a cartoon: "A picture swirls into the screen of a parrot out on the field singing razor blade songs" (137). Enraged, Big Nurse turns the set off, "and we're sitting there line-up in front of that blanked-out TV set, watching the gray screen just like we could see the baseball game clear as day, and she's ranting and screaming behind us" (138). As the first part of the novel ends, the group is self-conscious for the first time, watching a small blank screen out of which each man has been dragged into the world, white and shining, by Randall McMurphy.

As their first handshake telegraphs to Bromden, McMurphy's function is to feed his consciousness, to aid in psychic recovery: "My hand commenced to feel peculiar and went to swelling up out there on my stick of an arm, like he was transmitting his own blood into it. It rang with blood and power" (24). Paramount among his influences on Bromden is the recovery of memory. In *One Flew Over the Cuckoo's Nest*, Kesey suggests repeatedly that memory, knowing one's individual and collective pasts, is a key to any sense of present or future. For patients like Ruckly, "memory whispers somewhere in that jumbled machinery" (16). Significantly, the recovery of memory for Bromden is a process of reimagining the sources of his own pain and paralysis. McMurphy triggers him and, as the novel progresses, Bromden experiences vital parts of his past in flashbacks. Flashbacks are a familiar technique for the first-person novelist. They permit him to offer the reader a past for his characters, a sequence of motivation. But in addition, each time Bromden experiences these dreams of key moments in his past, he retrieves a part of himself from the fog and becomes more conscious. His flashbacks are poignant and often painful. They involve reenacting the oppression and destruction of his father by his mother, the wasting of his tribe by various U.S. government agencies, and his own paralysis and emasculation.

Very gradually, as Bromden reclaims his past, his sense of himself and of things beyond himself evolves. He perceives differently. For one thing, he is conscious of himself in relation to a larger world: "I realized I still had my eyes shut. . . . I was scared to look outside. Now I had to open them. I looked out the window and saw for the first time how the hospital was out in the country" (153). For another, he sees a more humanized existence around him. People are no longer cartoons: "For the first time in years I was seeing people with none of that black outline they used to have" (154). In fact, Bromden has almost ceased to see the world as a stream of aberrated and unrelated phenomena. He can form associations, in this context, the purely associative cognition demonstrated by Matterson suddenly becomes sensible: "'Mexico is . . . the walnut'. . . . I want to yell out to him Yes, I see: Mexico *is* like the walnut; it's brown and hard and you feel if with your eye and it *feels* like the walnut! You're making sense, old man, a sense of your own. You're not crazy the way they think. Yes, I see" (129). He can relate events in the present with his own past. At the ward windows, for instance, Bromden sees that "the stars up close to the moon were pale; they got brighter and braver the farther they got out of the circle of light ruled by the giant moon. It called to mind how I noticed the exact same thing when I was off on a hunt with Papa" (155).

So Randall McMurphy serves as an energy source and an inspiration to Bromden and his fellows. They become less lethargic and more interested in their own sexuality and physical existence. But mainly, they become able and willing to struggle for life. Through McMurphy's prodding and coaxing, they venture into the world outside, the occasion being a deep-sea fishing expedition. By this time, McMurphy has become aware of the paradox of his existence in the asylum. The inmates are voluntary admissions but lack the psychic abilities to sign themselves out; he is *committed* but can be released only on Big Nurse's judgment. What follows is a sequence establishing McMurphy as a kind of holy con man who "sells himself" by giving up his life for the patients on the ward. For if Kesey's protagonist is the true American hero, the confidence man, he is also an avatar, a Christ —the healer, literally a fisher of men. A pattern of Christ-like suffering is carefully wrought in the background of *One Flew Over the Cuckoo's Nest*. Early in his tenure on the ward, while examining the electroshock table, McMurphy is told: "You are strapped to a table, shaped, ironically, like a cross, with a crown of electric thorns" (67). Later, as he is about to receive his first shock treatment on that very table, he regards the graphite conductant: "Anointest my head with conductant. Do I get a crown of thorns? ... They put those things like headphones, crown of silver thorns over the graphite at his temples'" (270).

The fishing scene is an extended figure of Christ and his disciples, an instance of McMurphy as fisher of men. Here we see that McMurphy is Kesey's laughing Christ—profane, spontaneous, and above all loving, leading men not to immortality but back into this physical world. After a series of trials, the men are safely at sea on an old fishing craft. They repeatedly request McMurphy's aid in handling the boat and landing fish, but he laughingly refuses them. Imperiled by hostile men, seas, weather, and fish, they survive and flourish as a community. By the end of the trip, Bromden notices that the men have been energized by the trip, but the robust McMurphy looks "beat and worn out" (243). His men are psychically cannibalizing him. Slightly later, the Chief notes "the windshield reflected an expression that was allowed only because he figured it'd be too dark for anybody in the car to see, dreadfully tired and strained and *frantic*, like there wasn't enough time left for something he had to do" (245). And finally, part 4 of the novel concludes as directly as possible: "his relaxed, good-natured voice doled out his life for us to live, a rollicking past full of kid fun and drinking buddies and loving women and barroom battles over meager honors—for all of us to dream ourselves into" (245).

Near the end of the novel, after McMurphy has been quieted by repeated electroshocks and is about to be lobotomized, his purpose has become even clearer to Chief Bromden. By this time the Chief is fully conscious, able to articulate the peculiar insistence that his friend feels to defy Big Nurse and go the full route of consciousness reduction by lobotomy:

> We couldn't stop him because we were the ones making him do it. It wasn't the nurse that was forcing him, it was our need that was making him push himself slowly up from sitting, his big hands driving down on the leather chair arms, pushing him up, rising and standing like one of those moving-picture zombies, obeying orders beamed at him from forty masters. It was us that had been making him go on for weeks, keeping him standing long after his feet and legs had given out, weeks of making him wink and grin and laugh and go on with his act long after his humor had been parched dry between two electrodes. [305]

At this point, Bromden and the entire ward have changed radically. Following McMurphy's attack on Big Nurse and his subsequent lobotomy, many of the Acutes have signed themselves out or otherwise taken control of their lives. Big Nurse's domain is toppled, and Randall McMurphy's mind must be dimmed, extracted as fealty. Bromden performs a final action, the mercy-killing of the burned-out husk that remains of McMurphy. He quickly assimilates his master through a series of ritual actions. Like McMurphy, he becomes protean, a water force that breaks through walls of glass or ice. In a repetition of McMurphy's earlier actions, Bromden seizes the control panel and hurls it through the window—one of the many ritual cleansings and baptisms in the novel: "The glass splashed out in the moon, like a bright cold water baptizing the sleeping earth" (310). Bromden escapes northward, now a con man and storyteller himself, but we recognize at the novel's conclusion that the only certitude is Bromden's new consciousness. What lies ahead is at best tentative, but it is certain that Bromden has come through whole and sound:

> I might go to Canada eventually, but I think I'll stop along the Columbia on the way. I'd like to check around Portland and Hood River and The Dalles to see if there's any of the guys I used to know back in the village who haven't drunk themselves goofy. I'd like to see what they've been doing since the government tried to buy their right to be Indians. I've even heard that some of the tribe have took to building their old ramshackle wood scaffolding all over that big million-dollar hydroelectric dam, and are spearing salmon in the spillway. I'd give something to see that. Mostly, I'd just like to look over the country around the gorge again, just to bring some of it clear in my mind again.
>
> I been away a long time. [311]

Notes

1. The epigraph on page 161 is taken from Ken Kesey's *One Flew Over the Cuckoo's Nest* (New York: Viking, 1962): p. 8.

2. Tom Wolfe, *The Electric Kool-Aid Acid Test* (New York: Farrar, Straus & Giroux, 1968), p. 88.

3. John C. Pratt's introduction and chronology in Ken Kesey, *One Flew Over the Cuckoo's Nest; Text and Criticism*, edited by Pratt (New York: Viking, 1973), provide much of the available biographical information on Kesey. See also the special Ken Kesey issue of *Northwest Review*, published in book form as *Kesey*, edited by Michael Strelow (Eugene: Northwest Review Books, 1977).

4. Ken Kesey, *Kesey's Garage Sale* (New York: Viking, 1973): p. 7.

5. Kesey, *Sometimes a Great Notion* (New York: Viking, 1964).

6. Kesey and Paul Krassner, eds., *The Last Supplement to the Whole Earth Catalogue* (San Francisco: Portola Institute, 1971).

7. Kesey, *Kesey's Garage Sale*, p. iii.

8. Two "prayers" appear in *Kesey*, edited by Michael Strelow, pp. 99–166; Pratt's comments are also in "On Editing Kesey: Confessions of a Straight Man," in *Kesey*, p. 10. "Abdul and Ebenezer" appeared in *Esquire* (March 1976), pp. 55–59.

9. Kesey, "Letter to Ken Babbs," in *One Flew Over the Cuckoo's Nest,* edited by Pratt, p. 337. See also Malcolm Cowley's article, "Ken Kesey at Stanford," in *Kesey,* edited by Michael Strelow, pp. 1–4.

10. Kesey, *Kesey's Garage Sale,* p. 7.

11. Kesey, "Letter to Ken Babbs," quoted in *One Flew Over the Cuckoo's Nest,* edited by Pratt, p. 338.

12. Kesey, "An Early Draft of the Opening Scene of *One Flew Over the Cuckoo's Nest,*" in *One Flew Over the Cuckoo's Nest,* edited by Pratt, pp. 333–335.

13. Terry G. Sherwood, *"One Flew Over the Cuckoo's Nest* and the Comic Strip," *Critique,* 13 (Winter 1971): p. 97.

WILLIAM C. BAURECHT

Separation, Initiation, and Return: Schizophrenic Episode in One Flew Over the Cuckoo's Nest

Ken Kesey's *One Flew Over the Cuckoo's Nest* (1962) portrays sexual mythology as a primary motif in the individual's struggle for consciousness and to become free from institutional oppression in contemporary America. The use of a "schizophrenic episode" as a central stylistic and thematic device illustrates Kesey's idealized perception of modern heroism. Kesey portrays our national ideology of virile heroism in a story of democracy's triumph in true brotherhood. Two men. Chief Bromden and Randle Patrick McMurphy, come to love each other profoundly. Herein is the novel's radical departure from tradition. In our culture the portrayal of real love between men, not typical comradeship or male bonding, is difficult, if not nearly impossible, to achieve artistically and believably, because male affection is suspect.

The novel dramatizes a resurrection ritual through the narrator's *schizophrenic episode*. Kesey's central consciousness, Broom, is first of all a victim of racism. He is rescued by McMurphy, a messiah who shows him and the men in the ward the "way home." Chief Bromden repeatedly creates his own womb when he withdraws into his fog, wherein he is finally purified by the love of his messiah. Haunted by an image of his "giant" father, Broom must learn to accept his father as chief and refuse to replicate his father's dissipation from that "giant" into the racist culture's expected image of an alcoholic Indian. Broom's centering episode is in his discovery of true and unrestrained love for another

The Midwest Quarterly: A Journal of Contemporary Thought, Volume 23, Number 3 (Spring 1982): pp. 279–293.

male. At the novel's end Broom pursues an American pastoral ideal by fleeing north to Canada rather than remaining on the battleground that is mundane society. Broom rejects victimhood in a heroic male mode. He smothers the corpse-like martyr, McMurphy, in a lover-like embrace, smashes his way out of the asylum, and dashes north to open country. Some day Broom may return to the mundane world of America, without a woman, and become responsible for his brothers' welfare. If he returns he will be forced by history to engage in un-romantic political activism rather than in revolutionary, messianic, warrior-like activism. Sitting behind a desk with a pen is, after all, not the romantic image of heroism manning the barricades or leading the charge of comrades, illustrated so vividly by McMurphy's heroism. If Broom ever becomes a political activist, which he implies he may become, ending the novel with such a commitment would not structurally resolve, with literary tightness, the McMurphy-Broom love, nor would such an ending, although required by political realism, cor-respond to the mythology of male independent action. But the novel does end with a strong emphasis upon the central motif of male love. Finally, evil is located in clearly-defined external sources of oppression, rituals, and ideologies in American culture that are collectively called the Combine, the grim reaper of prevailing linear consciousness, in Kesey's transcendental world view.

　　One Flew Over the Cuckoo's Nest is a distinctly American novel because it is clear that no other culture could have produced it, given the novel's distinct mythology and ethos derived from the Western. Ken Kesey's work graphically portrays American masculinity snared in its myth of individual possibility, i.e. rugged individualism. Myth is a multifaceted cultural and psychic phenom-enon. In this essay I use "myth" both to mean a notion or half-truth which so captivates one's emotions that it becomes a religious verity and (in Richard Slotkin's words) an "intelligible mask of that enigma called the 'national char-acter.'" The American democratic dream renders one equal in *potentia* to all others. Accordingly, *One Flew Over the Cuckoo's Nest* is a tragic portrayal of a working-class hero's moral ascension and the implications for contemporary American males of that messianic encounter with society's limitations upon personal freedom. Ken Kesey endows his hero, Randle Patrick McMurphy, with mythic stature, using exclusively American literary allusions and associa-tions drawn from the Western novel and film, and from American folklore. As Dixon Wecter, in *The Hero in America* (1941), argues, the authentic American hero must be a man of the people and not one who sets himself up as above the people. A fact of the American character is that Americans trust only humanly flawed heroes, and simultaneously they look to those who inspire them to seek their potential and to those who give them hope.

　　Randle Patrick McMurphy is such a democratic hero, but he is not a *macho* archetype embodying the American male's capacity for violence and misogyny as most critics who have written about the novel contend. Rather,

McMurphy is something quite different, revealing both the dominant American male literary myth of "the territory ahead" and a repressed homoeroticism that exceeds in emotional intensity Leslie Fiedler's provocative, but accurate, thesis that male bonding in American literature (especially between a white protagonist and an ethnic minority companion) reveals a cultural denial of mature loving male relationships in which American men can engage. McMurphy does represent certain sexist and violent tendencies, which upon close scrutiny, however, are transcended by his symbolic heroism and his humanity. If this were not true, then it would be easy to categorize McMurphy as a reprehensible American male fantasy, a stereotype from out of that unique American creation, the Western.

On the other hand, McMurphy is an outlaw. It is understandable that American male mythology so admires and is so compelled by the ethos of the outlaw as hero because the United States is a nation founded by European outlaws and renegades, malcontents, and uncommonly stubborn and idealistic deviants who demanded something more than European institutions provided them (especially in the nineteenth century), who pursued their idealism, and who insisted that their wills were primary determinants of behavior. America, consequently, became the "City upon a hill," the *garden* in mythology, the retreat of plenty in a festering and hopelessly fallen world. The outlaw lives on the open road and thrives outside society's prevailing bourgeois institutions. Chief Bromden is also an outlaw; and when he escapes the ward, his "territory ahead" becomes Canada, because in the American male myth there must always be a place *outside to escape* to as man seeks freedom, self-integrity, and self-respect. The West is no longer a journey *outward*, a direction toward a frontier of sparsely inhabited space, it is a journey *inward* for Kesey, but also a journey above the forty-ninth parallel, where the garden may exist in myth because the people whom one will meet there are not absorbed in all of the same oppressive cultural assumptions and because there is much sparsely populated land with abundant timber, lakes, mountains, and wildlife.

Love, not power, glory, *machismo*, or the masculine imperial will, is the key to the meaning of *One Flew Over the Cuckoo's Nest* as an expression of a national male mythology. Climaxing in McMurphy's attack on Big Nurse, he totally forgets himself in his act of love for the men in the ward. His momentary insanity, in the vain attempt to exact revenge for Billy Bibbit's death, underscores the prevalence of injustice in society's dictation of behavioral norms and in man's helplessness to stand alone against those norms. No greater love hath any man than to give his life for his comrade or comrades. This is the key to Broom's "schizophrenic episode" and to the remission of his culturally prescribed insanity. Because Ken Kesey does not directly reveal McMurphy's thoughts and motives, one must examine the implications of what he does, and everything he does is in relation to Chief Bromden.

In the oral tradition of the tall tale, Chief Bromden tells us the story of McMurphy as he observes it. Its authenticity is established by his peripheral presence on the scene. He speaks to no one through most of the story except to McMurphy and, at the end, to the men. The tale filters through the Chief's schizophrenic consciousness. Unlike the tall tale which begins ex post facto, we have the feeling that Broom is telling us most of the story as it takes place; therefore we are more intimately drawn in. The tale is a resurrection myth whose central incident is a rescue, a typical motif of the tall tale. As a disciple, Broom, in a sense, recites the gospel of McMurphy according to Chief Bromden, or St. Bromden, if we are to assume that through his resurrection Bromden's salvation leads him to become a teacher of the gospel. Because of the story's length and its verbal and psychological complexity, it is, of course, not an orthodox tall tale, though largely dependent upon its tradition.

In lighting upon Bromden as a narrator, Kesey brilliantly created a tightly structured novel in which form and content are inseparable. The Chief as narrative consciousness accounts for the novel's understatement and for the universal suggestiveness regarding masculinity in American culture. Kesey believes that the Chief is a creation of Indian consciousness, a spiritual source with which Kesey had communed while writing the novel. Because Kesey had never known an Indian, he had no living model to imitate as he wrote the book. Kesey states that at first he credited Broom's creation to the mind altering, transcendental influences of peyote which he had used while writing. Later Kesey changed his mind, explaining that the Chief's spirit exists, and that he merely relayed the spirit's consciousness. Kesey thinks of himself as a *transmitter* rather than as a creator; this is in accordance with his transcendental consciousness.

> After years of getting off behind being prognosticator of what seemed to me a stroke of genius, if not a masterstroke, I was notified that a certain spirit was getting a little peeved at the telegraph operator for being so presumptuous as to take credit for messages coming in, as though the receiver were sending the signal.

What Kesey means here is that Chief Bromden was not a personal creation but a spirit of the Indian within American culture speaking through Kesey. The message he finally received from the spirit was: "I . . . am the entity that spoke through your words. It was my task to acquaint your people with this particular transgression upon the human soul. You availed yourself of the transmission. If you need something of which to be proud, be proud of this availability." I do not cite this to be accused of the intentional fallacy. The point is this, the metaphor (while, for Kesey, the spirit is probably *real*) excellently depicts the psychic consciousness of the artist. Kesey received the resonance of the male dilemma diffused throughout American culture from the consciousness (he calls it a spirit) which created Broom. The fact that Broom is an Indian adds dimension to the male dilemma, but, as in high art. Broom is more *everyman* than specifically Indian. The implications and motifs become universal. Ironically, in this tall tale an Indian is a hero, not just a supporting actor, a side-kick-Tonto, or an antagonist. Bromden's point of view gives thematic dimension as well as credence to the story.

What adds further dimension to the mythic interpretation of the novel are the parallels between a *Schizophrenic episode and a mythic hero journey*. Because of these parallels we can rely upon Broom's authenticity and the clarity of his truth, even though he is classified a schizophrenic by society. Joseph Campbell describes the parallels between the two phenomena in which the imagery is identical. He breaks the schizophrenic episode into five stages of imagery. The first stage is a "break away or departure from the local social order and context." The second stage is "a long, deep retreat inward and backward, as it were, in time, and inward, deep into the psyche." Third, a series of "darkly terrifying" encounters within the depths of one's private inner world follow. Fourth, for those who will spontaneously reemerge from their schizophrenic episode, "encounters of a centering kind, fulfilling, harmonizing, giving new courage," reintegrate the personality. Fifth, and finally, a rebirth journey into a new life integrated into reality ends the episode. These are the stages through which Broom has passed in the novel, and McMurphy is his centering force and his guide. The universal formula of a mythological hero journey is described by Campbell as separation, initiation, and return. Again, Broom takes this journey through McMurphy's tutelage, a role a psychotherapist frequently plays, or, in a primitive culture, a role played by a shaman.

As a prelude to Broom's rebirth as a man, he again begins to love another and himself. The simple act of receiving a package of chewing gum from McMurphy causes Broom to desist in his strategy of bizarre behavior that society labels schizophrenia. A simple act reveals McMurphy's loving and sensitive nature. He conquers Broom's fifteen years of silence. Broom's mask is lowered as he says "thank you." Brotherhood is what Broom most desperately needs to feel. McMurphy's act is a combination of *philia* (friendship, brotherly love) and *agape* ("love which is devoted to the welfare of the other"). Although one could argue that the underlying mythology in the novel is the traditional flight from women expressed in American literature and popular culture, the book graphically portrays as well the emotional withdrawal of men from themselves that they are encouraged to adopt. In his second novel, *Sometimes a Great Notion* (1964), Kesey focused upon the depth of homoeroticism within a family, which may be possible and is necessary if men are to adopt polymorphous emotional lives, but Kesey began his exploration of this phenomenon in *One Flew Over the Cuckoo's Nest.*

Broom immediately realizes the kindness, openness, and unselfishness of McMurphy's interest in him. Broom is so moved that he wants to say that he loves McMurphy, but society's restrictions upon the expression of homoeroticism is so relentless, intransigent, and punitive that Broom is unable to tell his friend the significance of receiving the package of gum. Broom tried to think of something to say to McMurphy, but the only thought which occurred "was the kind of thing one man can't say to another because it sounds wrong in words." Broom then explosively confesses his history, explaining the destruction and death of his "giant" father through alcoholism after society stole his way of life and denied the validity of what he was. This self-revelation fatigues Broom, who momentarily feels embarrassed and defensive. He tries to pass off what he has said as crazy. McMurphy ironically agrees that it *is* crazy, but says that it *does* make sense. Racism and economics make Broom's father's experience seem crazy.

Broom's bizarre behavior is a survival strategy that, like all behavior labeled *schizophrenia*, is invented in order to endure an intolerable situation. Psychiatrist R. D. Laing explains that the schizophrenic "cannot make a move, or make no move, without being beset by contradictory and paradoxical pressures and demands, pushes and pulls, both internally from himself, and externally from those around him. He is, as it were, in a position of checkmate." Temporarily, Broom publicly steps out of his adopted, protective role of schizophrenia. He realizes the truth of McMurphy's assurance that he is not actually crazy, that to the contrary, he is a victim.

Broom's blighted spirit then blooms with *philia* and *agape*, no longer is he defined only as a simple tool he constantly pushes to sweep clean the ward. He is elated and wishes to touch his new friend, but again taboo inhibits him from responding as his spirit urges. Broom wonders if he is homosexual but knows that it is a lie. He thinks, "That's one fear hiding behind another." (p. 210) The fear of latent homosexuality lurks behind the fear of wanting to embrace his friend as an expression of love, in order to show his appreciation and vulnerability, and to allow affection to pass between them physically. The root of this fear is the primary terror of males to express vulnerability, softness, and the need to be comforted. Men may lose face among other men if they display such human frailty. The male child is cast out, condemned under Medusa's gaze to maintain physical inviolability vis-a-vis other males. This taboo denies Broom the fullness of thanking his friend. "I just want to touch him because he's who he is," (p. 210) Therefore, one level of McMurphy as myth represents male love, *philia* and *agape*. He is the ideal friend, as well as a messiah, teacher, and democratic saint.

McMurphy is a fabulous character of mythic, heroic stature. Thus far critics have failed to comment upon the fact that *One Flew Over the Cuckoo's Nest* is an elaboration of a *fable*. The novel's title derives from a counting-out rhyme, partially quoted as the book's epigraph, in which a girl (significantly, because boys are not supposed to be helpless and need rescuing) is trapped in a cuckoo's nest and is plucked out by a goose. McMurphy, of course, is the "bull goose loony" who plucks the men (victims) out. As a title the rhyme works because the obvious colloquial definition of cuckoo is "crazy," and the nest is the asylum. But the rhyme's apt use is far more sophisticated and subtle. One must reconcile the nursery rhyme with the novel's meanings because not only is part of the rhyme used by Kesey in the title and epigraph, but on page 272 it is also quoted completely by Chief Bromden who lies in an isolation room after his last EST treatment, the only shock treatment he emerges from of his own volition. Because Broom, in this scene, recalls the rhyme and then never again reenters the fog of schizophrenia, the rhyme is a key to the myth in Broom's resurrection ritual. Broom tells us that he has always liked, even as a child, the goose who flies over the nest. The rhyme is a pleasant childhood memory of his grandmother and his native culture, and it is recalled when his mind is released from reality to freely associate. Myth intertwines with Broom's realistic memories, and the rhyme is most significant because it connects Broom with what he is, an Indian, with his dead grandmother whom he loves, with her culture, and with McMurphy. In the rhyme a mysterious girl, paradoxically a "fisherman" (Broom's heritage because his ancestors were fishermen), is in need of a savior. A victim or merely an innocent, she is saved by the goose who swoops down and plucks her out. Just so, Broom and the acutes on the ward are saved by their messiah, McMurphy, the American confidence man out of P. T. Barnum.

The rhyme, then, is a miniature fable. A fable is a story that satirically criticizes human folly, most frequently acted out by animals (but not exclusively) pointing out a moral. Not only does the child's rhyme suggest that *One Flew Over the Cuckoo's Nest* is fabulous, but also Kesey's careful use of animal imagery throughout supports this analysis. McMurphy is the "bull goose loony" as messiah. The men are rabbits and "dirty chickens" pecking each other to death. (p. 55) Finally, the rhyme is also significant because in a schizophrenic episode the mad journey often takes the schizophrenic deeply within himself into a cosmic realm where the person experiences ego loss within animal form, a phenomenon that parallels Joseph Campbell's description of the mythic hero journey.

In the beginning, Broom has taken refuge in "caginess," the ethos or rabbithood, and his psychic defense, which defines him as a schizophrenic, is the fog. Broom reasons that in modern society a man must be cagey in order to defend himself against violation and defeat, that fighting is pointless, perhaps suicidal. The cause of Broom's fog was an incident in World War II involving a helpless comrade. The war is the trauma, following upon racism that Broom suffered in the land of his ancestors, which pushes him over the edge. At Anzio, Broom as a warrior was compelled to listen to the death screams of another warrior who was tied to a tree in the blazing sun, but Broom was absolutely helpless because to attempt rescue was suicidal. The enemy lay waiting in ambush in a farmhouse near by. This traumatic horror creates the fog, Broom's spirit is crushed by guilt and impotence when he is trapped in the ultimate "double-bind," choosing death or choosing life at the expense of a fellow warrior's death. Broom's psychosis continually fogs him in; the fog is his troubled mind's creation, a symbolic equivalent of a shroud which protects him in self-isolation. The fog preserves his sense of freedom and integrity while it simultaneously buffers him from feelings of guilt for abrogating his responsibility to commune with other men and to be his brother's keeper.

In Broom's schizophrenic descent deep within his fragmented mind, his "darkly terrifying" encounters occurs within the bowels of a furnace room that he imagines within the asylum. Broom experiences men as robots whose entrails reveal "a shower of rust and ashes, now and again a piece of wire or glass." (p. 85) For Broom men have become so controlled by modern culture that they are mere electronic products. However, he never believes that he too is such a robot. Broom keeps his experience to himself because he knows that if he confided in anyone, even his fellow inmates, he would be told "a big machine room in the bowels of a dam where people get cut up by robot workers" doesn't exist. (p. 87)

The Chief's repeated withdrawals into the fog become both less terrifying and less comforting because McMurphy is working his magic as Broom's messiah. Love, *philia* and *agape*, draws Broom voluntarily out of his fog; this is his centering experience, which finally reintegrates his shattered ego and gives him new courage. As with schizophrenics who thus "heal," as it were, Bromden reemerges from the fog by choice. His last shock treatment was administered after he chose to join McMurphy in defense of George, the cleanliness fanatic. This act was Bromden's first willful decision to return permanently to the community of men. At this point, he is no longer concerned with threats to his ego and with self-exposure.

Joining his master, Broom emerges to fight in defense of his brothers. George is only his first public attempt to fight back. At the novel's end Broom seeks out his Indian brothers (no women are mentioned) in his village before fleeing to Canada. The male bond here is exclusive because in male mythology it is the warrior's bond in combat. Broom returns to society and his people as a warrior, a role still as important and respected in many Indian cultures in America as it is in the masculine mystique. Another minority male, "a Mexican guy," aids Broom without hesitation in his escape, lending him ten dollars and a jacket. Broom's new-found faith in his manhood and brotherhood is expressed in his intention to repay the man's hard-earned money. Through the coupling of love and communal responsibility, Broom is reborn a man and a warrior, after a prolonged schizophrenic episode. In pointed contrast, Cheswick, a suicide, is a victim of despair. Cheswick is disillusioned when he believes that McMurphy is only a self-interested confidence man. When a man is convinced that all are dreadfully alone and complete only for self-aggrandizement, the resulting despair, in Kesey's world view, may be fatal. McMurphy is a messiah because his ritual death lifts the acutes from their despair, and they return to the "sane" world of American society.

As the novel ends, the Combine still controls society through coercive, paternal cultural patterns. Broom's father was weakened and then destroyed by the intransigence of the Combine's racism. Consequently, Broom's father failed not only his people as their chief but also, and as importantly, his son in his collapse as protector and spiritual guide. Before his death McMurphy had replaced Bromden's lost father. In Bromden's lengthy schizophrenic episode he acts out his quest to know, honor, and love his father as himself and to experience brotherhood. By exorcizing the ghost of his withered father, Broom emerges healed; he becomes capable of assuming both the paternal role of an activist "chief" and the fraternal role of a caring comrade.

Romantic male myth (reflected in the novel's ideology and mythology) places man's "natural" home outside the settlement of civilization. Although McMurphy is Kesey's hero, Bromden is a survivor with the potential for heroism as he emerges from the asylum with a healthy, rebellious understanding of himself as a man and his society. Chief Bromden and McMurphy portray what is generally missing in the writing of American men, a genuine, profound male love that transcends friendship, male bonding, and comradeship in arms. This is Kesey's radical departure from American tradition. But, finally, one must admit that these men live without women, suggesting that the underlying mythic fear of women remains.

Separation, initiation, and return: Kesey's narrator self-defensively drifts off into his schizophrenic fog in order to preserve his fragile "sanity"; he centers in the "darkly terrifying" space of the human mind, and he ultimately emerges a potential hero, profoundly changed but willing and able to lead other men, possibly his people.

WORKS CITED

Baurecht, William C. "Messianic Masculinity: Myth of Freedom on the West." *Southwest Images and Trends: Factors in Community Development.* Susan Owings and Helen Bannan, Eds. Las Cruces: New Mexico State University, 1979.

———. "Romantic Male Deviance and the Messianic Impulse in American Masculinity: Case Studies of *Moby Dick, One Flew Over the Cuckoo's Nest,* and *Sometimes a Great Notion.*" Ph.D Diss., University of New Mexico, 1978.

Campbell, Joseph. *Myths to Live By.* New York: Bantam Books, 1973.

Fielder, Leslie A. "Come Back to the Raft Ag'in, Huck Honey." *An End to Innocence: Essays on Culture and Politics*. Boston: Beacon Press, 1955.

———. *Love and Death in the American Novel*. Rev. ed. New York: Stein and Day, 1966.

———. *The Return of the Vanishing American*. New York: Stein and Day, 1968.

Kesey, Ken. *Kesey's Garage Sale*. New York: Viking Press, 1973.

———. *One Flew Over the Cuckoo's Nest*. New York: Viking Press, 1962.

Laing, R. D. *The Politics of Experience*. New York: Ballantine Books, 1968.

May, Rollo. *Love and Will*. New York: Dell, 1974.

Slotkin, Richard. *Regeneration Through Violence: The Mythology of the American Frontier, 1600–1860*. Middletown, CT: Wesleyan University Press, 1973.

JANET LARSON

Stories Sacred and Profane: Narrative in
One Flew Over the Cuckoo's Nest

In his "wry codicil" to the "Definition of Man" which opens *Language as Symbolic Action*, Kenneth Burke observes that this symbol-using, symbol-misusing animal is "rotten with perfection." Goaded by Aristotle's principle of entelechy to make plans for our own completion—plans that could extend with "perfect logic" to our complete extinction (16–20)—we are storytelling animals and creatures who live in stories. Theologians have drawn upon such an understanding of human nature and culture to develop powerfully appealing accounts of life and faith as story. But what kind of stories shall we have? Ethicists David Burrell and Stanley Hauerwas write that

> a true story could only be one powerful enough to check the endemic tendency toward self-deception—a tendency which inadequate stories cannot help but foster. Correlatively, if the true God were to provide us with a saving story, it would have to be one that we found continually discomforting.[1] (111)

If the world is made not out of atoms but out of stories, what assures us that the narrative structures of our beliefs about God and ourselves bear truth and not fruit that is "rotten with perfection"? Northrop Frye has reminded us that while "truth and falsehood are not literary categories," for the critic

Religion & Literature, Volume 16, Number 2 (Summer 1984): pp. 25–42.

they "represent the directions or tendencies in which verbal structures go, or are thought to go" (17). If it is possible to identify a story form that tends toward truth, that works toward its liberation for the hearers, it would be both dialectical and dialogical. In this essay, I will be tracing the implications of such a story form in *One Flew Over the Cuckoo's Nest*.

Two distinct narrative expressions of *telos* together define the form of Ken Kesey's novel: myths, in a vitiated contemporary American mode, and parables, as understood chiefly but not exclusively from Jesus' dominant form of teaching in the gospels. Kesey exposes an idolatrous American archmyth and its parallel god-myth, but he also presses further to test the redemptive power of parable lived and told by his characters and through his book. While *Cuckoo's Nest* is not a Christian novel—for its wisdom is explicitly secular—its dynamic narrative structure models the possibility for genuine transcendence in this world and liberates its readers through a dialectic of myth and parable. In so doing, Kesey's novel imitates in its non-supernatural way the *"logons tēs pisteōs"* (words of faith) New Testament writers claim to tell and overturns the *"bebēlous kai graōdeis mythous"* (profane and old wives' fables) which St. Paul urges his fellow Christians to reject (I Tim. 4:7). It is only as McMurphy's own profane myths and those of the men in the institution are subverted through the power of parable that Kesey's transformed messiah can save and be saved from stories that are rotten with perfection.

In *The Sacred and the Profane*, Mircea Eliade has set forth the ancient function of myth to bring into the present, through the narration of the gods' creative acts, "the irruption of the sacred into the world... that *establishes* the world as a reality." This ontological function of myth is yoked to its cultural function: that "which narrates this sacred ontophany," which "alone reveals the *real*," becomes the paradigm for all important activities in a religious culture, vouching for what is done (97-98). Warner Berthoff emphasizes the "principle of generosity" in these basic functions of myth. Its chief purpose is

> not explanation (in the sense of interpretation) but *recovery, preservation, organization, continuance*. . . . The essential character of myth is plenitude and accommodation, above all the accommodation of the collective mind of men to their own incessant experience.

That accommodation is also personal: myths give individuals faces to put on. Thomas Mann, arguing for the need to assume an ancient mythic mantle, has called myth "the legitimization of life; only through and in it does life find self-awareness, sanction, consecration" (314–322).

In this personal appropriation of myth, one might discern the effort to achieve self-transcendence. Yet to the extent that one loses oneself in the legitimizing story—as Burrell and Hauerwas remind us that Albert Speer enclosed himself in the image of "Hitler's architect"—one can perfect the grand illusion, what Ernest Becker has called the "vital lie," with which we protect ourselves from the consequences of our own and others' acts (ch. 4). If myths are "organs of reality," in Ernst Cassirer's phrase, how can the reality thus created be judged for its truth? Sacred myth is not self-conscious; it cannot stand outside itself, for to the primitive mind enclosed in its myths, there is no other "real" place to stand. When personal myths are reinforced by all-embracing culture myths, it becomes considerably difficult for the unaided individual to achieve the critical standingplace of "self'-awareness." And for the society whose basis of integration is questionable, as Kenneth Burke cautions, cultural myths that give expression to this integration can become a social menace (*Literary Form* 314–322).

John Dominic Crossan has formulated structural definitions of myth and parable that, with qualifications, will prove particularly helpful in identifying the narrative structure of *Cuckoo's Nest*, in naming the kinds of stories told within this fiction, and in tracing their theological and ethical implications.[2] Drawing upon the work of Claude Levi-Strauss, Crossan describes what goes on in the deep structure of myth:

> an opposition between two terms that cannot be reconciled (binary oppositions) will be represented by two fictional surrogates, and these replacements will allow a reconciliation or mediation which the original pair could not receive.

Through this logic, the mediation may yield an actual "gain" in the story, like the recovery of the Golden Fleece, but the fictive gain is not crucial: "the whole process of mediation and reconciliation implies in itself a gigantic gain," for one establishes "in, by, and through myth the conviction that mediation is *Possible*" (*Interval* 51–53), In the realm of myth, dissonances are harmonized; the abstract pattern of rounded closure ensures belief in satisfying solutions in general. Crossan sees the danger in this; Berthoff, in his less skeptical conception of myth, calls it "organized plenitude" (282-83). But in the world of modern history, plagued by failed fictions, many myths do not preserve the plenitude their organization would seem to promise; these Northrop Frye in *The Secular Scripture* would consign to his category of "kidnapped romance," stories assimilated into ideology of the ascendant class and peddle for the mass consumption of docile citizens for whom these tales cannot really perform the profound functions of myth although they may seem to (26, 57). In a fractured and skeptical world, popular myths struggle to keep alive the belief in mediation and in rounded closure at the risk of mass delusion. It is these bogus myths that are exposed in *Cuckoo's Nest*.

In his typology of story, Crossan opposes parable to myth:

parable is always a somewhat unnerving experience. You can usually recognize a parable because your immediate reaction will be self-contradictory: "I don't know what you mean by that story but I'm certain I don't like it". (*Interval 56*)

Instead of reconciling contradictions, the logic of parable creates them within a given situation. At the heart of the parabolic event, "the *structure of expectation* on the part of the hearer and . . . *the structure of expression* on the part of the speaker" are diametrically opposed; in this battle of basic structures, the parable effects "the reverse of what the hearer expects" through a typical sequence of operations: Crossan calls them advent, reversal, action (*Interval* 66). The familiar situation in which, for example, Jesus' parables typically begin is shattered by what Crossan calls God's "advent," his act of sovereign freedom that upsets the hearer's cherished story, his righteous expectations, his ethical code. Advent brings a polar reversal of these expectations, and reversal initiates new action, "open[ing] up new worlds and unforeseen possibilities" for Prodigal Sons and their brothers, Publicans and Pharisees (*Parables* 34). To be truly human, Crossan says, "and to remain open to transcendental experience, demands a willingness to be 'parabled' . . ." (*Interval* 56)—not only in stories, but also in the surprising reversals of our temporal lives.

The relationship between myth and parable in Crossan's typology should now be evident: myth "establishes world. . . . Parable subverts world" (*Interval* 59). In the act of subversion, parable is not anti-myth but "shows us the seams and edges of myth":

To live in parable means to dwell in the tension of myth and parable. . . . [Parable] is a story deliberately calculated to show us the limitations of myth to shatter world so that its relativity becomes apparent. (*Interval* 56, 59–60)

If the storyteller begins to mediate the newly created contrast, "the story starts slipping . . . back into myth" (*Interval* 55). Correlatively, if the person who has been parabled begins reorganizing his life to achieve and sustain a static coherence, he too has slipped back into living by myth rather than remaining open to the experience of being "parabled."

This hardening of the outlines can make story idolatrous. As Paul Tillich argues in *Dynamics of Faith*, myths cannot be removed, for they are the language of faith; but they can be broken, so as to acknowledge their finite character. To break free of idolatrous faith, the modern believer must recognize the myth as a story which is not in itself sacred—and therefore no longer the story of traditional religious societies—but which points beyond itself as a provisional symbol of one's ultimate concern (48–54). In this way Tillich makes room for myth in the skeptical modern world. Parable, I would go on to argue, is a peculiarly appropriate narrative form in which to express a faith that is not wholly demythologized in Bultmann's sense, but that lives in tension with myth, that accepts its human stories as provisional and "broken." *One Flew Over the Cuckoo's Nest*, a novel that is critical of its own formulations, shows us that, particularly in a modern world ridden by bogus myths that make false promises to order our existence and bring delusive comfort, an appreciation of the parable's truth-bringing power becomes crucially important in our personal and collective lives. Further, for all its secular wisdom, Kesey's novel points to the power of the Christian story in particular by placing at the center a naturalized version of Jesus as the Parable of God.

In "The Nature of Art Under Capitalism," Kenneth Burke writes that art which makes for acceptance of its culture

> enables us to "resign" ourselves by resolving in aesthetic fusion trends or yearnings not resolvable in the practical sphere. . . . [But such art] tends to become a social menace in so far as it assists us in tolerating the intolerable. . . . at a time when the very basis or moral integration is in question. . . .

In such times art "must have . . . an element of suasion or inducement of the educational variety," that is, "a large *corrective* or *propaganda element* . . ." (*Literary Form* 320–321). The adjectives in Burke's statement suggest quite different narrative modes of inducement, "propaganda" being perhaps the least useful and certainly least attractive of forms. For if story is to save from delusion and corruption, its way of addressing the reader's experience must acknowledge its psychological and moral complexity—something propaganda cannot afford to do. The gain of parable as a corrective teaching device is that it is so constructed to induce us to change our expectations, experiencing them as lost in order to learn something entirely new.

Especially in its play and film versions, *One Flew Over the Cuckoo's Nest* has been taken by many as a propagandistic story for the flower-child revolution. But Kesey's book is much more than counter propaganda directed against America's dreams of order, The novel narratively exposes an American pseudo-myth of gain; it also challenges a conception of deity that is quite compatible with the American dream; the myth of an omnipotent sky-god who flies over the world, touching down just long enough to pluck out the "cuckoos." These challenges come through a transformational, shifting logic that generates the liberating power of Kesey's work, a dialectic of myth and parable. *One Flew Over the Cuckoo's Nest* exposes the relativity of story in a parabolic way, for the dialectical structure of the narrative constitutes an attack on the structure of expectation set up by the novel's own title. Through a process of story-reversals, or losses and gains, by which both readers and characters in the novel learn, Kesey persuades us to believe in the possibility of winning—through sacrifice, even death—an authentic transcendence within the natural order.

Before Chief Bromden even sees the newcomer, he hears the Word—a "loud, brassy voice" that "sounds like he's way above them, talking down, like he's sailing fifty yards overhead, hollering at those below on the ground. He sounds big . . . (*Nest* 10). For the Indian, McMurphy is a "giant come out of the sky to save us from the Combine," from all the social forces that crush men (255). At the opening of the novel, this red-headed hero appears to be the mythic figure which the title promises. Bursting into the deadly institutional quiet with an apparent hicrophanic surplus of being, Mac performs a larger-than-life role for the lifeless inmates, who crave a sense-making story that demands of them no personal change. While Kesey's culture-hero suffers initially from no explicit "Christ complex" like Nathanael West's Miss Lonelyhearts, McMurphy revels in his personal pop mythology, which stretches from the American past of the legendary logger, "the swaggering gambler, the big red-headed brawling Irishman," to the present of Superman, Captain Marvel, the Lone Ranger on "the TV set walking down the middle of the street to meet a dare" (189). Relishing himself as an emblem of "transcendent human possibility," in Terry G. Sherwood's phrase, Randle Patrick McMurphy at first takes on the lineaments of a "mythic Christ." Sherwood argues that the simplistic moral oppositions this heroic design requires prevent Kesey's novel from being a serious work; the book projects, like the comic strip, a world only as it ought to be (96-100). If *Cuckoo's Nest* remained thus enclosed in this pop-mythic pattern, it would indeed risk indulging a self-deceptively simple morality, for the sake of popular entertainment or counter-propaganda. But the "cartoon world . . . where the figures are flat and outlined in black," as Bromden calls it (31), is not Kesey's vision: it is his paranoid narrator's delusion. This structure must be broken if the whole saving story is to be lived and told.

As the Indian's "primitive" religious imagination suggests, the attraction of the McMurphy hero as a "giant come out of the sky to save us from the' Combine" is rooted in the appeal of ancient myth to a sick man terrified of formlessness. As his narrative opens Bromden sets the stage for nothing less than the primordial struggle between dragon and sky-god (Tiamat and Marduk, Cetus and Perseus) that in myths of the beginnings establishes the world (*Symbolic Action* 383).[3] Miss Ratched, who can blow herself up to more than human size in the Indian's imagination is the center of an evil techno-logical priestcraft, sitting "in the center of [a] web of watchful robot" (26), she inhabits a mechanical dragon's lair, where this female version "of the beast that was, and is not, and yet is" is as ontologically elusive as the dragon of the Apocalypse, to which Kesey refers in the novel's dedication. The head nurse of the ward is an opponent truly worthy of the larger-than-life McMurphy.

But the power of these opposing mythic terms must be diminished if the narrator is to get well. The archetypal enemy, the Combine, must be defeated *as an idea* (myth) because, representing all the ways "these things can be rigged" (27), it licenses Bromden's paranoid conviction that he is a victim who can at least play "deaf and dumb" safely in this enclosed fantasy. Bromden's image of his Champion as immortal hero must also diminish, change into mortal shape. The Indian puzzles over the logic of two possible answers to the question of identity: if Mac is One who "came out of the sky" he is surely the superhuman rescuer from the mythic Combine; but if Mac is "merely" human, surely he cannot save. Mac's continued presence in the institution as a real man who "is what he is" gradually subverts the Indian's imaginary world that dictates these false choices—these binary oppositions that prevent him from accepting the far more ambiguous. unfixed terms of historical experience. McMurphy comes to Bromden as parable by reversing these expectations: he is a "mere man" who redeems the time, rescuing other men not by touching down briefly in their world as a superhuman force, but by deeply enmeshing himself in their suffering experience. It is only as McMurphy becomes less mythic to the inmates and to himself that he *can* rescue them from the comfortable nest of their delusions and empower them to be what they are in the world as, it is.

Understanding the structure of these transformations is essential for seeing what kind of "Christ figure" McMurphy is and is not. Students of this novel have noticed many of Kesey's deliberate parallels drawn from the life of Christ. It is peculiarly appropriate, however, that these historical parallels "begin to emerge only in the last quarter of the book," as Theodore Ziolkowsky has observed (266, n. 19).[4] For by then Mac has moved away from his initial position as an ahistorical "mythic Christ" to become another kind of authentic messiah in human time. Just as Christ crucified, the Parable of God in the gospels, subverted the expectations of his world through the power of his weakness and the wisdom of his foolishness (I Cor. 1:20–25), so the parabolic McMurphy scandalizes the prevailing idolatries by succeeding ever more recklessly through failure, breaking Bromden's self-enclosing myth and becoming a parable for the men; he risks being martyred in the cause of his friends' liberation and is resurrected through the new life he brings to his followers—not, however, as a mythic Jesus or "Christ dream," but as a just and compassionate fellow human being. But he is no Son of God reincarnate in fiction; the Christlike pattern is complicated by the reality of his own resurgent sinning. If McMurphy becomes saving as he becomes parable for others, the others are also a needed parable for him. And McMurphy, unlike Nathanael West's false messiah, is willing to be parabled.

This is the central double reversal in the novel; bur *Cuckoo's Nest* overturns expectations more than once, and in more than one way. The mutual transformations of the men and of Mac are effected not by a single dramatic shift but, on a much more closely discriminated scale, through the repeated alternations of two distinctive forms of story logic. Again and again in the narrative parable (with its dynamic open structure of advent/reversal/action) breaks the perfect designs of resurgent popular myth (with its rounded closure), exposing the provisionality of story. This repeated dialectic eventually forms a pattern in the novel that makes moral and existential sense out of the discontinuities, regressions, dreamlike sequences, disjointed flashbacks, clearer memories, and stretches of forward-moving action that constitute the narrative complexity of Kesey's work. Each time parabolic breakage occurs, expectations are overturned, values are redefined, plans are changed, emotional security is upset, and fresh action is forwarded for a while until the delusive certainties of the men's and McMurphy's myths reassert their old seductions. These alternations in the action are accompanied by the actual storytelling of myths and parables, with their different rhetorical situations and effects. And yet, even though the narrative movement of *Cuckoo's Nest* depends upon the breakdown of stories that foster mere acquiescence, Kesey remains tolerant of the human need for legends and mythic play-acting as his characters live through the pain of coming to awareness. This tolerance I do not sense in Crossan's treatment of myth. More usefully, Kenneth Burke writes that along with efforts to change the structure of society

> must go the demand for an imaginative equipment that helps us to make it tolerable while it lasts. Much of the "pure" or "acquiescent" art of today serves this invaluable psychological end. For this reason the great popular comedians or handsome movie stars are rightly the idols of the people (*Literary Form* 322)

For such reasons does the heroic McMurphy legend linger through the last pages of the novel. But it is embedded in Kesey's dynamic fictional world of provisional stories that undergo continual reformulation; and in the concluding paragraphs, myth does not have the final word,

Even at the novel's opening when Mac is most celebratively identified with popular mythology, his parabolic potential for the men is evident. With his unexpected laughter and songs, he threatens "the whole smoothness of the outfit" (39), as though he were pure subversion aiming at "simply the actual *disruption* of the ward for the sake of disruption" (25). After the first group therapy session, Mac unsettles the inmates' theories of Big Nurse as either the "tender angel of mercy. Mother Ratched" or as "the juggernaut of modern matriarchy" (58, 68) and sets out to expose the seams of her myth: he is going to "Bug her till she comes apart at those neat little seams, and shows, just one time, she ain't so unbeatable as you think" (72). By the end of Part 1 he has done it, but the reversal and new action come not quite in the way anyone expects.

Mac's small successes in early skirmishes with Big Nurse are entertaining, but he cannot diminish her power by his own pop-myth performances: he must first change the men's image of themselves. (As Crossan says; "It takes two to parable" [*Interval 87*]). Mac then tries to teach these losers that they can "win" at the gaming table; to their myth of total failure, he opposes the antimyth of capitalistic success. But an antimyth does not disturb the hearer's structure of expectation; and this one is only another version of the institution's myth of the powerful against the weak. Besides, the men play only for paper money and a poker-table peripety. When the odds are seriously against them in a real power-game (as in the first vote on the World Series), the men back down. What they must learn is a different kind of heroic winning that challenges the myths of power and gain by transforming the meaning of failure.

An unexpected parabolic event points this way when McMurphy, typically inviting bets and bragging of his legendary strength, tries to lift the control panel in the tub room. No emblem of transcendent possiblity now or a TV hero, Mac shows himself a man with a body shaken by strain who has the courage to try even though "he *knows* he can't lift it," even though *everybody* knows he can't" (121). Mac thus begins to take on the lineaments of a new kind of "gambling fool " As the inmates' images of him change, the way is opened for their expectations of themselves to change, and for action on their discovery that risking oneself is also a way of succeeding as a human being.

This acted parable has almost immediate results on the men Mac has been "trying to pull . . . out of the fog" (132). Their second, successful vote on the baseball game, a gesture of independence from ward policy, initiates a rapid series of reversals, losses, and gains. By the time the outraged Ratched comes apart, making her lose control has become much less important than the men's gain of a new structure of expectations. Better than actually watching the old World Series on television, the men "see" a new "world"—their new communal assertion and collective laughter. And now Mac sits next to an empty TV screen, entertaining them not with pop-culture antics in place of TV's mass media fantasies but with parabolic stories: true accounts of efforts to win that had turned out losses which Mac laughs at now, and stories about losers who, even "blindfolded and backwards," had defeated the expected winners (152). As Part I closes, the Indian has ventured outside the enclosure of his fantasy to see the whole absurd scene objectively and to laugh at it. If his hero has outwitted an enemy, the victory has came not on the terms of myth but on the unsettling terms of parable. Bromden's willingness to be thus parabled signals his capacity for healing—and for telling the whole story.

Part II begins by working out the ironies of a nice counterpoint: Nurse Ratched seeks now to expose the seams of McMurphy's myth ("a Napoleon, a Genghis Khan, Attila the Hun") with an antimyth that this "mere man" will sooner or later prudently enclose himself in self-interest (146); meanwhile,

Mac's actual generous presence on the ward *as* a mere man has an increasingly salutary effect on his "buddies." Even with the tragic results of Mac's temporary defection in Part II, when he retreats self-protectively and a disillusioned Cheswick lunges into the deep water to his death, we see Mac's lasting influence as parable for the men: they still gaze at him with a look "like they wished things didn't have to be this way" (165). And just when they have nearly given up on their champion, he breaks their structure of expectations again by recklessly running his hand through the Nurse's spotless window. By this foolish gamble, Mac risks not financial loss or limited physical pain as before, but permanent commitment in an institution for the insane.

The works that follow this perilous victory are his increasingly daring therapies for the men, culminating in the fishing trip. Their biggest risk, the journey repays them with both successes and failures as they learn to laugh at the chaos they make in their struggles with the deep. By Part III McMurphy has grown to be considerably more real than an emblem of sheer transcendence. That complexity is now reflected in the unfolding of Bromden's fuller humanity as a courageous *and* compassionate human being. Already Mac has made the Indian "bigger" in personal power than his fatalistic fantasies had allowed, but such power carries with it the danger of psychopathy; Bromden's consciousness as a social being must be empowered too. Appropriately, this expansion is not manifested in clear vision alone, which might still imply the passive attitude of a wise but uninvolved onlooker; awareness, as Burrell and Hauerwas observe, is more like speaking than like seeing. In Part III what Bromden discovers is that he must talk to save himself and others. He must venture out of the fog to name his experience in the existentially open territory of dialogue. Parable, which depends upon a dynamic relation between teller and listener in a way myth does not, helps to prepare Bromden for this engagement with others in the fluid space of social relationships.

Bromden's first social challenge is the reconstruction of his personal story for another. McMurphy helps the Chief to find his voice by telling a boyhood story of his own about the "worth" of speaking out despite its material "cost" (206–207). Bromden acts on this surprising parable by talking about his own past and discovers that for the loss of what is not true in his myth of the White Man's exploitation and the Red Man's total weakness, he gains both sympathy and judgment from his listener. McMurphy is there to question, to ask for clarifications, to object, to empathize through dialogue as well as through story that is dialogical. Dialogue and dialectic clarify and refine thought; and during a silence when Bromden is arguing internally, he follows the sequence he has learned through speaking with another person, three times making a statement, questioning it, correcting it, and affirming a restatement, working toward a truer account of his history (210). Yet their midnight talk ends in fantasies as McMurphy spins a yarn about a wild Heaven in which Bromden is the superlatively sexual hero. The Indian needs such stories, mingled with the laughter that acknowledges their provisionality, as old expectations of himself are reversed and he works toward clearer consciousness.

With the spoken word, Bromden's narrative in real time properly can be said to begin. His action in open time—with an uncertain future—flows from this point in the novel. His first words had been an involuntary "Thank you" for a stick of gum; speaking also brings Bromden out into the world of others where there are both gifts and demands. Much earlier in the book, the befogged and paralyzed cigar-store Indian had seen faces floating by asking him for help: "I can't do nothing for you either, Billy," he had imagined himself saving. "You know that. None of us can. You got to understand that as soon as a man goes to help somebody, he leaves himself wide open. . . . Put your face away, Billy" (131). Nevertheless, the faces had kept "filling past"—for, as Martini (hallucinating bodies in the showers) says, "They need you to see thum" (176). Bromden has been trying to put the faces away by making them into mere signs that read "I'm tired" or "I'm dying of a bum liver" (131). The impact of McMurphy's parabolic presence is to liberate the faces from these signs so that they take on fully human dimensions for the Indian, who also gains a face of his own that is no longer trapped screaming behind mirrors. As his narrative in open time begins, Bromden sheds mythological thinking to become a human being present for others.

In Part IV as the men return toting salmon like "conquering heroes," Mac threatens to turn back again into myth, into a friend too good to be true, like Jesus or Santa Claus (243–249). Big Nurse determines to destroy the men's new heroism by launching her final attack on the McMurphy legend, whose terms have significantly shifted from "Attila the Hun" to "martyr" and "saint" (252). Harding offers a weak defense with the demoralizing theory that there are neither gifts nor givers but only "the dear old capitalistic system of free individual enterprise, comrades," and its "good old red, white, and blue hundred-percent American con man" (254), This "whole bit" is not adequate to explain their friend; and the cynical Harding desperately needs more. But as the men ask, "What's in it for or Mack?" (250); McMurphy re-enacts the opportunistic role of "Nobody's fool" with which he has been charged, and the capitalistic counter-myth seems to be winning again.

The men's mythic expectations are once more shattered when Mac steps forward to defend a vulnerable inmate from the cruel pranks of the aides. The importance of this moment as parable for the men is underscored by Bromden's response. By joining Mac in a fray which neither can finally win, Bromden shows that he has gained the compassion to identify with others' losses, as well as the courage to throw himself into an open situation "without thinking about being cagey or safe or what would happen to me," thinking only about "the thing that needed to be done and the doing of it" (258).

Reversal has led to action, and when the action is punished by Electro-shock Treatment, the impact of the parable is not lost. In the foggy aftermath, it is by reordering fragments of his past largely in parabolic patterns that Bromden painfully reconstructs his identity toward the clear moment of his full awakening. The hunting incident with his father which he recalls, the memory of his white mother's challenge to the old Indian ways, and the stories of his grandmother's life/death/resurrection follow in his mind as a lifelike sequence of losses and gains, the ambiguous contradictions he must face in his continued living (271–275). When he emerges as an openly speaking and hearing member of the human community after this, the Chief is capable of his own liberation.

As the men's transformation in the background and Bromden's in the foreground show, the combat at the heart of *Cuckoo's Nest* is not simply, as it first appears, the opposition of Champion and Enemy (the sky-god myth), or People against the Institution and Machine (the Combine myth), or the Weak against the Strong (Harding's rabbit myth), although these conflicts are anchored in real power relations in the book. The central conflict is between the men's endemic tendencies toward self-deception and their capacities for generating truer, more adequate stories about themselves and their world. And just as parable is "story grown self-conscious and self-critical" (*Interval* 57), so Bromden's dialectically constructed narrative increasingly becomes aware of itself. While he does not simply demythologize McMurphy's story—for remnants of legend linger in the descriptions of Mac's last performances—the transformed narrator's very awareness that the pop myths are broken testifies to the saving power of Mac's parable for his friends.

In *Cuckoo's Nest*, master and disciples become transformed in the encounter with each other. The men are also an "advent" for McMurphy that turns his familiar world upside down and challenges him to new and unforeseen acts, Mac too needs to be parabled; the protective "cartoon world" of his shallow individualist persona must be transformed if he is to enter the multidimensional human community. The sign of his grace is that McMurphy is open to the reconstitution of his image and to the lesson of limit, indeed to the lesson of his own mortality.

Introducing himself through his master-image—"McMurphy, buddies, R. P. McMurphy, and I'm a gambling fool"—he does not at all hide the fact that he has come not to *be* a sacrifice but to "trim you little babies like little lambs" (11–12). A "smart gambler," Mac plans to "look the game over awhile before [drawing him] self a hand" (47). But the game he sees is not what he expects. Although he has begun in the spirit of enterprise he later laughs at "how funny the whole thing is" (113); and by the end of Mac's first parabolic encounter with the men, he feels "he's been trapped some way" (69). The surprising crazy story of the patient's utter defeat forces him to listen to their expressions of suffering, and he watches Harding with "puzzled wonder . . .

like it's the first human face he ever laid eyes on" (60). After the first revelatory group therapy session, he begins examining his values and later dreams night after night not of signs but of individual faces.

Mac keeps drifting back into old games of self-interest even as he moves toward his redemption from that capitalistic world. His first savior role is the perfect "con" (getting what he wants while making others think they are getting what they want): he will become the Champion of this pitiful circle without taking risks, by gambling on a sure thing. [Ironically, this is his disciples' own game of self-protection (78). In Part II the tables are turned on him: by coming to him like he is "some kind or savior," he says, without warning him of the "risk [he] was running," the men have "conned of R. P. McMurphy." Stepping right out of this deep water, he tells his buddies: "Yon got in swallow your pride sometimes and keep an eye out for old Number One" (182). Yet he cannot achieve insensibility to the men's continuing need. Nor can he find a harmonizing explanation for their shocking news that they are voluntary inmates: this scandal to his winning principle he cannot "seem to get straight in [his] mind" (185). If Mac is to be saved and saving, he must, as the resident doctors say, "give up his bit," reverse his master-image, and become a "gambling fool" who wins by losing. When he runs his hand through the glass at the end of Part II, he breaks his own self-encapsulation in an individualist myth; the man dedicated to "gambling on all levels" has escalated the perils and redefined the meaning of his vocation.

That he has not entirely disengaged himself from the gambler's dream of gain is evident yet in Part IV when McMurphy exploits Bromden's new physical strength by persuading the men to bet on it. When Bromden scruples to refuse his share of the winnings, the baffled McMurphy asks, "Now what's the story?" His comrade steps in a parable: "We thought it wasn't to be *winning* things . . ." (257). In the next critical scene, Mac acts on Bromden's "story" by defending the helpless George from the cruel aides, just as Bromden acts on the parable Mac has been for him. The ring of expectant faces goads McMurphy to make an irrevocable choice against the remnants of his master-image, for he knows he cannot finally win. As his "helpless, cornered despair" (261) forecasts, he seems to know that this event will lead him to give his last gift, his life.

Thinking forward to the end of the story, Bromden muses that "it was like he'd signed on for the whole game and there wasn't any way of him breaking his contract" (296). In this new "world series," McMurphy had also *been* signed on and the stakes are very high. The suicides of Cheswick and Billy Bibbit are sobering proof that Mac has risked, as Nurse says, "Playing with human lives—gambling with human lives"; but it is not, as she further charges, because Mac thinks himself "to be a *God!*" (304). For her psychopath theory is only another version of *her* dream of manipulation. It also implies an inadequate conception of deity as transcendent power, rather than as the par-adoxical God of the Bible who requires sacrifice and is himself the satisfying sacrificial love—that courageous compassion which Mac has in his imperfect way imparted to the others because he has risked participating in their reality. Now, his last desperate gamble with his own life is an act of justice as well as an act of love that consummates his incarnation from mythic into mortal shape, an obedience unto death for the friends "making him do it" (304).

Billy's suicide is a harrowing parabolic event that launches Mac's fi-nal reversal. It also shows us that the revolution of consciousness which we have attended through the book is not in itself enough. Hearing Nurse's self-legitimizing explanation moments after Billy's death, Mac instantaneously grasps the reality of human limit: people are not inviolable, and institutional stories have real power over people's lives. Billy's self-deception had been an enemy, but Nurse Ratched is an enemy too, not just a paranoid projection. McMurphy's lunge to strangle her makes a frontal attack on an institutional lie, tackling the larger structure of untruth which has victimized Billy and in which the Nurse plays the leading role. Accepting his parable, McMurphy is drawn swiftly to his death. The men, accepting theirs, venture out not at all assured of their futures, but strong enough to try living their lives outside the mythic entrapments of the institution.

Bromden's triumphant leap from the asylum with all the symbolic force of a resurrection from the tomb may seem to turn the parable of McMurphy back into myth. But Kesey does not perfect the form of his story by harmo-nizing all the contradictions his work has raised. His conclusion is poised on a paradox of death/life that opens up the story for the survivors; and some of the remaining details and ambiguities suggest a conclusion appropriate to the dynamic provisionality of all the novel's storytelling and to its own narrative structure.

Bromden's escape coalesces two opposed images that have been kept separate through most of the book: images of lifting associated with mythical transcendence (only a hero of legendary strength could have lifted the control panel that Bromden lifts) and images of shattering associated with parabolic breakage (only one who now sees himself as human can shatter this prison and enter the contingent human world). The event occasioned by lifting and shattering is both transcendental and descendental: he flies, he falls. "The glass splashed out in the moon, like a bright cold water baptizing the sleeping earth," he writes (310). Joyously celebrating beauty, he is also reminded, with deliberate invocation of the sacrament, that one enters a new life by being baptized into a death.

As the narrative nearly slips back into myth, Bromden nonetheless goes on to show us that he has entered no legendary life outside the contingencies of human time; rather, in his ending he is finally aware of himself as a temporal being. The entrapping mythic present of his opening paranoid formula, "They're out there," has been replaced by the sense of the past now measured and assessed: "I been away a long time" (311). Leading up to these last words, he thinks through his plans in the closing paragraphs and imagines that the world he will encounter is neither entirely in the grip of a Combine conspiracy nor better than it really is. Aiming to "look over the country" in order to "bring some of it clear" in his mind, Bromden heads toward whatever is "out there"—the tragedy of Indians who have "drunk themselves goofy" and the comic absurdity of Indians spearing salmon again in the dam's spillway—in the provisional, surprising world (311).

Bromden heads toward the highway "in the direction I remembered seeing the dog go" to hitch a ride toward home (310). The memory recalls Bromden's first time at the symbolic window in an important prefiguring scene that had mingled threat with promise. In the tranquil autumn night, a flock of Canada honkers were crossing the moon, led by one that looked like "a black cross opening and closing." When the geese pass out of sight, a dog continues loping in their direction "steady and solemn like he had an appointment." A car's headlights loom; Bromden sees the "dog and the car making for the same spot of pavement." What had happened next he never knew, for he had been taken away from the window (156–157).

Recalling this earlier passage is an appropriate way for Kesey to open the end of his novel. Bromden will have to live in the tensions that have moved his narrative forward, with its combat between closed and open forms of living and of telling and with its many conflicts between disillusion and believing, sin and regeneration, dying and living. Kesey's work has a complex structure with many crossings and re-crossings, most fundamentally a dialectic between the tragic and the comic in a tale of loss and gain. Across its moon flies not a sky-God, transcendent and distantly beautiful, but a black cross, opening and closing, moving into the dark.

Notes

1. I am indebted to professor Walter R. Bouman for his paper. "Piety in a Secularized Society." Read at Valparaiso University in 1977, which called my attention to "Self Deception and Autobiography . . ." and to John Dominic Crossan.

2. The adequacy of Crossan's definition of parable to describe the actual *Parabolē* of Jesus has been debated. See, for example, *Semeia* 1 (1974) and John Cobb. What ever its technical limitations of applicability to the gospel stories, however, Crossan's understanding of parabolic story and action does accord with the design in the gospels of Jesus as the Parable of God and, in kesey's novel, of McMurphy's story.

Parabolē encompasses many kinds of figurative language: although metaphor is part of the event of Jesus' parables through which consciousness is transformed, I do not treat metaphoric structure in this essay.

3. Burke cites ten elements from the earliest known type of "combat myth" which are present in the opening episodes of *Cuckoo's Nest*.

4. See also David M. Graybeal and George M. Boyd.

Works Cited

Becker, Ernest. *The Denial of Death*. New York: Free Press, 1974.

Berthoff, Warner. "Fiction, History, Myth: Notes Toward the Discrimination of Narrative Forms." *Interpretation of Narrative: Theory and Practice*. Ed. Mortan W. Bloomfield. Cambridge Harvard University Press, 1970.

Boyd, George M., "Parables of Costly Grace Flannery O'Connor and Ken Kesey." *Theology Today* 29 (1972): pp. 161–171.

Burke, Kenneth. *Language as Symbolic Action*, Berkeley: University of California Press, 1996.

———. *The Philosophy of Literary Form*. Berkeley: University of California Press, 1973.

Burrell, David, and Stanley Hauerwas. "Self-Deception and Autobiography: Theological and Ethical Reflections on Speer's *Inside the Third Reich*, "*Journal of Religious Ethics* 2 (1974).

Cobb, John. *Orientation by Disorientations, Presented in Honor of William A. Beardslee*. Ed. Richard A. Spencer. Pittsburgh: Pickwick Press, 1980.

Crossan John Dominic. *The Dark Interval: Towards a Theology of Story*. Niles, Illinois: Argus, 1975.

———. *In Parables: The Challenge of the Historical Jesus*. New York: Harper and Row, 1973.

Eliade, Mircea. *The Sacred and the Profane*. Trans. Willard R. Trask. New York: Harper and Row, 1961.

FRED MADDEN

Sanity and Responsibility:
Big Chief as Narrator and Executioner

In more than twenty years since its publication, *One Flew Over the Cuckoo's Nest* has elicited continuing critical debate about McMurphy as the novel's hero. Readings fall roughly into two camps: one, because downplaying aspects of McMurphy's racism, sexism, and paternalism, proves of him as a vital, positive figure and the novel's hero; the other, condemning McMurphy, attacks Kesey for glorifying a despicable individual. Those readers who affirm McMurphy's heroism argue that he valiantly confronts the forces of dehumanism and mechanism in our society—forces represented by what Big Chief calls the "combine." But even recent readings that praise McMurphy have the task of either palliating or ignoring what have been seen as McMurphy's racist and sexist biases.[1] Readers condemning McMurphy have pointed both to his language (he calls blacks "coons" four or five times and Washington "a nigger") and to his actions (he seems to take sadistic pleasure in bloodying Washington's nose in a basketball game and in hitting the orderly in the shower room). Other readers have accused McMurphy, and Kesey himself, of sexist attitudes: the "bad" women (Big Nurse, Billy's mother, and Harding's wife) are bitches, and the "good" women are prostitutes with hearts of gold. Readings that emphasize racist and sexist attitudes blame Kesey for creating stereotypical characters who are used to convey a white macho-paternalism that degrades women and blacks.[2]

Modern Fiction Studies, Volume 32, Number 2 (Summer 1986): pp. 203–217.

Emphasis on either McMurphy's positive character traits or his negative ones is largely responsible for the novel's continuing controversy. Readers, lining up on one side or the other, have produced an interpretative stalemate. However, a shift of critical perspective from McMurphy to Big Chief provides a way around this deadlock. For such a reading, Big Chief must be seen as the novel's central character whose narrative records his own movement toward self-reliance and sanity.[3] But, second, this seemingly positive narrative reveals the ward members' and Big Chief's manipulation and destruction of McMurphy.

Most readings render the plot of the novel in approximately the following form. McMurphy arrives on a static ward where all the ward members have been cowed into conformity. He immediately wants to challenge the power of Big Nurse—first as a means of winning a bet but later in behalf of the ward members. Just before Cheswick's suicide, however. McMurphy finds out that Big Nurse has control over the length of his stay in the asylum. So he decides to conform. But after a time he begins to understand that his rebellion is terribly important to the ward members, and so he resumes his challenge to Big Nurse's control. He succeeds until he fights Washington for attempting to abuse George, another ward member. As a result of this confrontation and of his refusal to conform to the rules of the ward, he receives a number of shock treatments. Finally after Billy Bibbit's suicide, McMurphy cannot control his hatred of Big Nurse, whom he attempts to strangle. This act of rebellion gives Big Nurse the power to order McMurphy's lobotomy. When McMurphy is brought back to the ward, Big Chief smothers him because the Chief feels that the lobotomized form is not really McMurphy and that Big Nurse will use it as an example to make her ward members conform. After he kills McMurphy, Big Chief escapes from the hospital to spread McMurphy's word of rebellion against conformity. Such a summation of the novel's plot relies heavily on McMurphy as the central character and hero, making Big Chief McMurphy's sidekick—a sort of Tonto figure.

There is, however, evidence against this reading of the novel. In an interview after the release of the film version of *Cuckoo's Nest* (during the production of which he "walked off the set" in disagreement with Milos Forman), Kesey stressed that "it's the Indian's story—not McMurphy's or Jack Nicholson's" (Grunwald 4). Kesey's insistence was not simply the result of his disagreement with Forman. While working on *Cuckoo's Nest*, Kesey wrote that he wanted to create a narrator "who leaves the ground and breathes in print" (Tanner 23). In a letter to Ken Babbs, Kesey suggested the examples of Holden Caulfield, Benjy Compson, Gulley Jimson, and Humbert as the type of character he wanted to create with Big Chief (Tanner 23). These characters filter events and control the way in which these events reach the reader—as, in fact, Big Chief's consciousness does. *Cuckoo's Nest*, then, needs to be seen in a tradition of novels that present limited and sometimes unreliable points of view.

Not only does Kesey argue against McMurphy's being taken for the central character, but it also seems doubtful that Kesey advocated the type of rebellion McMurphy advocates. An interview after the film was released indicates Kesey's own emphasis:

> Kesey: No, listen what this country needs is sanity. Individual sanity, and all the rest will come true.
>
> *Argus:* "Bullshit!"
>
> Kesey: You can't do it any other way. You work from the heart out, you don't work from the issue down.
>
> *Argus:* You don't think it's a heartfelt thing, making revolution. You don't think it means anything? . . .
>
> Kesey: I had to spend six months in jail, taking all the stuff you're talking about first hand, over and over, until you realize that what they want you to do is what you're doing. . . . As long as that action is taking place, as long as you take up the gauntlet, you'll have somebody to slap you. (Kesey, *Kesey's Garage Sale* 205)

The "individual sanity" expressed here is a position closer to Big Chief's at the end of the novel than to McMurphy's during it.

Of course it still may be argued that without McMurphy's sacrifice, Big Chief never would have achieved the sanity he does. As valid as such an idea may first appear, it is qualified *throughout the novel* by Kesey's treatment of McMurphy. In an interview in 1963, Kesey's words seem echoes of Emersonian self-reliance: "Look. I don't intend to let anybody make me live in *less* of a world than I'm capable of living in. Babbs once said it perfectly: *A man should have the right to be as big as he feels it's in him to be.* People are reluctant to permit this" (Lish 18). At first McMurphy seems to be "big" from the Chief's point of view, but by the end of the novel, his cap is "too small" for the Chief to wear. McMurphy does not become increasingly self-reliant as the novel progresses; rather, he becomes increasingly dependent on the ward members for direction. McMurphy may seem to achieve a kind of heroism *as defined by the members of the ward*, but the reader is meant to judge McMurphy's "sanity" (in response to the ward's wishes) as a loss of "individual sanity." The ward members first "con" and then "sacrifice" McMurphy in their attempt to overcome Big Nurse:

> We couldn't stop him because we were the ones making him do it. It wasn't the nurse that was forcing him, it was our need that was making him push himself slowly up . . . rising and standing like one

of those moving-picture zombies, obeying orders beamed at him from forty masters. (304)

McMurphy's description as a zombie emphasizes his conformity to the wishes of the ward members. How admirable can McMurphy be when the reader remembers Big Chief saying, at the beginning of the novel, that the black aides, like McMurphy in the above passage, operate "on beams" (their beams from Big Nurse) and that the wheelchair Chronics are "obedient under [Big Nurse's] beam" (29)? By the end of the novel, McMurphy is as obedient to the desires of the ward as the Chronics and blacks were to Big Nurse's desires at the novel's beginning. For Kesey, any sort of conformity means a loss of individual sanity.

In commenting on *Cuckoo's Nest,* Kesey has repeatedly stressed "conditioning" as important (Grunwald 2). McMurphy is conditioned by the ward members into accepting his role as hero and with it the eventual necessity of strangling Big Nurse:

> We made him stand and hitch up his black shorts like they were horsehide caps, and push back his cap with one finger like it were a ten-gallon Stetson, slow, mechanical gestures—and when he walked across the floor you could hear the iron in his bare heels ring sparks out of the tile. (305)

Not only do the ward members condition McMurphy to accept his role they also make him take on the image of the cowboy hero. This transformation, however, is not entirely successful because McMurphy's gestures are "mechanical"—a word that does not link him to the prohuman, anticombine forces he is often seen as representing. If anything, the word "mechanical" might be seen as linking McMurphy with his opponent and supposed opposite—Big Nurse, whom Big Chief described early in the novel as a "watchful robot" (an image similar to "zombie") that looks after its network of wires "with mechanical insect skill" (26).

In contrast to Big Nurse's and McMurphy's acquiescence to group pressure suggested in the dehumanizing imagery above is Big Chief's "humanizing" ability to make his own choices by the end of the novel. These choices reflect a growing self-reliance that comes out of a matrix of attitudes in opposition to those producing conformity.* Some of these attitudes come from his family. His Papa says, "if you don't watch it people will force you one way or the other into doing what they think you should do, or into just being mule-stubborn and doing the opposite out of spite" (198). The Chief's father implies that a person is controlled either in conformity to the wishes of others or *in rebellion* against them. He goes on to illustrate this apparent paradox by pointing to one of the Chief's uncles, who became a lawyer "purely to prove he could, when he'd rather poke salmon in the fall than anything" (198).

By the end of the novel all the characters, except Big Chief, either conform to society or become "mule stubborn" and rebel against it. Judging from the comments of the Chief's father, none of these characters has made an individual choice. Early in the novel, Big Chief is "stubborn," pretending to be deaf and dumb because he feels that people will not listen to him anyway. McMurphy, as well, can be seen as stubborn when he arrives on the ward:

> "Ya know, ma'am," he says, "ya know—what is the ex-act thing somebody always tells me about the rules. . . ."
> He grins. They both smile back and forth at each other, sizing each other up.
> ". . . just when they figure I'm about to do the dead opposite." (24)

In this passage, McMurphy limits his individual choice because he *reacts* to Big Nurse rather than acting as an individual. But what is also telling is the equation of McMurphy and Big Nurse, smiling back and forth, "sizing each other up."

Kesey presents a number of comparisons between these "supposedly" strident opponents. Both must exert self-control to play by the rules of their "battle." Although Big Nurse calls McMurphy "a manipulator," she herself is "a manipulator" par excellence who continually acts to expert her power and control over others. Nevertheless, her power is revealed as an illusion as the novel progresses. In reality, Big Nurse acts as an agent who enforces a conformity to the rules of "outside society," whereas McMurphy becomes an agent of conformity to the wishes of the ward members' "inside society." Both are used by their respective societies, which deny their individuality and pit them against one another as combatants. Their similarity is stressed in the aftermath of their final "showdown": Big Nurse's face is described as "bloated blue" after she has nearly been strangled, and McMurphy's eyes have purple bruises around them after his lobotomy (306, 307). The similar bruises result from their socially imposed roles rather than from the exercise of individual choice.

Of course, Big Nurse may have lost any chance for individuality long before she ever heard of McMurphy. But McMurphy is given a chance to see the importance of retaining his identity, a chance he fails to take advantage of. After McMurphy learns that Big Nurse controls his length of stay in the asylum, he decides to conform to her demands, becoming what the ward members call "cagey." Although McMurphy's retreat from rebellion may be viewed as a loss of personal courage or as a structural device to heighten the action, this retreat also allows him to have glimpses of his "bind": if he conforms to Big Nurse's demands, he loses his status as ward "hero"; if he rebels against her, he may be committed forever. Kesey, however, wants the reader to see that either choice will limit McMurphy's overall freedom because external pressures, rather than McMurphy's own internal preferences, are forcing him to choose.

McMurphy's "bind" is illustrated after McMurphy meets Harding's wife:

> "What do you think?" Harding says.
> McMurphy starts. "She's got one hell of a set of chabobs," is all he can think of. "Big as Old Lady Ratched's."
> "I didn't mean physically, my friend, I mean what do you—"
> "Hell's bells, Harding! What do you want out of me? A marriage counsellor? All I know is this: nobody's very big in the first place, and it looks to me like everybody spends their whole life tearing everybody else down. . . ." (174)

Like Harding, the ward members want "something out of" McMurphy and use their group pressure to tear him down, an action that seems paradoxical because they also idealize him. But in this novel, being idealized is dangerous. As his conversation with Harding continues, McMurphy begins to realize the danger of and pressure behind the ward's admiration of him. So he "glares" at "the other patients" and yells "All of you! Quit bugging me, goddammit!" (174).

The conflict between individual choice and social pressure is crucial to the novel. For Kesey, any kind of social pressure can "condition" the individual and destroy his freedom of choice, as McMurphy begins to see in the ward member's behavior:

> "Hell's bells, listen to you," McMurphy says. "All I hear is gripe, gripe, gripe. About the nurse or the staff or the hospital. Scanlon wants to bomb the whole outfit. Sefelt blames the drugs. Fredrickson blames his family trouble. Well, you're all just passing the buck." (181)

McMurphy even goes on, a few lines later, to suggest that getting rid of Big Nurse would not get rid of "the deep down hang-up that's causing the gripe" (*Cuckoo's Nest* 181).

The reason behind this "deep down hang-up" is something that Mc-Murphy in not able to realize because he cannot see the full extent of the seductive power of social control. McMurphy is able to understand that the ward members as individuals lack self-reliance and also that, as a group, they are conning him:

"I couldn't figure it at first, why you guys were coming to me like I was some kind of savior. Then I just happened to find out about the way the nurses have the big say as to who gets discharged and who doesn't. And I get wise awful damned fast. I said , 'Why those slippery bastards have *conned* me, snowed me into holding their bag. If that don't beat all, conned ol' R. P. McMurphy.'" (182)

But McMurphy assumes that the ward members "con" him so that they can take Big Nurse's pressure off themselves. When he finds that most of the Acutes are voluntary and can leave whenever they want, he gets a "puzzled look on his face like there's something that isn't right, something that he can't put his finger on" (182). What McMurphy cannot understand is the ward's responsibility, as a group, for reinforcing its patients' feelings of powerlessness, feelings that do not arise simply from Big Nurse's authoritarianism.

When Billy Bibbit blames his own voluntary commitment on the fact that he is "not big and tough" and does not have "the guts," McMurphy "turns round to the rest of the guys and opens his mouth to ask something else, and then closes it when he sees how they are looking at him." The ward members stand in front of McMurphy, their "row of eyes aimed at him like a row of rivets" (185). This image, in part, conveys the social pressure and guilt "aimed" at conditioning McMurphy's behavior. But the Image carries more sinister associations as well. A few pages earlier, the "metal door" of the shock shop looked "out with its rivet eyes" (269). Through this association Kesey suggests that McMurphy is receiving the ward members' version of "shock therapy." The patients want McMurphy to conform to their expectations in the way that electroshock in the novel is used as a means to make deviants conform to "outside" society.

After the ward's "treatment," McMurphy embraces the role of savior that the group has presented to him, a role that leads ultimately to his lobotomy. In fact, McMurphy's individuality undergoes a "lobotomy" as the result of group pressure long before Big Nurse orders the actual one. Kesey underscores the callousness of McMurphy's manipulation when the whole ward passively watches his being subdued by the orderlies after he has attempted to strangle Big Nurse. The ward knows he is headed for an actual lobotomy, but not one of them helps because such an action would force them to admit that they are responsible for McMurphy's position. In an attempt to deflect this responsibility, Big Chief often calls the struggle between Big Nurse and McMurphy a "game." For the ward members this contest, among other things, provides excitement in their otherwise dull lives.

Only three of the twenty Acutes who condition McMurphy to accept his role as ward hero remain to find out what happens to him. It might be argued that it would be too depressing for them to see McMurphy after his lobotomy, but their deflection of responsibility from the person they have victimized, conned, and manipulated points out the negative feelings Kesey has about the final effects of "social conditioning." What Kesey is advancing, cynically and unromantically, is the necessity for a person to look after his own individuality. It seems likely that Kesey sees McMurphy as a more positive figure when he first arrives on the ward than when he sacrifices himself for the ward members at the end.

McMurphy's problems are both his lack of awareness of the dangers of social control and his unwitting acceptance of some forms of it. Early in the novel he is "a moving target that's hard to hit" (89). But later he becomes "a fool" because he is conned by others into ignoring his own individuality. As Big Chief says, "You got to understand that as soon as a man goes to help somebody, he leaves himself wide open" (131). Such a message is undoubtedly unpleasant to people who would like to believe in sacrifice for the sake of others; Kesey's novel, however, contains no such "elevated message."

What, after all, has McMurphy's "rebellion" accomplished? Billy Bibbit and Cheswick have killed themselves, and all the Acutes except Scanlon, Martini, and Big Chief discharge themselves from the ward before the lobotomized McMurphy returns. For those who have left, "the game" is over. They have, in a sense, "won" in pitting their warrior against Big Nurse. But there is no solid evidence that any of the discharged patients has taken responsibility for his role in McMurphy's destruction Nor is there evidence that any of the ward members has become sane. Some have simply transferred themselves to other wards. Harding's return to his wife gives no indication that any of his problems have cleared up. Although they have discharged themselves, Sefelt and Fredrickson are still faced with the "double bind" of epileptic fits or rotting gums. Though the composition of the ward has changed, nothing significant has happened to any of the ward members—except Big Chief.

Big Chief is Kesey's most complex creation in *Cuckoo's Nest* because he is both a character in his own right and one whose perspective controls the reader's. Although the Chief cannot be termed a character who intentionally attempts to deceive, he is a character whose insanity *and humanity* cause him to distort facts in ways that disclose Kesey's preoccupation with people's dehumanization of themselves and others.

Big Chief's distorted perspective reveals truths about the extent of dehumanization on the ward because much of his bizarre behavior is an attempt to avoid this dehumanization. His "deaf and dumb act" offers him a way out of degrading situations, but the problem with this tactic becomes evident to Big Chief when he finds the alienation of the "fog" more frightening than the hostile environment of Big Nurse's ward. In avoiding the outside world and retreating into the "fog," the Chief comes up against the terrifying sense of being alone without identity.

As Big Chief moves toward sanity, he begins to break out of the bind of having to choose either the hostile world or his own alienation. McMurphy, as a catalyst, may be partially responsible for prodding the Chief toward recovery, but Kesey wants the reader to see that Big Chief's sanity results from his own actions, especially after his last electroshock treatment when the Chief knows he "had them beat" (276).

There is, however, for the Chief no quick avenue to sanity, which seems to come mainly from his increasing sense of responsibility for his own actions. His first significant act is his vote in favor of the World Series. Initially the Chief attempts to believe that McMurphy is making him raise his hand by means of "wires." But immediately after making this assertion the Chief takes responsibility and says that he "lifted it" himself (136). This first acceptance of responsibility leads to others: his decision to go on the fishing trip, his support of McMurphy in fighting the orderlies, and his quick recovery from his last shock treatment.

What often happens, however, is an attempt by readers to give McMurphy exclusive credit for the Chief's growing sanity. Yet Big Chief is the only one of the ward members who gains his sanity. If McMurphy acts as a catalyst, to sanity, all of the other Acutes presumably should have benefited as well. Only the Chief, however, is meant to be seen as sane at the end.

Read carefully, the novel reveals the pattern of Big Chief's slowly growing sanity independent of McMurphy's aid. Twenty pages alter he has voted in favor of the World Series, the Chief gets out of bed alone to look at the autumn night. Here he begins to recapture some of his former feelings about nature as he watches a dog wander about in the moonlight. That the dog is run over by a car reinforces the images of the power of the machine over the organic world, but the event doesn't distress Big Chief. In fact, the extensively birthmarked nurse who puts the Chief to bed might seem less sane than he does. This whole incident is independent of McMurphy's presence and points to Big Chief's growing individualism.

Immediately alter the above incident, McMurphy begins to "get cagey" because he learns that Big Nurse has control over his length of commitment. In relationship to the pattern of the novel Kesey is suggesting that Big Chief is increasingly able to strengthen his self-reliance while McMurphy loses his: specifically, when McMurphy capitulates to the pressure of the ward members and becomes their leader once again at the end of this section (189–190).

In the next section, when McMurphy becomes the ward's leader once again, the Chief begins to remember his childhood in detail, independent of McMurphy's, or anyone else's, influence. Because these rather lengthy memories (197–203) precede McMurphy's offer of gum (205), it seems likely that they can be seen to have some influence on Big Chiefs decision to speak. Take for instance a passage that occurs seven pages before the Chief speaks:

"I lay in bed all night . . . and thought it over, about my being deaf, about the years of not letting on I heard what was said and I wondered if I could ever act any other way again" (197-198). The memory that follows this quotation bears directly on the reasons why Big Chief began his "deaf and dumb" act; it is his memory of when he was treated as "invisible" by the federal agents who wanted the Chief's tribal land. After the memory, he is already predisposed to begin talking when he finds Geever taking the gum from under his bed. Such an argument does not deny McMurphy as a catalyst agent, but rather it emphasizes Big Chief's active part in preparing himself for sanity.

Big Chief's active role is most clear when he has his last electroshock treatment, after which he is able to speak to others and no longer feigns deafness—a change meant to indicate his growing sanity and ability to cope. Surprisingly little attention has been given Big Chief's fragmented thoughts immediately before his recovery from his last electroshock treatment. If, however, these thoughts are seen in the context of Big Chief's attempt to find a viable individualistic option for his life, the section makes sense. As the Chief searches his memory, images of dice coming up "snake-eyes" indicate his rejection of possible options:

> My roll, *Faw,* Damn. Twisted again. Snake eyes.
> The schoolteacher tell me you got a good head, boy, be something. . . .
> Be what, Papa? A rug-weaver like Uncle R & J, Wolf? A blanket-weaver? or another drunken Indian?
> I say, attendant, you're an Indian, aren't you?
> Yeah, that's right.
> Well, I must say, you speak the language quite well.
> Yeah.
> Well . . . three dollars of regular.
> They wouldn't be so cocky if they knew what me and the *moon* have going. No damned regular indian . . .
> He who—what is it?—walks out of step, hears another drum.
> Snake eyes again. Hoo boy, these dice are *cold.* (274)

In this passage Big Chief rejects the standard options, from rug-weaver to alcoholic, available to an Indian in white or Indian society. At the end of the passage he also rejects his possible role as rebel (intimated by the paraphrasing of Thoreau's words). Ultimately Big Chief docs not want to be cast in the role either of conformist or of rebel because both end with "snake eyes."

If Big Chief rejects both conformity and rebellion, what option is left for him? Here the dice imagery is important because at the end of the section the Chief sees that he has been loading the dice against himself (275). Only after this realization can he "work himself out of the shock treatment. When he takes responsibility for his own actions, he knows he has "them beat" (275).

After his recovery from this, his last shock treatment, the Chief is able to see McMurphy from a less idealized perspective. He becomes aware that McMurphy forces himself to continue to take shock treatments because "every one of those faces on Disturbed had turned toward him and was waiting" (276). Although McMurphy attempts to pose as a heroic figure who can take anything that Big Nurse "dishes out," Big Chief sees through the role: "But every time that loud speaker called for him to forgo breakfast and prepare to walk to Building One, the muscles in his jaw went taut and his whole face drained of color, *looking thin and scared*—the fact I had seen reflected in the windshield on the trip back from the coast" (276–277, italics mine). Group pressure forces McMurphy to play the role of hero, but the result is the draining of his individuality.

When Big Chief returns from his last electroshock treatment, he begins to understand the power exerted on him by the ward members. They begin to look at him as a hero: "everybody's face turned up to me with a different look than they'd ever given me before" (277). And, as a result, Big Chief begins to realize "how McMurphy must've felt all these months with these faces screaming up at him" (277). The ward members are ready to see the former "deaf and dumb Injun" as a glorious "Wildman," but Kesey's point is that neither of these roles reflects the Chief's real self. "Injun" and "Wildman" are roles that the group defines or has defined.

Perhaps Big Chief is the only character who actually maintains an awareness of his personal involvement in the process of playing roles at the end of the novel. To a large extent this awareness is the result of watching McMurphy become trapped by his roles. It is not by chance, then, that Big Chief kills McMurphy. It is not a mercy killing as some readers have argued, or an act of love, or a murder of the Chief's former self.[5] The murder is best understood in light of both group pressure and individual realization. It is the Chief's last action as part of the group, and through it Big Chief is able to understand fully the extent to which McMurphy and he have been manipulated by the ward members. This awareness of the power of groups allows him to free himself from the members and to define himself as an individual.

As one of the ward's members. Big Chief acts in the manner of a priest/executioner of a primitive society. The title of the novel is derived from a nursery rhyme, and as Bruce Carnes notices, counting rhymes were often used by "primitive tribes" to "select the human sacrifice offered to appease a wrathful god" (15). The idea of a sacrifice is apropos: not in order to "appease a wrathful god" but rather as the result of the ward members' need to manipulate and destroy a victim both as a demonstration of their own power and as a way to scapegoat the guilt resulting from the destruction of the individual.

The notion that Kesey intended McMurphy as a sacrificial victim finds support in the novel. When McMurphy returns from the lobotomy, Big Chief denies that the lobotomized form has a name—a denial comparable to a ritual common to sacrifices: the victim's namelessness before sacrifice. Big Chief, however, attempts to argue that McMurphy's form will be used by Big Nurse as an example to others of what happens to those who buck the system. In reality, the ward members themselves are more responsible for McMurphy's destruction than Big Nurse is.

Big Chief, however, is more than simply an executioner performing the will of the ward members who have sacrificed McMurphy's individualism to their own manipulative needs. Earlier in the novel, Big Chief had seen McMurphy as "a giant come out of the sky to save us from the 'Combine'" (255). Later he sacrifices "this giant" not to the "Combine" but to fulfill the collective will of the ward members, which is inseparably his own. It is immediately after he kills McMurphy that Big Chief realizes the extent of his own manipulation and his responsibility in McMurphy's death.

It is interesting that Big Chief deflects this realization from direct expression:

> I lay for a white, holding the covers over my face, and thought I was being pretty quiet, but Scanlon's voice hissing from his bed let me know I wasn't
> "Take it easy, Chief," he said. "Take it easy. It's okay." (309)

Big Chief's crying here might be explained as the result of his grief over having to destroy the lobotomized form of his onetime friend and leader, McMurphy. But more is suggested if Big Chief's reaction is connected with his description of the actual murder:

> The big, hard body had a tough grip on life. It fought a long time against having it taken away, flailing and thrashing around so much I finally had to lie full length on top of it and scissor the kicking legs with mine while I mashed the pillow into the face. I lay there on top of the body what seemed days. Until the thrashing stopped. Until it was still a while and had shuddered once and was still again. (309)

What is noticeable about this description is its dehumanization of McMurphy, who is referred to as "it" or "the body." Here Big Chief, fulfilling his role as the ward member's priest/executioner, has completely dehumanized another human being. Viewed in the context of Big Chief's murder of McMurphy, it might seem ironic that so much attention has been paid to McMurphy's sexist and racist postures in the novel. They may be indefensible, but in the novel their expression as an indication of an individual's prejudice and stereotyping might be judged as less menacing and destructive than the type of dehumanization that is socially enforced.

In killing McMurphy, Big Chief has, as the ward's "representative," direct experience of the power of a social group over an individual. He has been both a participant in exerting the group's power and a witness in recording the effect of that power on the individual. He cries after McMurphy's death because he realizes that both he and McMurphy not only have been used by the ward members but also have accepted the roles that the members have provided for them—executioner and victim. In rejecting McMurphy's cap as too small, Big Chief also rejects his attachment to any social role because it can lead only to the roles of victimizer or victim. In his rejection of the social role that led to McMurphy's lobotomy and murder, Big Chief proves that he is "bigger" than any of the other characters. He is able to understand the terrible power of groups and, more than that, the power of the individual to reject social control. It is this second realization that leads to his escape from the institution and his freedom.

Such an escape, as uplifting as it might appear in relationship to the assertion of an individual's freedom, is not without qualification in the novel. A question might be raised about what exactly Big Chief escapes to. There is some suggestion that he might become like the other Indians who "are spearing salmon in the spillway" below the "big hydro-electric dam," an image of the survival of individualism under the immensity of the technocratic superstructure of American society. However, his main preference is "to look over the country around the gorge again" because, as he says, "I been away a long time" (311).

On the surface, this rather tentative ending, bordering on nostalgia, does not seem a potent enough answer to the socially destructive forces that Big Chief escapes. But the Chief's last line, "I been away a long time," also echoes Huck Finn's last line, "I been there before" (Clemens 299).[6] And likewise, Big Chiefs escape to The Dalles may be reminiscent of the impossibility of Huck's complete escape from social forces by being "ahead of the rest." But the connection between Huck Finn and Big Chief is not simply one of tentative escapes. Both are storytellers who recount their pasts and, in so doing, reveal their inability to escape. In each novel the reader is given little about the possibilities of each of these characters' lives after their respective escapes to freedom. The only definite action is the narration of the story itself. However, there is a paradox in the telling of each story because in doing so the narrator still is tied the social forces he has supposedly escaped. On one level, the narration recounts an individual's escape. Simultaneously, on another level, the narration repeals an individual's inability fully to escape because the individual independence that is formed in repudiation of society is also inextricably linked to it.

In *Cuckoo's Nest* the Chief's growth in his sense of responsibility for his own actions leads ultimately to his escape from the asylum. But that same responsibility carries with it the burden of guilt for his role in murdering Mc-Murphy. The individual responsibility that allows Big Chief to escape also binds him to his past actions in the asylum. When Big Chief played deaf and dumb at the beginning of *Cuckoo's Nest*, he may have swung from his alienation in the "fog" to his fear of the hostile world of the ward, but he did not feel any guilt. Guilt, however, drives Big Chief's narration, which must finally be seen as confessional: "It's gonna burn me just that way, finally telling about all this, about the hospital, and her, and the guy—and about McMurphy. I been silent so long now it's gonna roar out of me like floodwaters..." (8). The "truth even if it really didn't happen" is the Chief's final inability to escape the ward because his shadowy sense of freedom at the end is irrevocably tied to his escape from the asylum. The act of murder that allows the Chief to realize his own and McMurphy's manipulation at the hands of the ward members is the same act that, because of his newly acquired sense of responsibility, produces the guilt that drives the narration. By the end of the novel Big Chief has traded his initial freedom from guilt (due to his personal denial of responsibility for his own actions) for a freedom from social control (due to his acceptance of responsibility and its attendant guilt). It is perhaps fitting then that Big Chief's narration should begin as if he were once again back on the ward.

WORKS CITED

Barsness, John A. "Ken Kesey: The Hero in Modern Dress." *Bulletin of the Rocky Mountain Modern Language Association* 23 (1969): pp. 27–33.

Baurecht, William C. "Separation, Initiation, and Return: Schizophrenic Episode in *One Flew Over the Cuckoo's Nest.*" *Midwest Quarterly* 23 (1982): pp. 279–293.

Beidler, Peter G. "From Rabbits to Men: Self-Reliance in the Cuckoo's nest.:" *Lex et Scientia* 13 (1977): pp. 56–59.

Benert, Annette. "The Forces of Fear: Kesey's Anatomy of Insanity." *Lex et Scientia* 13 (1977): pp. 22–26.

Boardman, Michael M. "*One Flew Over the Cuckoo's Nest:* Rhetoric and Vision." *Journal of Narrative Technique* 9 (1979): pp. 171–183.

Bross, Addison C. "Art and Ideology: Kesey's Approach to Fiction." *Lex et Scientia* 13 (1977): pp. 60–64.

Carnes, Bruce, *Ken Kesey.* Boise State University Western Writers Series 12. Boise: Boise State University Press, 1974.

Clemens, Samuel L. *Adventures of Huckleberry Finn.* 1885. New York: Norton, 1977.

De Bellis, Jack. "Alone No More: Dualism in American Literary Thought." *Lex et Scientia* 13 (1977): p. 73.

———. "Facing Things Honestly: McMurphy's Conversion." *Lex et Scientia* 13 (1977): pp. 11–13.

Falk, Marcia Y. Letter. *New York Times* 5 Dec. 1971. Rpt. in *"One Flew Over the Cuckoo's Nest": Text and Criticism.* Ed. John C. Pratt. New York: Viking, 1973: pp. 450–453.

Forrey, Robert. "Ken Kesey's Psychopathic Savior: A Rejoinder." *Modern Fiction Studies* 21 (1975): pp. 222–230.

Gallagher, Edward J. "From Folded Hands to Clenched Fists: Kesey and Science Fiction." *Lex et Scientia* 13 (1977): pp. 49–50.

Grunwald, Beverly. "Kesey: A Sane View from *Cuckoo's Nest.*" *Women's Wear Daily* Dec. 1975: pp. 1–3.

Hardy, William J. "Chief Bromden: Kesey's Existentialist Hero." *North Dakota Quarterly* 18 (1980): pp. 72–83.

Herrenkohl, Ellen. "Regaining Freedom: Sanity in Insane Places." *Lex et Scientia* 13 (1977): pp. 42–44.

Hort, Leslie. "Bitches, Twitches, and Eunuchs: Sex Role Failure and Caricature." *Lex et Scientia* 13 (1977): pp. 14–17.

Hunt, John W. "Flying the Cuckoo's Nest: Kesey's Narrator as Norm." *Lex et Scientia* 13 (1977): pp. 26–32.

Kesey, Ken. *Kesey's Garage Sale.* New York: Viking, 1973.

———. *One Flew Over the Cuckoo's Nest.* New York: Viking, 1962.

Leeds, Barry H. *Ken Kesey.* New York: Ungar, 1981.

Lish, Gordon. "'What the Hell You Looking in Here For, Daisy Mae?' An Interview with Ken Kesey." *Genesis West* 2 (1963): pp. 17–29.

Martin, Terence. "*One Flew Over the Cuckoo's Nest* and the High Cost of Living." *Modern Fiction Studies* 19 (1973): pp. 43–55.

Murphy, Kevin. "Illiterate's Progress: The Descent into Literacy in *Huckleberry Finn.*" *Texas studies in Literature and Language* 26 (1984): pp. 363–387.

Sasoon, R. L. Rev. of *One Flew Over the Cuckoo's Nest. Northwest Review* 6 (1963): pp. 116–120.

Sherwood, Terry G. "*One Flew Over the Cuckoo's Nest* and the Comic Strip." *Critique,* 13 (1971): pp. 96–109.

Sunderland, Janet R. "A Defense of Ken Kesey's *One Flew Over the Cuckoo's Nest.*" *English Journal* 61 (1972): pp. 28–31.

Tanner, Stephen L. *Ken Kesey.* Twayne's United States Authors Series 444. Boston: Twayne, 1983.

Waldmeir, Joseph J. "Two Novelists of the Absurd: Heller and Kesey." *Wisconsin Studies in Contemporary Literature* 5 (1964): pp. 192–204.

THOMAS J. SLATER

One Flew Over the Cuckoo's Nest:
A Tale of Two Decades

When adapting Ken Kesey's *One Flew Over the Cuckoo's Nest* for the screen, Milos Forman faced one very significant problem: the novel's narrator is a paranoid-schizophrenic who sees things that nobody else can. Seen through the eyes of the six-foot-eight American Indian named Chief Bromden, *Cuckoo's Nest's* main setting of mental ward at the Oregon State Hospital becomes a surrealistic world controlled by hidden wires and fog machines that help the head nurse and her staff to work their will on the patients. Although the Chief's vision is comic and absurd, it also reveals the reality of the world and the events that take place. As he accurately notes, "It's the truth, even if it didn't happen" (Kesey 1962, p. 13).

Forman also faced the problem of making Kesey's liberal early-sixties' theme of fighting conformity relevant to the mid-seventies. Forman had to make the story contemporary without losing its essence. He was successful mainly because he gave the novel's unusual narrative perspective to his camera and transformed Kesey's mythic characters and surrealist setting into human beings in a unique but recognizable world.

To many readers, the novel's apparent hero is Randle Patrick McMurphy, a big, boastful Irishman who lies his way into the Oregon State Hospital to escape the drudgery of a prison work farm. Once there, he leads the patients in a fight against the hospital staff's attempt to impose mind control. The

Film and Literature: A Comparative Approach to Adaptation, Eds., Wendell Aycock and Michael Schoenecke (Lubbock: Texas Tech University Press, 1988): pp. 45-58.

narrator, Chief Bromden, sees McMurphy as a hero because he merely laughs at the whole situation on the mental ward instead of living in fear.[1] Through his swaggering, boastful nature and his defiance of conventions despite the consequences, McMurphy eventually helps instill the other men on the ward with the confidence to face life again. He creates a virtual metamorphosis in his fellow patients, which leads the Chief to present him in mythic terms.[2]

For example, the Chief's depiction of McMurphy as a Christ figure is blatantly obvious. McMurphy comes into the ward, gathers his followers about him, instructs them in how to live, and then sacrifices himself for them even though he has done nothing wrong. He dies merely because he is a threat to the status quo. The Chief leaves no doubt about his analogy when he includes a description of the electroshock therapy table as looking like a cross (Kesey 1962, p. 64) and of himself as wanting to touch McMurphy merely because "he's who he is" (Kesey 1962, p. 188). A fishing trip that McMurphy organizes is also directly out of the Christ story. McMurphy leads his twelve followers out to sea and goes down into the hold, but when chaos breaks out on board, he is forced to come back up and calm everything down (Kesey 1962, pp. 191–218). The Chief completes the analogy by saying that the last time any of them saw him conscious "he let himself cry out" (Kesey 1962, p. 267).

Despite this convincing portrait, McMurphy is not really the man that the Chief presents him to be. Throughout the novel, Kesey subtly undercuts the Chief's biased presentation of McMurphy as a mythic figure. At midpoint in the story, McMurphy learns that Nurse Ratched (the ward's controller and novel's villain) has the power to keep him in the hospital as long as she wants. He first responds by fully cooperating with her so that he can gain his release (Kesey 1962, pp. 148–149). But then he changes his mind and spends the rest of the novel doing exactly what he wants, consciously antagonizing Big Nurse (Ratched's nickname). The Chief never explains why McMurphy becomes rebellious again, but he does reveal several factors operating on his hero's mind at that point in the novel. McMurphy feels responsible for the suicide of fellow patient Charlie Cheswick (Kesey 1962, p. 151), and he also discovers that the other men are in the hospital only because they do not have the courage to be on the outside (Kesey 1962, p. 168). McMurphy therefore realizes that conformity and fear are interrelated, feeding on each other and producing the kind of hollow men that Nurse Ratched desires.

Thus, when McMurphy once more defies Nurse Ratched, he is acting under strong feelings of guilt and doubt. Just when Nurse Ratched believes that she is in full control of the ward, McMurphy deliberately smashes her office window, an act that the Chief relates in mythic terms as a calculated act of self-sacrifice (Kesey 1962, pp. 171–172). Most likely, McMurphy is attempting to redeem himself and preserve his self-identity. The Chief notes that Nurse Ratched felt she had gained a "final victory" (Kesey 1962, p. 172). McMurphy is mainly fearful of losing his own soul, and he is not basically concerned with saving others.

Nurse Ratched is also a larger than life character in the novel. The Chief pictures her as a machine who sits at the center of a system (which he calls "The Combine") that operates both outside and inside the ward to keep people contentedly going about their business without complaint. The Chief sees her battle with McMurphy as a struggle between two large conceptions of what America is, and his hero's one chance of victory is to get Nurse Ratched to recognize her own humanity.

At the end of the novel, Kesey undercuts the mythic stature of both McMurphy and Ratched when fellow-patient Dale Harding denies that McMurphy is a Christ-figure while at the same time denying Big Nurse a chance to regain her power. She feels that if she can make an example of McMurphy, the ward will return to its former routine. Taking over the words of Christ, she tells Harding that McMurphy is going to return: "I would not say so if I was not positive. He will be back" (Kesey 1962, p. 268). Harding responds, "Lady, I think you're so full of bullshit" (Kesey 1962, pp. 268–269). By finally dispelling the notion of McMurphy as Christ, Kesey makes it clear that the novel's true hero is the Chief himself. Throughout the novel, the Chief undergoes a complete spiritual transformation and is ready at the end to continue struggling against society's oppressiveness, but not by adopting McMurphy's recklessness. He represents a middle path between these two extremes and exemplifies Kesey's message of individual responsibility. The Chief's story represents the end of one phase of his battle and the beginning of another.[3]

Milos Forman remains true to the spirit of Kesey's novel by keeping his basic message but renovating the story to make it relevant to the mid-seventies. In the film, Forman's camera appropriately takes over the narrative perspective of both the Chief and Ken Kesey. Like the Chief in the novel, the camera presents McMurphy as a mythic figure while, at the same time, undercutting that notion. In the end, the viewer must realize his own responsibility for going beyond the philosophies of both McMurphy and Nurse Ratched. Once again, the Chief provides the final example to be followed.

In contrast to the book, the movie establishes the Chief as the only character that McMurphy sets free because he is the only one who has gained the courage to act on his own. Forman gives the story a contemporary meaning by showing it as a struggle for power among McMurphy, Ratched, and Harding. On its surface, Forman's film appears to have a conservative message because the hero is battling an oppressive social system dominated by a woman and a homosexual (Dale Harding), but his film is neither sexist not anti-gay. His depiction of all three characters as failing to achieve or maintain power because of their very lust for it presents his true theme. Forman shows that people who strive for power are susceptible to their own human weaknesses, a fact that everyone needs to realize. In the end, each individual must work towards his or her own freedom or remain entrapped by the whims of those in power.

Forman begins by translating the Chief's characterization of McMurphy as a mythic hero onto the screen. The opening shot shows the red light of daybreak glowing out over a dark mountain. The music starts with the sound of an American Indian drumbeat, which is joined by a gentle folk guitar and a mournful harmonica that also has a mocking tone to it, like something has passed but does not really merit deep sympathy. Emerging from the deep shadows of the mountain are the headlights of the police car bringing McMurphy from the prison camp to the hospital.

In this one shot, Forman creates McMurphy as a mythic figure. McMurphy represents the freedom and elemental forces associated with the American wilderness. The mountain becomes an important symbol of manhood. When the Chief is ready to leave the hospital at the end of the film, he tells the comatose McMurphy that he is "big as a damn mountain." The native and folk music associates McMurphy with the basic instincts of Americans who are closely related to the land and do not have much power, people such as American Indians, farmers, and mountain people. The harmonica sounds like a lament, but McMurphy is not a character who would mourn anything and so the slightly mocking tone is appropriate. When the Chief makes his escape at the end, the harmonica tune becomes a brief, joyously orchestrated crescendo before lapsing again into a gentle murmur. The music thus emphasizes Forman's theme that the human spirit can, at times, overcome despair and burst forth in triumph.

For the second shot of the film, Forman pans from a window inside the hospital ward across the bed of one of the patients and on through the room. The shot is from the viewpoint of a patient who could have been watching the car coming and then turned to look back across the room. Scattered patches of red light coming from the window break the darkness of the ward, like sunlight seen from under water. Forman maintains the association of the red light with freedom and the idea of the men being kept like fish in an aquarium throughout the entire film. The ward's red exit signs constantly beckon the men towards a different world, one whose uncertainty makes them reluctant to leave their safe confines, despite the abuse they suffer.[4]

Forman's starting the shot from the barrier formed between the two worlds by the wall and the opposite movement of the camera from the opening shot further support his quick division of the world in the film between the outside and the inside. This division docs not exist in the novel, where the Combine operates everywhere. In the film, McMurphy enables the men to experience freedom and dignity by taking them away from the hospital by involving them in sports such as basketball and fishing. McMurphy starts simply, within the ward. When he arrives, four of the men, Charlie Cheswick (Sidney Lassick), Billy Bibbit (Brad Dourif), Harding (William Redfield), and Martini (Danny DeVito) are playing cards.[5] McMurphy gathers his first follower by flashing his own deck of pornographic playing cards at Martini and luring him away. This action demonstrates that McMurphy is presenting the men an alternative reality more appealing to them than anything they have experienced before. Forman, however, has already begun to undercut McMurphy. When the police first take the handcuffs off him, McMurphy begins jumping around and screeching like a monkey. The action is funny, but it also shows that an uncontrolled nature is not completely desirable. Society has good reasons for taming the forces with which McMurphy is associated. But, in the mental hospital, it has gone too far. The film, therefore, like the novel, must demonstrate that a middle path between the extremes of Mc-Murphy and Ratched does exist.

McMurphy is also a Christ-figure in the film, but Forman suggests the idea much more subtly than the Chief does in the novel. He shows McMurphy on the ward for the first time exercising with the other men before the daily therapy session. Forman shoots him from behind as McMurphy stands briefly with his arms stretched out in the crucifix position. The camera angle is significant because it emphasizes that McMurphy is not conscious of others seeing him as a Christ-figure. In the film, he never shows any intention of playing the hero. He makes all of his challenges to Nurse Ratched when he has no knowledge of her power to keep him institutionalized indefinitely. He acts openly only because he does not understand the risk he is taking.

For example, during the scene in which McMurphy tries teaching the Chief (Will Sampson) how to play basketball, Forman demonstrates the enormity of his spirit in comparison with the other men. McMurphy climbs onto the shoulders of another patient, Bancini. When Bancini begins to run around, McMurphy starts screaming. "Hit me, Chief! I'm open." His voice fills the soundtrack, giving the impression that he is now the dominant force at the hospital, but Forman's camera is on Nurse Ratched watching from an omnipotent position inside the hospital. She maintains the power and McMurphy's optimism is false, Once again. Forman uses the perspective of another patient, this time one who is standing on the sidelines, whose simple vision both supports and undercuts McMurphy's lofty stature.

In the fishing trip sequence, Forman undercuts McMurphy through a combination of the camera's point of view and an alteration in the narrative structure. In this scene, Forman strongly emphasizes the idea that the men are taking on new identities. McMurphy manages to confiscate a rental boat by telling the harbor manager that the men are doctors from the mental hospital. Forman captures the men in individual shots as McMurphy introduces them, and they all look suddenly sophisticated.[6] McMurphy gets the men

started fishing and then goes below deck with his girlfriend. Martini immediately leads the men up front to try to peek in the windows. Chaos erupts
when Cheswick turns around, sees no one on deck, and leaves the steering
wheel. The boat starts going crazy, McMurphy comes up on deck, and Taber
(Christopher Lloyd) hooks a fish. All of the men struggle together to bring it
in while Harding and Cheswick fight over the steering wheel. Forman pulls
up to a high shot to show the boat going in a circle, thus communicating one
of the problems with McMurphy's influence. Though the men are feeling
free, McMurphy is actually leading them in circles. They are merely bouncing
from Nurse Ratched's control into his.

In this shot, Forman copies the Chief's narrative perspective in the book
exactly. The difference is that the Chief interprets what he sees in purely opti-
mistic terms, whereas Forman's shot captures the full complexity of the situation. Although he is a part of the group, the Chief also imagines himself high
above the men and sees their laughter crashing in waves on shores all over the
world (Kesey 1962, p. 212). In the film, the Chief is not even on the boat, a
fact relevant nor only to Forman's change of narrator, but also to his alteration
of the story to emphasize his own distinct themes. In the novel, the fishing
trip and the basketball game between the patients and the aides both lake
place after McMurphy has already learned about Nurse Ratched's power over
him. Forman places both events before McMurphy's discovery of this fact.
Thus, McMurphy is not taking a conscious risk in the film; he is acting out
of a pure desire to prove himself to the men and have some pleasure, feeding
his own ego and libido at the same time. Kesey makes the trip a major step
in McMurphy's aid to the Chief's transformation, but Forman replaces the
theme of spiritual growth with an examination of individuals in a struggle for
power. The three characters who seek it, McMurphy, Ratched, and Harding,
all fail, leaving each of the men ultimately responsible for facing the world
on his own.

By showing that he never consciously plays a hero's role, Forman undercuts McMurphy's mythic image thoroughly. In the novel, when McMurphy
smashes the glass in Nurse Ratched's office window, the Chief describes him
as carefully contemplating his action beforehand. In the film, McMurphy acts
out of anger while surrounded by chaos. Taber has been carried away screaming after being burned by a cigarette that became lodged in his pant cuff, and
Cheswick is hollering to get his confiscated cigarettes back. McMurphy first
tries to silence him, but then goes in frustration to smash the window.

Similarly, at the end of the novel, McMurphy simply chooses not to leave
the ward, and the Chief once again allows for the possibility that McMurphy's
act is a heroic gesture. Forman shows McMurphy as unable to leave; when the
aides arrive in the morning, he is still passed out on the floor from the previous night's party. Forman's shot of him lying there summarizes his conception

of the character. The empty liquor bottle next to him, its former contents a source of both liberation and entrapment, is a reflection of McMurphy himself. Without self-control, the spirits of both have been wasted.

When McMurphy finally attacks Nurse Ratched, he is again acting impulsively. Shortly before, he is about to escape when Billy Bibbit's body is discovered. McMurphy's girlfriends call from outside the open window, but he cannot keep himself from returning to the scene. Nurse Ratched attempts to reassert the old order, and McMurphy, realizing that he is losing his power, attacks. Even if his action is interpreted as a sacrifice, his own lack of conscious behavior has created the entire situation in the first place Ultimately, McMurphy has no one but himself to blame for his suffering.

Jack Nicholson deserves much credit for creating McMurphy as a powerfully ambiguous character, both appealing and repulsive.[7] When he acts like a baboon upon entering the hospital, Nicholson indicates that McMurphy is a character who lives on his own level of existence. This factor is the source of both his power and his downfall; he fascinates everyone, but no one can figure him out. All the patients think he is crazy for acting as boldly as he does, but follow him as if he were sane. All the doctors, and Nurse Ratched, believe he is sane, but treat him as it he were crazy. Meanwhile, the audience must question who is really mentally ill, the patients or the staff. Nicholson illustrates the power in McMurphy's own brand of insanity in one key scene.

McMurphy's attempt to lift a shower control panel seems idiotic at first. He begins by taking some deep breaths, working himself into a frenzy, and uttering some gibberish as if he were speaking in tongues. As he strains to lift the panel, every vein in his arms and neck seems to pop up. He is clearly entering his own distinct reality. When he fails and challenges the other patients for not even trying, he gains the admiration of his fellow patients. By contrast, Forman questions McMurphy's sanity most at a time that appears to be his peak. At the end of the party he creates on the ward, the night before he is supposed to leave, McMurphy sits down to wait while Billy Bibbit goes to make love to the prostitute, Candy (Maria Small). The ward is in chaos, and the men are all drunk. It is McMurphy's moment of triumph. He gazes around with a self-satisfied smirk on his face. The camera holds him in a long close-up, forcing the viewer to stop to consider the image deeply. McMurphy's destructiveness does not make him an admirable figure to follow.

If McMurphy's ideal world is one of complete disarray, Nurse Ratched's is one of total order. Forman reveals this aspect of her personality in his first shot of her entering the ward. She wears a black cape and bat that forms a perfect color balance between herself and the three black aides, who all wear starched white uniforms. Later, Forman uses red light, which indicated a new day dawning for the men in the opening shot of the film, to represent the entrance to what Nurse Ratched considers to be freedom. Significantly, the hallway of the ward is lined with jail cells filled with men probably considered to be hopeless cases. The dominant empty whiteness represents the blank future toward which the hospital methods are leading the men. In one shot, a bright rectangular white light shines at the end of the hall, an image of the future. In contrast with McMurphy, Nurse Ratched promises a future devoid of life and, color; however. Forman never makes Nurse Ratched into a mythic figure. Instead, she is a very human character whose evil is greater than she realizes. She is as unconscious of her destructiveness as McMurphy is of his positive aspects.

The combination of Forman's camera and Louise Fletcher's performance truly defines Nurse Ratched as a person whose initially good intentions have been transformed into oppressiveness.[8] Because she is not a character of mythic proportions, Nurse Ratched is never called Big Nurse in the film. She is even referred to by her first name, Mildred.

Forman presents Nurse Ratched as a character who genuinely believes that she has the patients' best interests at heart, and Louise Fletcher offers no hint that the situation might be otherwise. The most obvious example of her nonmaliciousness occurs at the staff meeting when the doctors are trying to decide what they will do with McMurphy. When Nurse Ratched calmly states that they should not pass on their problem by sending him back to the prison farm, the camera is unable to capture a note of malice. Her statement that she thinks they can help him is made away from the camera and is dramatically ambiguous.

In this scene, Forman's camera once again correlates exactly with the Chief's perspective in the novel, and the film is again more complex because Nurse Ratched is seen as a human being. The Chief's view of her is clearly dehumanizing. He imagines her taking a sip of coffee and setting the cup smoldering from the heat of her lips (136). The novel then requires the reader to discern between the Chief's point of view and reality. Nevertheless, Bromden clearly presents Nurse Ratched as a mechanistic villain. In the film, Nurse Ratched does not blatantly overrule the other doctors' diagnosis as she does in the book. Instead, they ask for her opinion as a skilled professional. The viewer must ponder what is wrong about her judgment, which seems perfectly logical. The distinction between Nurse Ratched as the villain and McMurphy as the hero becomes significantly blurred.

Paradoxically, even through Forman's Nurse Ratched is more human, she is also more evil. In the novel, the Chief describes her as only the Combine's representative (Kesey 1962, p. 165). In the film, there is no Combine. Nurse Ratched is the sole barrier between the men and the outside world, a fact that Forman strongly emphasizes when she returns to the ward in the morning after the party. She and the aides stand opposite the patients, forming a human wall between the men and the red exit sign beckoning them towards the outside.

Forman's presentation of Nurse Patched as the evil oppressor left him vulnerable to being accused of sexism, as Ken Kesey had been earlier.[9] Kesey escapes the charge by virtue of the fact that not endowing Nurse Ratched with masculine qualities would completely ruin his novel's comic structure.[10] But, superficially, Forman seems to go even further in his antifemale imagery. Except for Nurse Ratched's young impressionable aide, the other women in the film are either sexual treats and builders of male egos or castraters. The prostitute whom McMurphy takes along on the fishing trip and later brings onto the ward for the party represents the woman as treat. McMurphy first introduces her to the others by saying, "Boys, this here is Candy." Candy's function is obviously to help turn boys into men, and she succeeds with Billy Bibbit. When McMurphy is about to leave the hospital at the end of the party, he stays only because Billy wants a quick "date" with Candy. Through Billy, the other men also gain maturity. They eagerly wheel him up to the room where Candy awaits. McMurphy affirms the act's communal nature when he tells Billy, "I've got twenty-five dollars that says you burn this woman *down* Eliminated from the film are references to the Chief's mother as the cause of his father's drinking and to Billy's mother as the cause of his shyness. Forman thus avoids any attacks on motherhood. He also removes from the story the young, intelligent, and humanitarian head nurse of another ward who completely opposes Nurse Ratched's methods.

Discarding the Chief as narrator necessitates these changes. The camera can only present what it sees, and no dialogue informs the audience about the patients' backgrounds. Using the camera as narrator also accounts partially for Forman's creation of Dale Harding as a more negative character than he is in the book. In both works, Harding is a weak-spirited homosexual, but Kesey explains that his personal problems originated from social factors when he was very young. He is intelligent, and McMurphy has no trouble accepting him.

Forman makes him a negative figure because he challenges McMurphy for power, counseling conformity to Nurse Ratched's wishes. Every time McMurphy attempts something new, refusing to take his medicine, trying to get the World Series on television, stealing the hospital bus, or organizing the patient's basketball team, Harding either opposes him or goes along very reluctantly Harding is in a leadership position, running the patients' games and speaking like an intellectual at the first group therapy session, but he is intimidated by Nurse Ratched, and all his talk is meaningless. He is weak because he is more committed to holding empty power than to resolving his personal problems and becoming a real leader. Harding frustrates the other patients, particularly Taber, because he wants to keep their respect without taking any chances.

After McMurphy's attempt to lift the control panel, Harding realizes that he has lost his leadership position. In the next scene, he reluctantly joins the vote to watch the World Series on television. But Harding never gives up his desire for power. When McMurphy receives his lobotomy, Harding immediately attempts to take his place and destroy the masculine image that the men are trying to hold on to. But the men will not let him, even though he alone acknowledges that McMurphy has finally been defeated for good. Harding is not McMurphy either as a card dealer or as a leader. In the end, he is still trapped inside his personal weaknesses by his desire for power. In the final shot of him, Harding is standing behind an iron gate, a picture representing his state of mind, as the Chief runs off into the night.

McMurphy continually challenges Harding's masculinity and insults him throughout the film. On the fishing boat, when he is introducing all the other men to the dock manager as doctors, he introduces Harding as mister. McMurphy is also constantly asserting his own sexual prowess, such as when he returns from electroshock therapy and tells the men, "Next woman who takes me on is going to light up like a pinball machine and pay off in silver dollars." McMurphy is thus a sexual hero as well as a spiritual one, and Forman is thereby able to satisfy his audience's contrasting desires for rebellion and reassurance. Through his revolt against bureaucratic control and association with freedom, McMurphy is a sixties' hero; but through his reassertion of a traditional social hierarchy, he is definitely one for the seventies.

Yet, the film does by no means condemn homosexuals. During the party sequence, when McMurphy seems to be firmly in charge, Forman does show homosexuality as acceptable. McMurphy calls Harding by his first name, Dale. Forman presents Fredrickson (Vincent Schiavelli) and Sefelt (William Duell), who are together throughout the film, as clearly homosexual. They dance together during the night, and aides push their beds apart the next morning. Scanlon also demonstrates deviant sexuality at the party by putting on a dress and nurse's cap. McMurphy never objects to Fredrickson, Sefelt, or Scanlon because they never challenge him. Scanlon has only one line in the whole film. Harding's offensiveness, therefore, is dearly because of his desire for power, and in this respect he is no different from either Nurse Ratched or McMurphy.

In *One Flew Over the Cuckoo's Nest*, Milos Forman manages to capture many important popular attitudes of the immediate post-Watergate era. His presentation of three characters who each fail in their struggle for power because of personal weaknesses matches the public's dominant beliefs about the fall of Richard Nixon. People did not tend to blame the political system for Watergate, but they did generally distrust social institutions. *Cuckoo's Nest* reflects this attitude, and Forman's emphasis on individual responsibility fit the "Me" decade's concern with personal development perfectly.[11]

Forman's presentation of the outside world supports his theme of each person being responsible for working towards his or her own freedom. Forman's camera again parallels the Chief's narration in the novel by revealing more about the world than most of the other characters seem to realize. Unlike those in the novel, however, Forman's references are very brief and require more interpretation from the viewer.

When the men go out on their fishing trip, they see mostly deserted streets. The few people who are around are as lifeless as the chronics on the ward. One couple has pulled a pair of folding chairs up to a television set playing in a department store window. They turn their backs on life in order to enjoy the culture presented to them. Forman thus presents television as another dictator of the social order.

When the men arrive at a trailer park to get McMurphy's girlfriend, an old man stares blankly at the camera. Upon their return from their fishing trip, a number of people line the dock, staring at the men just as blankly. These are people, young and old, who have been worn down, who go places to observe life rather than experience it themselves. When they are no longer able to do that, they just sit and stare. The vision that Forman thus presents of America in October of 1963 is not one filled with the optimism of the Kennedy Administration's Camelot, but of stifled individuals for whom being on the outside is no guarantee of freedom. Forman captures the social conformity that Kesey was attacking in his writing, and he does not pretend that McMurphy's victory would make much difference in it.

As indicated in the film's opening, McMurphy represents the unbridled freedom of the American wilderness. His opponent, Nurse Ratched, represents a highly structured and institutionalized social system, one that is concerned with men only as physical beings who need to perform as required without complaining. When the Chief throws the water control panel through a window at the end, he produces the unity of body and spirit for which McMurphy was striving. Hearing the crash, Taber wakes up and gives a triumphant yell; but he and the other men still remain inside the ward. Each of them, like each viewer, must take the first steps towards freedom on his own and be prepared to keep fighting to preserve it. *One Flew Over the Cuckoo's Nest* expresses many of Milos Forman's long-held beliefs about power and feelings of compassion for the people who lack it.[12] By capturing the spirit of Ken Kesey's novel while also giving its meaning a contemporary significance, Forman gained a popular audience and established himself as a prominent film adaptor of contemporary American works.

NOTES

1. Ronald Wallace explains the comic structure of Kesey's novel, arguing, "What McMurphy learns in the course of the novel is how to control and direct his laughter, how to use it as an effective counter to repression and sterility. What he really learns, and nearly masters, is the typical pose of the comic spirit" (97).

2. Donald Palumbo traces the metamorphosis McMurphy produces in the other patients.

3. Wallace concludes,

The final result of the Chief's new knowledge is the novel itself. Bromden learns to perceive his life as a comic fiction and to transform that fiction into art. Laughing at himself and his society, he writes a novel that makes the reader laugh, thus perpetuating his own comic vision. Form and content merge as Bromden writes a book in praise of laughter that itself induces laughter. (112)

4. Stanley Kauffmann gives Forman particular credit for his control in these opening shots and also heaps praise on Nicholson.

5. Casting the patients was crucial to Forman: "Since [they] have few lines to say, [the] audience must remember each simply by their look" (Burke, "The Director's Approach," 15).

6. Michael Wood finds Forman's theme of individual responsibility clearly expressed in the scene of the men boarding the boat (4).

7. Pauline Kael provides significant insights into jack Nicholson's careful handing of the McMurphy role, showing how Nicholson created ambiguity while avoiding the temptation to flaunt his shrewdness.

8. Alejan Harmetz explains the importance of Louise Fletcher's contributions.

9. Robert Forrey delivers charges of racism and sexism.

10. Ronald Wallace gives a significant defense of Kesey.

11. Social and political analysts verify Forman's assessment of the struggle for power and social institutions as matching public attitudes at mid-decade. For analysis of public opinions about Nixon and social institutions, see Muzzio (161) and Carroll (235).

12. Josef Skvorecky quotes Forman as saying,

I think all that which is noble, and which has remained in art and literature since ancient times . . . and which also is significant for strong contemporary works of art, has always concerned itself with injuries and injustices perpetrated against the individual. There, at the bottom of all those great works, are the injustices, which no social order will eliminate. Namely, that one is clever and the other is stupid, one is able and the other is incompetent, one is beautiful while the other is ugly, another might be honest, and yet another dishonest, and all of them are in some way ambitious. And it indeed does not matter that we are arriving at eternal themes. (84)

Works Cited

Buckley, Tom. 1981. "The Forman Formula." *New York Times Sunday Magazine*, 1 March: pp. 28, 31, 42–43, 50–53.

Burke, Tom. 1976. "The Director's Approach—Two Wives." *New York Times*, 28 March 2: p. 15.

Carroll, Peter N. 1982. *It Seemed Like Nothing Happened: The Tragedy and Promise of America in the 1970s.* New York: Holt Rinehart, and Winston.

Forrey, Robert. 1975. "Ken Kesey's Psychopathic Savior: A Rejoinder." *Modern Fiction Studies* 21.2: pp. 222–230.

Harmetz, Alejan. 1975. "The Nurse Who Rules The 'Cuckoo's Nest.'" *New York Times*, 30 Nov 2: p. 13.

Kael, Pauline. 1975. "The Bull Goose Loony." *New Yorker,* 1 Dec.: pp. 131–136.

Kauffmann. Stanley. 1975. "Jack High." *The New Republic* 13 Dec.: pp. 22–23.

Kesey, Ken. 1962. *One Flew Over the Cuckoo's Nest.* New York: New American Library.

Muzzio, Douglas. 1982. *Watergate Games: Strategies, Choices, Outcomes.* New York: New University Press.

Palumbo, Donald. 1983. "Kesey's and Forman's *One Flew Over the Cuckoo's Nest* "The Metamorphosis of Metamorphosis as Novel Becomes Film." *CEA Critic* 415.2: pp. 25–32.

Skvorecky, Josef. 1971. *All the Bright Young Men and Women: A personal History of the Czech Cinema.* Toronto: Peter Martin Associates, Ltd.

Wallace, Ronald. 1979. *The Last Laugh: Form and Affirmation in the Contemporary American Comic Novel.* Columbia: University of Missouri Press.

Wood, Michael. 1976. "No But I Read the Book." *New York Review of Books,* 5 Feb.: pp. 3–4.

THOMAS H. FICK

The Hipster, the Hero, and the Psychic Frontier in One Flew Over the Cuckoo's Nest

In "The White Negro" Norman Mailer describes the "hipster" as a philosophical psychopath living on the fringes of society: "One is Hip or one is Square... one is a frontiersman in the Wild West of American night life, or a Square cell, . . ." (339). Mailer's essay is a characteristically American attempt to define possibility as the product of stark opposites. Hip and Square quite explicitly translate into contemporary and psychological terms the opposing forces that have been the basis for much of our greatest literature: civilization and wilderness, Aunt Sally and the Territory.

The internalization of geography is an attempt to compensate for the disappearance or degeneration of a literal frontier. The West may still offer freedom, but in addition it frequently represents an exhaustive emptiness, or else (telescoping freedom and repression) inspires madness—both a consequence and a rejection of restrictive society. Nathanael West's *The Day of the Locust* (1939) is the classic portrayal of emptiness and despair erupting into violence on what was once the frontier, the California toward which Jack Burden drives, in Robert Penn Warren's *All the King's Men* (1946), feeling that he is "drowning in West," in a motionless "ooze of History" (288). Five years later, J. D. Salinger's Holden Caulfield (*The Catcher in the Rye*, 1951) dreams of fleeing to a rustic cabin to live a sequestered life with his girl. Yet when he goes West it is not to freedom but to recover his shattered nerves in the rela-

Rocky Mountain Review of Language and Literature, Volume 43, Number 1/2. (1989): pp. 19–34.

tive restriction of a Hollywood sanitorium. But if, as these novels suggest, the West provides no ready-made opportunities for escape, there is another intangible and portable frontier which can be maintained by constantly calling attention to the defining extremes of freedom and restriction.[1] The modern frontiersman invests his energy in disruption rather than flight: he must be a fighter, not for the sake of violence or of winning permanent victories but for the clearer distinctions and hence greater freedom that conflict engenders.[2] Yet this investment in a conflict from which there is no easy flight often demands an emphasis on personal inviolability—on the public to the exclusion of the private man—which can be a condition of defeat.

Ken Kesey's *One Flew Over the Cuckoo's Nest* (1962) concerns just such a man, one whose successes and failures can help us to understand the special demands of the psychic frontier. *Cuckoo's Nest* takes place in an Oregon insane asylum—a version of Holden's sanitorium. In *The Closed Frontier* Harold Simonson remarks that "one way of escaping nineteenth-century conventions was to go west, another way was to go 'beyond'" (140).[3] Randle Patrick McMurphy, the protagonist of *Cuckoo's Nest*, does both. A footloose westerner, he ostentatiously transgresses the limits of society, much like Kesey himself, whose destination—Furthur [sic]—was emblazoned on the Pranksters' bus. McMurphy teaches the inmates of the insane asylum to create their own truths and identities, but to do so he must share himself and inevitably compromise his own.

Committed to the asylum as a psychopath, McMurphy is a down-home hipster who vitalizes the sterile ward with the energy of his language. "Some thief in the night boosted my clothes" (93), he explains to Nurse Ratched when he appears the first morning wrapped in a towel (with his white whale undershorts beneath). The Nurse's confusion inspires McMurphy to more elaborate jive, a burst of verbal energy that cuts through the inert institutional vocabulary: "'Pinched. Jobbed. Swiped. Stole,' he says happily. 'You know, man, like somebody boosted my threads.' Saying this tickles him so he goes into a little barefooted dance before her" (94). And McMurphy makes his presence felt with fancy footwork as well as fancy talk, on his first day dancing away from the aides with all the grace and savvy of a street fighter and politician: "One of the black boys circles him with the thermometer, but he's too quick for them; he slips in among the Acutes and starts moving around shaking hands before the black boy can take good aim" (12). His beautifully choreographed entry—the physical counterpart of his verbal maneuvers—confirms the source of his strength: reaction, not just motion. His physical vitality expresses a love of struggle, of the conflict from which his identity as hipster takes form. Later, when he has become the acknowledged bull goose loony, Chief Bromden (chin jerking with emotion) accuses him of "always *winning* things" (257), to which McMurphy wearily responds, "Winning, for Christ-sakes. . . . Hoo boy, winning" (258). Of course he *does* win, and shamelessly, but the pot is the excuse for the process, the joyous feints and games.[4]

The centrality of process rather than goal can be seen in the relative weakness of the fishing expedition and final party, scenes that offer a telling contrast with the dominant narrative rhythm of parry and thrust. Both belie the energy of conflict because they seem to promise not temporary respites but permanent victory. Under McMurphy's tutelage, the fishing trip begins with the Acutes' invigorating and self-promoting confrontation with two predatory service station attendants, and McMurphy successfully outmaneuvers the captain of the boat, who refuses to take the group out without proper authorization. But the fishing scenes drag, for all their consistent good humor, prize flounders, bruised nipples, and brotherhood. The fish are no Moby Dicks (as big Nurse seems to be) and offer only dumb resistance. The ward party at the end of the novel is unsatisfactory for similar reasons: no idyll of strife, the celebration consists of dull stories, flabby fun, and saccharine brotherhood.[5] Though ill at ease outside the intense but narrow range of ecstatic battle, in these episodes Kesey nevertheless makes a gesture toward static joy, perhaps from a lingering respect for the unhip notion of success. The celebrations are not without merit; there *are* moments of rest in even the most driven of lives. Such consummations, however, are important as the beginning of a new cycle, not the completion of an old. We see McMurphy perfectly at rest only when marshaling his energy for the final, stylized assault on Big Nurse: "He closed his eyes and relaxed. Waiting, it looked like" (303). Waiting, of course, to *begin* for the last time. And his loss is ultimately the inmates' victory, and his death offers the chance for a new beginning, as the successful and very different *Liebestod* between Bromden and McMurphy makes clear.

McMurphy most clearly reveals his dedication to process through his stories, which stand equally opposed to institutional stasis and to private revelations. In his stories and scarcely-believable brags— his self-conscious construction of a public self—McMurphy exemplifies the therapeutic aggression that affirms personal integrity by claiming absolute possession of personal materials. Soon after McMurphy arrives, one of the inmates calls him a "backwoods braggart" (56). Although the remark is intended to be cutting, it contains much truth: like his frontiersmen ancestors, "McMurphy" is as much a fiction as a fact. Unlike the mute, stuttering, or squeaky-voiced inmates, McMurphy knows that how big you are depends in part on how big you sound: Chief Bromden, six-foot-eight and silent for the last twenty years, is a pigmy. In conformity with this conviction, McMurphy's therapy for the inmates consists as much of talk as of action; he teaches them to replace an imposed identity with an imagined identity of their own creation. As Billy Bibbit grins and blushes, McMurphy invents him a personal history worthy of a salacious Mike Fink:

Billy 'Club' Bibbit, he was known as in them days. Those girls were about to take off when one looked at him and says

"Are you the renowned Billy Club Bibbit? Of the famous fourteen inches?". . . "And I remember, when we got them up to the hotel, there was this woman's voice from over near Billy's bed, says, "Mister Bibbit, I'm disappointed in you; I heard that you had four—four—for goodness *sakes!*" (98–99)

Later, on the way to the fishing excursion, McMurphy helps the inmates capitalize on what they had always thought a weakness. When two service station attendants try to take advantage of them, the inmates (with McMurphy's help) affirm their manhood by posing as criminally insane. "You see that freckle-faced kid there?" McMurphy says.

Now he might look like he's right off a Saturday *Evening Post* cover, but he's an insane knife artist that killed three men. The man beside him is known as the Bull Goose Loony, unpredictable as a wild hog. You see that big guy? He's an Indian and he beat six white men to death with a pick handle when they tried to cheat him trading muskrat hides. (224)

The Acutes learn, as Harding puts it, that "mental illness [can] have the aspect of power, *power*" (226), or, more generally, that one should have confidence in the self one chooses to invent. McMurphy's lies reveal hypocrisy even as they assert independence. He is the antithesis of those passive victims—suburbanite or institutional drudge—who are no more than blank screens for the receipt of others' projected desires and expectations. This crucial difference is made clear when McMurphy refuses to let Nurse Ratched thwart his plan to watch the World Series: "It didn't make any difference that the power was shut off in the Nurses' Station and we couldn't see a thing on that blank gray screen, because McMurphy'd entertain us for hours, sit and talk and tell all kinds of stories . . ." (152).

"Bull sessions" led by the bull goose loony provide an antidote to the "Therapeutic Community" (an intensified version of the outside world) which is ostensibly intended to help the inmates adjust to normal society but is actually devoted to destroying personal integrity by defining the individual as common property. The philosophy of this community, as Bromden understands it, is "Talk . . . discuss, confess . . . Help yourself and your friends probe into the secrets of the subconscious. There should be no need for secrets among friends" (47). The result of such talk, however, is the "pecking party" that thoroughly unmans Harding, already the least confident of the group.

Wayne Public Library
461 Valley Rd.
Wayne, NJ 07470
(973) 694-4272
www.WaynePublicLibrary.org

Item ID: 32352051622535
Author: Bloom, Harold.
Title: Henry David Thoreau's Walden
Date due: 7/17/2015,23:59

Item ID: 32352054610982
Author: Bloom, Harold.
Title: Ken Kesey's One flew over the cucko
o's nest
Date due: 7/17/2015,23:59

Thank you.

McMurphy's entertaining gab is diametrically opposed to the generic "honesty" of institutional therapy, which can blur personal boundaries and leave one vulnerable to assimilation by repressive organizations like Bromden's "Combine." If McMurphy sometimes seems two-dimensional—a cartoon cowboy—it is neither because Bromden sees him as a superhuman savior, nor because of a weakness in Kesey's powers of characterization, but because McMurphy stands resolutely opposed to any violation of the inner man. In particular, he humorously but firmly rejects Big Nurse's cold, relentless probing, her insistence that the private self is community property, and that as such, it should be reduced to "phrenic this or pathic that" (288), the simultaneously impersonal and cheaply revelatory language of psychiatry. McMurphy's lack of conventional psychological complexity, his insistent exteriority, is in fact a defense rather than a denial of the private individual.

Candy's presence in the novel raises an issue that grows from the peculiar demands of McMurphy's character. Robert Boyers accuses Kesey of "porno-politics": the substitution of a sexual paradise for a difficult-to-achieve political vision (45). For all the talk, however, adult sexuality, like politics, is conspicuously absent from the novel. If, as Terence Martin has noted, the primary motive of female tyranny is to make men into little boys ("High Cost" 45), it is even more centrally the men's motive to remain boys on their own terms. Like so many American classics, *Cuckoo's Nest* is a boy's book, and paradise is surprisingly asexual, if not strictly bachelor as in many other American novels. McMurphy's women are appropriately boys' companions; although Candy and Sandy are physically robust and sexual women, in every other way they are good bad *girls*, hardly more substantial than promiscuous versions of Cooper's chaste and often infantile blond heroines.[8] The paradoxical climax of the final party is not Billy Bibbit's deflowering or Sefelt's astonishing epileptic orgasm, but the transformation of Sandy and McMurphy from adult lovers into "two tired little kids" (296). Despite all his whoring, McMurphy has in this case much in common with the chaste Natty Bumppo, for his virility too (as Leslie Fiedler says of Natty) is ultimately "not genital but heroic" (*Love and Death* 211). It is true that Nurse Ratched, Billy Bibbit's mother, and Vera Harding embody the dual threats of regimented society and family and are the focus of a conventionally ghoulish misogyny. Yet women can also serve the cause of freedom, at least when they do not demand the commitments of adult relationships or marriage. The two types of women embody the polarities of Hip and Square, spiritual frontier and confinement, upon which the world of *Cuckoo's Nest* is predicated. *Cuckoo's Nest* effectively draws upon the energy of opposition by presenting sex not as orgiastic but as offering the opportunity for both aggressive confrontation and strategic retreat.

McMurphy's sexuality complements a personal consistency that obliterates the distinction between past and present. Returning from the fishing trip, for example, he stops by his childhood house and tells the men of his own sexual initiation. Seduced at ten by a prepubescent whore, in retrospect McMurphy marvels at how little difference there is between girls and women, between his boyhood and adulthood: "'Jesus, nine years old' he said, reached over and pinched Candy's nose, 'and knew a lot more than a good many pros'" (245). At ten he was already a little McMurphy and his woman a whore in a child's body, just as Candy (no more proficient for all her professional experience) is a child playing prostitute. We should be prepared, as McMurphy is, to accept the rag flying above the house as a remnant of the same dress (a token of his conquest) that he threw out the window years before. Past and present merge for the seamless man.

Although McMurphy's apparently inexhaustible vitality accounts for a great deal of the novel's appeal, *Cuckoo's Nest* is concerned with depletion as well as renewal, the second term in the hipster's equation and one horizon of the spiritual frontier. It soon becomes clear that McMurphy's commitment to telling stories for others, as well as for himself, is a dangerous undertaking. As the inmates drive home from the fishing trip, Chief Bromden remarks that McMurphy's "relaxed, good-natured voice doled out his life for us to live, a rollicking past full of kid fun and drinking buddies and loving women and barroom battles over meager honors—for all of us to dream ourselves into" (245). One does not, however, dole out one's life—and especially one's fictional public life—with impunity. Unlike the others, Bromden notices that the relaxed voice comes from a man who is "dreadfully tired and strained" (245).

McMurphy, who comes in bigger than life and restores the inmates' power, ends as a clockwork version of his former self, his defeat the fitting— even affirmative—conclusion to a life lived consistently on the very edge of experience. Only superficially predicated upon an orgiastic vision. *Cuckoo's Nest* stresses a perpetual search rather than the definitive climax—a vision, finally, of strife rather than of fulfillment or mechanical immortality. And while McMurphy's extraordinary physical presence is undeniable, his legacy is to be found as much in Harding's effort to make his thin voice "sound like McMurphy's auctioneer bellow" (306) as in the chief's successful attempt to throw a control panel through the asylum's barred window and escape. The language of the "backwoods braggart" is an intentional violation of taste and credibility; and because opposition rather than truth is its goal, such language can end, like the braggart himself, only in total collapse. Just before McMurphy gets up wearily from his corner for the final round with Big Nurse, Chief Bromden reflects with profound insight into the logic of hip that "the thing he was fighting, you couldn't whip it for good. All you could do was keep on whipping it, till you couldn't come out any more and somebody else had to take your place" (303).

McMurphy's defeat is the result of an engagement that for all its emphasis on parry and thrust is predicated upon a monolithic heroism, upon a stable identity or *point d'appui* from which physical and verbal sorties can be made, and part of Kesey's strategy is to play this integrity off against another more conflicted version of heroism frequently associated with the frontier. McMurphy is among the "negative heroes" whose function, Terence Martin writes, "is to measure the world in which we live by the worlds in which they are unable to live" ("Negative Character" 232), Yet not all negative heroes are so depleted, even when, like Nathan Slaughter (in Robert Montgomery Bird's *Nick of the Woods*, 1837) or Natty Bumppo in Cooper's *Leatherstocking Tales,* they devote themselves as required by convention to their genteel charges. Of course neither Natty nor Nathan had to survive on the psychological frontier of modern American life; their wilderness offered possibilities for escape that McMurphy, in a madhouse backed up to the very western edge of the continent, does not have. But there is a more fundamental difference between these two types of hero: unlike McMurphy, Nathan and Natty find power in division, their doubleness conserving and purifying a strength otherwise dissipated in commitment to others. Nathan is both a violent Indian killer (the mysterious "Jibbenainosay") and a pious Quaker so solemn that he is a source of amusement to the rough frontiersmen. His blood-curdling psychopathic hipness depends upon the opportunities for evasion provided by his social persona. And Natty has the Great Serpent to assume part of the burden of violence. But McMurphy has only himself.

The double hero exemplified by Natty and Nathan—men who may have both their public spectacles *and* their private lives—defines a tradition of American heroism to which McMurphy offers an alternative, with its own rewards and dangers. The contemporary version of the divided man is the comic book superhero (e.g., Superman, Batman, The Incredible Hulk) whose doubleness is a way of re-creating the moral equivalent of the wilderness by concentrating social constraints in one identity while leaving the other free to act out dreams of force in a world purified of human commitments.[7] The conflicting pulls toward community and self that ultimately drain McMurphy's energy are distributed between the two selves of the double hero; like Nathan Slaughter, the modern superhero can alternate between the spectacularly public (Superman) and entirely private (Clark Kent), and so preserve his powers without compromising his self. One may describe the typical comic book superhero as both square and hip at the same time: transformation rather than sustained force is the key to the superhero, who radically cons the world each time he changes from pipsqueak to savior.

In *Cuckoo's Nest* Kesey makes use of the divided hero in order to define by contrast the special qualities of his integral and undivided man. The influence of the comic book on Kesey's art has been discussed many times,[8] but it is important to note that McMurphy is only half of a "superhero." Unlike Superman or Captain Marvel (Kesey's favorite), McMurphy is an undivided man, and his engagement cannot be interrupted with a SHAZAM![9] The centrality of this energetic wholeness is confirmed rather than undermined by the relative weakness of Bromden's efforts to convey a sense of his hero's private self. At times, Bromden remarks, McMurphy would do things

> that didn't fit with his face or hands, things like painting a picture at OT with real paints on a blank paper with no lines or numbers anywhere on it to tell him where to paint, or like writing letters to somebody in a beautiful flowing hand. How could a man who looked like him paint pictures or write letters to people, or be upset and worried like I saw him once when he got a letter back? (153)

One answers that he must not, a response demanded by the categorical nature of Bromden's praise: "He's what he is, that's it. Maybe that makes him strong enough, being what he is" (153). The sudden revelation of McMurphy's painting, anonymous correspondence, and flowing penmanship rounds off an angular—even abrasive—personality, substituting arts and crafts for craftiness. It is a rare evocation of McMurphy's carefully concealed private identity, significant in its very implausibility. And while McMurphy does become more frantic as his commitment to the inmates increases, it is only because he cannot draw upon this other side. Without the saving options of flight to the frontier or refuge in an anonymous private identity, his single self can only snap.

McMurphy's death is a direct consequence of his successful efforts to establish a community of men, a success demanding forms of personal commitment in conflict with his essentially public nature. When McMurphy wins his first major bet with the inmates by cracking Big Nurse's icy facade, he is given an important but unrecognized lesson. As he sits before the blank television screen, Nurse Ratched screams, "You're committed, you realize.... Under jurisdiction and *control*..." (138). One by one, the inmates drop their work and join him to listen to his stories. The nurse means that he cannot voluntarily leave the asylum, as most of the other inmates can. And indeed, the prospect of this "commitment" is what first causes McMurphy temporarily to knuckle under to the nurse's authority. But the other form of commitment—to *others*—that this scene strongly evokes is more dangerous, and is finally McMurphy's triumphant undoing. As John Wilson Foster points out, McMurphy and Big Nurse are from the same world and play by the same rules (116). Incarceration can be circumvented. But McMurphy's growing commitment to replenish the imagination and the self-confidence of those who join him in front of the TV set cannot.

McMurphy's revolution succeeds. But by turning rabbits into men he thereby negates the very terms of his freedom. McMurphy is destroyed not by the Combine but by the united needs of the inmates—a "combine" of a very different sort. After Billy Bibbit's suicide, Bromden watches McMurphy girding himself for the final round: "We couldn't stop him because we were the ones making him do it . . . [I]t was our need that was making him push himself slowly up from sitting.... rising and standing like one of those moving-picture zombies, obeying orders beamed at him from forty masters" (304). Before McMurphy's arrival, Chief Bromden had watched Big Nurse "sit in the center of her network with mechanical insect skill" (26); now the inmates have spun their own kind of web, beaming commands which, though charged with love, work contrary to a consistently dramatized sense of radical individuality, of power in *difference*.

The last pages of the novel are spent dismantling the web of concerted action strand by strand. The inmates rapidly disband: only half a sentence is given to the departure of Sefelt, Fredrickson, and three others. Anything but occasions, these departures stand in telling contrast to the massive presence of the two celebrations, as well as to the jarring sentimentality of Sandy's and Turkel's earlier escape across the "wet, sun-sparkled grass" (298). Picked up by his bitchy wife, Harding is concerned above all with the *style* of his departure, just as McMurphy had earlier put himself wholly into the style of his entrance. As Harding explains, "I want to do it on my own, by myself, right out that front door, with all the traditional red tape and complications. I want my wife to be here in a car at a certain time to pick me up. I want them to know I was *able* to do it that way" (293). Harding does not deny the possibility of more substantive confrontations, but for the moment he means only to construct a public self to shield his private integrity. He engages the rituals of society without yielding to them, like the chief's uncle who becomes a lawyer, Bromden remarks, "purely to prove he could" (198). This might be McMurphy's motto. To prove, without thought of past or future, of reputation or permanent gain—*purely* to prove—is to find a force beyond the power of society to cast human energy in the form of mechanism or to reduce the private man to public formulae. Bromden learns from McMurphy that freedom can be achieved only through renewed gestures of mastery, and that energy must not be enshrined as a *fait accompli*. McMurphy is a savior without being a saint.

Despite his obvious physical courage, McMurphy's gestures of mastery are primarily verbal; fittingly, the major legacy of McMurphy's death is the chief's transformation from mute to storyteller. After the lobotomy, McMurphy lies with his eyes "open and undreaming" (309), emptied not just by the operation but by the transmission of imaginative energy, a gradual process whose effects the chief noticed on the way back from the fishing expedition. The chief is the primary recipient of this transmission; he is so full of his story that it seems about to roar out of him "like floodwaters," and he can say, with a true artist's sensibility, that "it's the truth even if it didn't happen" (8). Like McMurphy himself, the chief has learned to distinguish between the facts that lie and the lies that save. It is important to keep in mind that Chief Bromden's story, like one of McMurphy's extravagant boasts, is a tall tale; he re-creates both McMurphy and his own madness from a position of recovered sanity and creative energy. The chief seldom portrays his past psychosis in convincing clinical terms; he consistently veers toward the extravagant. When Bromden describes his hallucinations and fears, the dominant impression is not of madness but of art, as we can see even in brief comments like this one, about a chronic: "At the old place he stood so long in one spot the piss ate the floor and beams away under him and he kept falling through to the ward below, giving them all kinds of census headaches down there when roll check came around" (15). Despite the horror behind such passages, the tone is comic, even celebratory: the dumb Indian can really talk.

The necessary complement of the chief's newly acquired imaginative freedom is the possibility of perpetually renewed flight, of feints and strategic retreats in the interest not of winning for good, but of winning the freedom to enter the fight once again. Bromden's exuberant escape (after smothering his shorted-out savior) is a fitting counterpart to McMurphy's evasive entrance: "I remember I was taking huge strides as I ran, seeming to step and float a long ways before my next foot struck the earth. I felt like I was flying. Free" (310). In flight, Bromden joins those American heroes who typically achieve their stature on the run, like Nathan Slaughter, who is laughed at in the settlements but inspires fear when stalking through the woods at twilight, "as tall and gigantic . . . as the airy demon of Brocken" (125).[10] Bromden finds freedom in movement, and thereby insures future confrontations and other chances to tell stories. As a professional wrestler, the identity McMurphy tentatively suggested to him earlier, Bromden hitchhikes north. McMurphy has not only made Bromden big again, he has shown him how to tell a story. Bromden survives.

Yet in some ways the novel turns away from the opportunity to clinch the value of those acts of imaginative aggression—tall tale and brag—that confirm personal integrity. Before McMurphy drew him from the fog, Bromden would sometimes imagine himself into the painting of a tranquil mountain landscape (a gift of the man known as "Public Relations") from which he could look back at a safely contained ward: "It's a real nice place to stretch your legs and take it easy" (122). The last paragraphs of the novel provide a similar frame, PR for a primitive isolation at odds with the predominant values of sophisticated struggle on the hipster's new frontier:

I might go to Canada eventually, but I think I'll stop along the Columbia on the way. I'd like to check around Portland and Hood

River and The Dalles to see if there's any of the guys I used to know back in the village who haven't drunk themselves goofy. I'd like to see what they've been doing since the government tried to buy their right to be Indians. I've even heard that some of the tribe have took to building their old ramshackle wood scaffolding all over that big million-dollar hydroelectric dam, and are spearing salmon in the spillway. I'd give something to see that. Mostly, I'd just like to look over the country around the gorge again, just to bring some of it clear in my mind again. I been away a long time. (311)

This vision of extraordinary innocence seeks to rehabilitate the individual by diminishing the value of conflict. The language does emphasize possibility ("I might . . . I think . . . I'd like . . . I'd like"), and the boys indeed seem victorious. The battles with Big Nurse, however, did not make the opposition less threatening but more a force to be engaged even at the expense of one's life. Indeed, McMurphy warned the Acutes against those who, like Big Nurse, want to win by making others weaker rather than making themselves stronger. Yet the last paragraphs do precisely this; the Combine is reduced to a humming shell, and while the Indians' laid-back rebellion has a certain miniature charm, it evokes none of the aggressive excess that defines McMurphy's hipper brags and stories, and, certainly, none of the comic horror that characterizes Bromden's inspired and self-liberating tales of the Combine. Indeed, Bromden's final words—I been away a long time—not only resurrect family (albeit bachelor and native) but imply that victory waits complete in a sentimental past, a product of nostalgia rather than invention. By de-emphasizing the language (if not the fact) of conflict Kesey replaces the hipster with the noble savage, and evokes a dusty vision of the western hero to which McMurphy has thus far offered a modern alternative.

Gary Lindberg remarks that Jack Kerouac and Ken Kesey are both attracted to "centers of energy, buoyancy, and faith" (270). This is for the most part true. In a moment of uncharacteristic introspection, Raoul Duke (in Hunter Thompson's *Fear and Loathing in Las Vegas*) recalls the euphoria of riding up to La Honda, the home of Ken Kesey and the Pranksters:

There was a fantastic universal sense that whatever we were doing was *right*, that we were winning . . . And that, I think, was the handle—that sense of inevitable victory over the forces of Old and Evil. Not in any mean or military sense; we didn't need that. Our energy would simply *prevail*. There was no point in fighting—on our side or theirs. (68)

As we have seen, however, this Emersonian optimism is balanced by a pessimism as deeply rooted and formative. The language of the modern frontiersman, as Mailer notes, is "the language of energy, how it is found, how it is lost" (349). In *The Dharma Bums*, for example, Jack Kerouac's hobo narrator, prevented by the police from camping on the pure white sand of a dry river bottom, thinks, "The only alternative to sleeping out, hopping freights, and doing what I wanted, I saw in a vision would be to just sit with a hundred other patients in front of a nice television set in a madhouse, where we could be 'supervised' (96). Pessimism—even paranoia—calls attention to the possibility of confinement, to one of the opposing terms which define a psychic frontier. Further, in the modern American novel failure can be as much a sign of grace as success: it substantiates the threat of repression and legitimizes the quest for purity. In *Cuckoo's Nest* McMurphy pays the steep but unavoidable price of monolithic heroism on the modern frontier: he chooses to share himself and in the end must pay with his life. *Cuckoo's Nest* is a powerful novel which effectively translates into contemporary terms the enduring American concern with a freedom found only in—or between—irreconcilable oppositions.

NOTES

1. Henry David Thoreau (expert in "home-cosmography") was one of the first exponents of internalized geography. A true rebel if no literal frontiersman, he understood the importance of boundaries and restrictions in defining freedom of language and action. In *Walden* he wrote

> *Extra vagance*! it depends on how you are yarded. The migrating buffalo, which seeks new pastures in another latitude, is not extravagant like the cow which kicks over the pail, leaps the cow-yard fence, and runs after her calf, in milking time. I desire to speak somewhere without bounds. . . . (324)

2. Richard Slotkin describes the development of the American hero from the Indian captivity narratives and particularly from the Boone literature, which differs from earlier descriptions of America as Eden because "the final vision of paradise is seen growing out of a savage combat" (277). This hero is "the lover of the spirit of the wilderness, and his acts of love and sacred affirmation are acts of violence against that spirit and her avatars" (22).

3. "Leslie Fiedler, noting that Columbus, dreaming of a western passage to India, was considered mad, remarks that "it is only a step from thinking of the West as madness to regarding madness as the true West" (*Return* 185). My position, however, is closer to Tony Tanner's in *City of Words*. Tanner writes that Norman Mailer tries to maintain a "tottering freedom by not capitulating to the patterns and powers on either side of him [i.e., political and demonized ordering of reality], walking his own line in a bid to defy conditioning" (371). The same is true of Kesey, who tries to make a home in Edge City, "poised *between* social identity and dissolution, a sort of third area between structure and flow" (390). Tanner's analysis suggests that it is important to distinguish, as Fiedler does not, between liberating and restrictive

"madness." The psychotic, writes Mailer, "lives in so misty a world that what is happening at each moment of his life is not very real to him" (344), whereas the psychopath knows only the intense reality of each successive moment. We should remember that the "psychopathic" Irishman saves the psychotic Indian narrator, who is much further gone in the "West" than he.

4. Only the Combine inevitably wins. Harding quickly informs McMurphy that Big Nurse "always wins, my friend, always. She's impregnable herself . . . (70). Later Bromden says, "To beat her you don't have to whip her two out of three or three out of five, but every time you meet. And as soon as you let down your guard, as soon as you lose *once*, she's won for good. And eventually we all got to lose" (109). The truth of this is no reason for capitulation; McMurphy teaches the inmates the importance of *trying*, not winning.

5. Joseph J. Waldmeir accounts for the deficiencies of this episode by arguing that Kesey "is trying to show that the form of protest which the party represents will no longer work" (201)

6. The only other sympathetic woman, the Japanese nurse on the Disturbed Ward, is also clearly a child, physically if not emotionally. Bromden describes her as "about as big as the small end of nothing whittled to a fine point" with a "little hand full of pink birthday candles" (265).

7. For a more complete discussion of the relationship between the frontier hero and the comic book superhero see Fick.

8. See, for example, Fiedler (*Return* 184), and Sherwood.

9. In *Sometimes a Great Notion* Kesey calls attention to the superhero and his divided existence. While going through his comic book collection. Lee Stamper reflects upon the source of Captain Marvel's power:

> [He was] still my favorite over all the rest of the selection of superdoers. Because Captain Marvel was not continuously Captain Marvel. No. When he wasn't flying about batting the heads of archfiends together he was a kid about ten or twelve named Billy Batson, a scrawny and ineffectual punk who could be transformed, to the accompaniment of lightning and thunder, into a cleft-chinned behemoth capable of practically *anything*. . . . And all this kid had to do to bring off this transformation was say his word: Shazam . . . maybe it wasn't really Captain Marvel that was my hero; maybe it was Billy Batson and his magic word. (142)

On Kesey's own identification with superheroes, see Wolfe (especially 40–41, 52).

10. See also Saul Bellow's *Henderson the Rain King* (1959), which ends with Eugene Henderson's remark that "I felt it was my turn now to move, and so went running—leaping, leaping, pounding, and tingling over the pure white lining of the gray Arctic silence" (341). Henderson, like Chief Bromden, is a big man (and a brawler) whose spirit has been restored to a size commensurate with his physical bulk.

Works Cited

Bellow, Saul. *Henderson the Rain King*. New York: Viking, 1959.

Bird, Robert Montgomery. *Nick of the Woods; or, The Jibbenainosay; a Tale of Kentucky*. Ed. Curtis Dahl. New Haven: College and University Press, 1967.

Boyers, Robert. "Attitudes toward Sex in American 'High Culture.'" *The Annals of the American Academy of Political and Social Science*, 376 (March 1968): pp. 36–52.

Fick, Thomas H. "A Killer and a Saint: The Double Hero in America." *Studies in Popular Culture*, 8 (1985): pp. 71–78.

Fiedler, Leslie. *Love and Death in the American Novel*, Rev. ed. New York: Stein and Day, 1966.

———. *The Return of the Vanishing American*. New York: Stein and Day, 1968.

Foster, John Wilson. "Hustling to Some Purpose: Kesey's *One Flew Over the Cuckoo's Nest.*" *Western American Literature*, 9 (1974): pp. 115–129.

Kerouac, Jack. *The Dharma Bums*. New York: New American Library, 1959.

Kesey, Ken. *One Flew Over the Cuckoo's Nest*. 1962. Ed. John Dark Pratt. New York: Viking, 1973.

———. *Sometimes a Great Notion*. New York: Viking, 1963.

Lindberg, Gary. *The Confidence Man in American Literature*. New York: Oxford University Press, 1982.

Mailer, Norman. "The White Negro." *Advertisements for Myself*. New York: G. P. Putnam's Sons, 1959.

Martin, Terence. "The Negative Character in American Fiction." *Toward a New American Literary History: Essays in Honor of Arlin. Turner*. Ed. Louis J. Budd, Edwin H. Cady, and Carol L. Anderson. Durham: Duke University Press, 1973.

———. "*One Flew Over the Cuckoo's Nest and the High Cost of Living.*" *Modern Fiction Studies*, 19 (1973): pp. 43–55.

Sherwood, Terry. "*One Flew Over the Cuckoo's Nest* and the Comic Strip." *Critique*, 13 (1971): pp. 96–109.

Simonson, Harold P. *The Closed Frontier: Studies in American Literary Tragedy*. New York: Holt, 1970.

Slotkin, Richard. *Regeneration Through Violence: The Mythology of the American Frontier, 1600–1860*. Middletown, CT: Wesleyan University Press, 1973.

Tanner, Tony. *City of Words; American Fiction 1950–1970*, London: Jonathan Cape, 1971.

Thompson, Hunter S. *Fear and Loathing in Las Vegas: A Ravage Journey to the Heart of the American Dream*. New York: Popular Library, 1971.

Thoreau, Henry David. *The Illustrated Walden*. Ed. J. Lyndon Shanley. Princeton: Princeton University Press, 1973.

Waldmeir, Joseph J. "Two Novelists of the Absurd: Heller and Kesey." *Wisconsin Studies in Contemporary Literature*, 5 (1964): pp. 192–204.

Warren, Robert Penn. *All the King's Men*. New York: Harcourt, 1946.

Wolfe, Tom. *The Electric Kool-Aid Acid Test*. New York: Farrar, 1968.

ROBERT P. WAXLER

The Mixed Heritage of the Chief: Revisiting the Problem of Manhood in One Flew Over the Cuckoo's Nest

Ken Kesey's novel *One Flew Over the Cuckoo's Nest* challenges us with the issue of mixed heritage through Chief Bromden's half-breed status. In this we confront the most significant and unsettling conflict of the text. Although few critics have focused on the issue it is complex enough to have been a part of American fiction throughout the twentieth century. Like Faulkner, Kesey sets his character on a symbolic search for the Father: that is, the spark of manhood within himself that flares at the traditional gender definition. The search is complicated, however, by the father's minority status which gives the mother social supremacy. Moreover, Kesey further hinders the search by making the dominant system throughout the story a demanding and outwardly oppressive matriarchy. The combined elements of gender and mixed heritage form the point, I believe, that makes the novel problematic, not only for the reader, but for Kesey himself.

In an important sense, the family is always the matrix for social and individual identity. We are our family. And in such a context, we need to ask how Chief Bromden can possibly gain back his manhood, in a sense rediscover "the name of the father," when he is rooted in a family which has denied that name, privileging instead the name of his white mother (Bromden). Chief Bromden's problem, in this sense, is the difficulty he faces in attempting to recover the roots of his Native American identity, the identity

Journal of Popular Culture, Volume 29 (Winter 1995): pp. 225–235.

151

of his father, that male Indian identity buried deep along the Columbia River in the Dalles.

What the critics seem to have avoided when discussing *One Flew Over The Cuckoo's Nest* is that Bromden's "mixed heritage" is at the root of the Chief's problem of identity, accounting, to a large extent, for his schizophrenic narrative. More specifically, the Chief's family history puts him in the precarious position of a son who believes that his roots can only be discovered through his father, a man with an ethnic minority status. The Chief is a son, in other words, attempting to achieve manhood in a world dominated by women in general (one version of the classic story of the American boy), but specifically by a white mother. As Terence Martin has put it: "The female reduced the male—the white reduced the Indian. The Chief has only to think of his parents to know the legacy of his people" (45). The Chief, that Vanishing American as Kesey calls him, must rediscover not only his legacy as a Native American, but the very roots of his manhood by thinking back through his father, that is through the place of the father, the original territory of the Native American man now overrun by whites. That act of white imperialism in terms of the novel is represented in the first instance by his mother. In this context, we can assume that the Chief's problems would be very different if his mother had been an American Indian.

In a sense, Kesey has given us an Oedipal story with a twist rarely explored by white American novelists, especially before the early 1960s when *Cuckoo's Nest* was written. In the simplest Freudian version of the Oedipal story, if the son is to achieve manhood, he must symbolically kill the father and marry the mother. But what if the father, a member of an ethnic minority, has been marginalized by the mother, a member of the dominant culture? How then does the son recover the authority and power of the father? And how does the son rejuvenate desire for the mother, especially when that mother, in the mind of the son, has become an abstraction, a repressive symbol of the majority culture? These are questions that critics rarely discuss when talking about *Cuckoo's Nest*, yet they are questions central to a full understanding of the novel. They raise issues that help to illuminate the relationship between the racial and sexual identity of the Chief and his narrative perceptions. They help the reader to understand the Chief as an embattled self and as a Vanishing American male.

When the Chief first introduces Big Nurse to the reader, for example, she is carrying her woven wicker bag made by Indians but used by her to carry the tools that she manipulates to maintain her dehumanized control over the ward. Like the Chief's mother, Big Nurse uses the Indian, but is not of the Indian. Yet the reader also realizes immediately that "those big, womanly breasts" (Kesey 5) hidden beneath her starched exterior make Big Nurse something other than a bureaucratic automaton. Those breasts eventually, and inevitably, will need to be exposed. For the Chief, Big Nurse is an abstraction, a projection of the symbolic power that stripped his father of his name, but beneath her starched uniform she must also be a reminder of the carnal body of his origins.

For the Chief though, it is clearly not the memory of his mother that gives him any comfort, but the early childhood memories of bonding with his father. When Big Nurse sends the black boys to shave the Chief at the beginning of the novel, for example, the Chief thinks of his father, their hunting trips in the early morning fog in the Dalles. For the Chief it is the father who is associated with the womb-like protection of the fog—a temporary, but ultimately unsatisfying, retreat from the threat of Big Nurse's attempts at symbolic castration. In this opening scene, Big Nurse is clearly in control, forcing the Chief away from any possibility of manhood as "she jams wicker bag and all into Chief Bromden's mouth and shoves it down with a mop handle" (Kesey 7).

When Randle Patrick McMurphy appears in the ward, however, the Chief is reminded of the strength of his father: "He talks a little the way Papa used to, voice loud and full of hell . . ." (Kesey 11). And, as those familiar with the novel know, McMurphy takes on the role of the father for Bromden in order to get Bromden to emerge from the womb-like protection of that fog, to move the Chief to name and remake the father in himself.

Throughout the novel, McMurphy creates strategies (from games to gambling to fishing trips) to get the Chief to understand his full potency, for it is only then that he can name his father. As the Chief finally tells McMurphy, "My Papa was a full Chief and his name was Tee Ah Millatoona. That means The-Pine-That-Stands-Tallest-on-the-Mountain, and we didn't live on a mountain. He was real big when I was a kid. My mother got twice his size" (Kesey 186). Not surprisingly, shortly after this naming, Big Nurse orders a lobotomy for McMurphy, who is then brought back to the ward, "wheeled in this Gurney with a chart at the bottom that said in heavy black letters, MCMURPHY, RANDLE P. POSTOPERATIVE" (269). Like the Chief's father before him, McMurphy has been symbolically castrated here by a white woman and the white establishment. He has become an impotent member of Big Nurse's symbolic order. Only the abstraction of his name remains, controlled by Big Nurse herself.

In this context, the Chief knows that Big Nurse has silenced McMurphy just as the Combine had silenced his father. Big Nurse can now use McMurphy's name for her own purposes, bringing that name under her authority, making that name part of her matriarchal system. In effect, the same thing had happened to the Chief's father when he married the white woman named Bromden. That name became the family name, the father giving up his authority as the mother continued to grow in size. From the Chief's perspective, these events must have led to his belief that the world was dominated not only by whites, but by a matriarchal structure, one that blocked him from easily rediscovering the manhood embodied within his father. At the same time, the Chief also knows that McMurphy "wouldn't have left something like that sit there in the day room with his name tacked on it for twenty or thirty years so the Big Nurse could use it as an example of what can happen if you buck the system. I was sure of that" (270).

Throughout the novel, the Chief legitimately believes that it is not the name of the father, but Big Nurse, the name of the mother, that defines and represents the ruling symbolic order. His father is "the Other," existing at best at the margins of Big Nurse's discourse, a discourse that the Chief imagines eventually, through his schizophrenic projections, as the abstract order of the Combine itself.

The reader is faced then with a dilemma at the center of Kesey's novel. Not only must the son separate from the mother, but she is being represented within the family romance as the one that needs to be killed, for she is the one who dictates law. The implication, in a larger sense, is that males with fathers of ethnic minority status married to mothers from the dominant culture must travel a difficult and radically indirect route to achieve manhood. In a somewhat confusing pattern, Kesey suggests that sons of "mixed heritage," especially with mothers from the dominant culture, may not be able to achieve manhood in American culture.

It is as if Kesey is suggesting, like Jaques Lacan, that adulthood is achieved by the son when the child moves into the system of language and culture, a symbolic order, that has been defined and represented by the father. For Kesey, however, the dominant discourse experienced by the Chief is the symbolic order controlled by Big Nurse. Into this enters McMurphy and there he is comfortable. It seems he is able, not only to function along the lines of control as established by Big Nurse and her system of language, but also to out-smart her by using her own rules. Outside the showers McMurphy willingly engages in spirited verbal fencing with Big Nurse over the propriety of wearing nothing but a towel in the hall. In an act of complete compliance to Big Nurse's wishes, thereby the controlling language, McMurphy drops the towel, effectively following the rules and challenging them at the same time. McMurphy, through his ability to recognize and function within Big Nurse's discourse, takes the place of the Chief's father and does what he could not do; McMurphy demonstrates how to use the language of the matriachy to control a dominant female. The Chief, unfortunately, cannot place himself in the context of the father's discourse. As a result, at best, the Chief is "the Other" in a system controlled by the white woman, his mother, Big Nurse herself. The Chief suffers from a lack of voice and language for these reasons.

In this context, we can first believe that there is a possible way out for the Chief. The American Indian voice, like the voice of women in America, can be defined as a voice of the body, a voice distinct from the abstract law. It is, in a sense, a voice of plenitude and joy, a celebration of the fullness of the body. As Helene Cixous puts it in the context of women: "Let masculine sex-uality gravitate around the penis, engendering this centralized body (political economy) under the party dictatorship. Woman does not perform on herself this regionalization that profits the couple head-sex, that only inscribes itself within frontiers. Her libido is cosmic, just as her unconscious is worldwide…. She goes on and goes on infinitely" (87–88).

Such a voice does not pound to a climax, nor drive to a determined point, but it does offer the richness of intimate experience. In terms of the 1960s, we might understand it best as a voice of polymorphous eroticism. In terms of *Cuckoo's Nest*, it is a voice that the Chief might discover at the mar-gins of Big Nurse's own rigid discourse, a voice of the body and of his own past, the voice of the counter-culture itself. But to discover such a voice, the Chief must also abandon binary thinking about gender. He must substitute phallic power for the polymorphic erotic.

In such a context, we can understand the basic dilemma that the Chief faces and the contradiction in Kesey's own vision. For Kesey has within the logic of the novel legitimately established the father within the family ro-mance as "the Other" equivalent to an ethnic minority overpowered by the dominant culture within the social structure. And he has posed the interest-ing question of how a son in such a situation can achieve manhood. How-ever, at the same time, Kesey refuses to deny the binary mode of Western thinking about gender, and in fact he sets up an ideological fiction (Big Nurse) that allows him to blame women and to avoid any analysis of patri-archy. "Somehow, in the confused vision of the author and playwright, the refusal of women, an oppressed class, to utterly submit to male-oriented social structures is identified with the attack of white males, the oppressor class, on people of color" (Falk 221–222). It is as if Kesey recognizes that "the Other" must create a discourse and a life of process, a playfulness of the body, a polymorphous eroticism. Yet, at the same time, he accepts the binary thinking of Western consciousness. Kesey seems to embrace a style of polymorphous eroticism, but he will not give up the American myth of nineteenth century individualism, a myth which includes the privileging of the male and the celebration of phallocentrism.

Through much of the novel, McMurphy seems to adopt a strategy that encourages the playfulness of the polymorphous erotic body. Like the coun-ter-culture hero that he is, McMurphy wants the Chief to feel the joy of life by expressing the natural playfulness of his own self. As he puts it early in the novel: "Yes sir, that's what I came to this establishment for, to bring you birds fun an' entertainment around the gamin' table" (Kesey 12). And the biggest bird of all, the Chief, will eventually not only go on a lark (the name of the boat on which McMurphy takes "his crew" fishing), but learn to fly without fear over that abstract symbolic order called the Cuckoo's Nest.

But at the same time, Kesey seems to insist on a conventional sense of manhood, manhood rooted not in the discourse of the polymorphous erotic body, but in the abstract language of the symbolic order, a form of phallocentric power. In such a system, meaning always operates within a hierarchial language system. Oppositions are established, and manhood is won when the male presence governs the female absence. In the end, Kesey, too, seems governed by this kind of thinking.

Kesey might like it both ways, but the result is that the Chief's narrative vision, rooted in his mixed heritage and half-breed status, necessarily remains confused and incomplete. Confronted with Big Nurse and her social order, the Chief is powerless. Like the other characters of the novel he has to "either conform to society or become 'mule stubborn' and rebel against it" (Madden 207). He is immobilized.

As a substitute father for the Chief, McMurphy helps him re-write the story of his father by opposing the rigidity of Big Nurse's rules with his own sense of bodily energy. McMurphy, as Kesey would say, goes with the flow, and that flow is the natural rhythm of uncalculated sexual energy, the rhythm of the body and of the land, a rhythm which in itself could help to eliminate the hierarchy constructed within the symbolic order. When Big Nurse attempts to rob McMurphy of his name at the beginning of the novel, for example, she does it within a context that insists upon the fixed structure of her rules. "Please understand, I appreciate the way you've taken it upon yourself to orient with the other patients on the ward, but everything in its own good time, Mr. McMurry. I'm sorry to interrupt you and Mr. Bromden, but you do understand: everyone . . . must follow the rules" (Kesey 28). McMurphy responds with a wink and a grin, resisting her formulation and simultaneously beginning to empower the Chief.

McMurphy also uses the power of touch to help effect this transformation. As the Chief describes it: "I remember (his) fingers were thick and strong closing over mine, and my hand commenced to feel peculiar and went to swelling up out there on my stick of an arm, like he was transmitting his own blood into it. It rang with blood and power. It blowed up near as big as his, I remember" (Kesey 24). And McMurphy's laugh, too, becomes part of an expansive expression of bodily plenitude: ". . . free and loud and it comes out of his wide grinning mouth and spreads in rings bigger and bigger till it's lapping against the walls all over the ward" (Kesey 16).

Kesey seems to offer through McMurphy's gestures the joy of the language of the body and of plenitude that McMurphy himself is capable of creating. It is the joyful language that we might imagine the Native American Indian had when he was still close to the natural world, living near the flow of the Columbia River along the Dalles. Such a language is clearly a threat to the rigidity of the symbolic order controlled by Big Nurse. It is the language of "the Other," an articulation of pleasure like the high school carnival that McMurphy discusses with Dr. Spivey, a celebration of polymorphous eroticism that undercuts the monolithic structure of the dominant culture. Most importantly, such a language does not suggest a phallocentric strategy, but, as Cixous puts it, a joy of the body that could go on and go on infinitely.

Yet McMurphy also reminds the Chief that a man, like a pine on the tallest mountain (Tee Ah Millatoona), must grow big and stand erect in order to defeat the control of the white matriarchy. And it is this kind of image of phallic power rather than the image of polymorphous eroticism that finally dominates the novel. The Chief's narrative story is filled with the language of play, the poetry of the land, even the playful rhymes of his grandmother (Porter 16–17). "McMurphy was teaching me. I was feeling better than I'd remembered feeling since I was a kid, when everything was good and the land was still singing kid's poetry to me," the Chief can claim at one point in his story (Kesey 216). But in the end the story drives toward a climax and so becomes a plot structured in typical phallocentric terms, undercutting the counter-cultural voice.

At this level, *Cuckoo's Nest* moves close to the traditional Oedipal narrative concerned with the son's desire to replace the father and gain the phallocentric power as part of his inheritance. Even in this context, however, Kesey makes the narrative problematic. In order to return to his Native American roots, the Chief cannot marry the mother; he must eliminate her. To marry the mother in terms of the Chief's narrative structure would be to lose the name of the father again. In fact, as Kesey has defined the terms of the narrative, there is, ironically, no way for the Chief to achieve manhood without attempting to destroy the mother. For Kesey, marriage is an impossibility. Manhood for the Chief can only be achieved by a frontal attack on Big Nurse.

The climax of McMurphy's battle against Big Nurse then, as it is filtered through the consciousness of the Chief, becomes unfortunately, but by necessity, an act of violence. McMurphy's "red fingers" penetrate "the white flesh of her throat" in an act equivalent to rape; yet there is a hint of how it might have been otherwise as Big Nurse's breasts are for a moment revealed; "the two nippled circles started from her chest and swelled out and out, bigger than anybody had ever imagined, warm and pink in the light . . ." (Kesey 267). The image here is of the world of the mother, the feminine body as the Chief would like it to be. But McMurphy's violent attack undercuts such an image, aggravating instead the divisions in the battle of the sexes. Such violence does allow, however, the Chief to attempt to bring to closure his own Oedipal struggle.

When McMurphy is returned to the ward after his lobotomy ordered by Big Nurse, the Chief finally decides to kill him, a killing that not only clearly represents a transfer of sexual energy from McMurphy to the Chief, but also one that signals that the Chief has now assumed the place of McMurphy, his substitute father.

As the Chief describes the killing: "The big, hard body had a tough grip on life. It fought a long time against having it taken away, flailing and thrashing around so much I finally had to lie full length on top of it and scissor the kicking legs with mine while I mashed the pillow into the face. I lay there on top of the body for what seemed days, until the thrashing stopped. Until it was still a while and had shuddered once and was still again. Then I rolled off" (Kesey 270). In a poignant blending of homoerotic love and death, the substitute father is sacrificed for the son so that the son can become the father and so preserve the name of the father. But we must still ask: what precisely has the Chief with his mixed heritage gained in this struggle for manhood? And what does he still lack?

In one sense, the Chief has become McMurphy, although he realizes that in some ways he is bigger than McMurphy. McMurphy's cap is too small for him, for example, and the Chief can lift Big Nurse's control panel which McMurphy could not budge. Like McMurphy, the Chief has become a con artist able to survive on the road as he heads for the Columbia Gorge to see "if there's any of the guys (he) used to know back in the village" (Kesey 272). But if the Chief has saved the name of McMurphy, he has not recovered the place of Tee Ah Millatoona, nor has he come to terms with his white mother. This is particularly disturbing because, as Jack Hicks has said, "Kesey suggests repeatedly that memory, knowing one's individual and collective pasts, is a key to any sense of present or future" (Hicks 173).

Admittedly the Chief has found a voice that allows him to articulate his experience; yet as he says: "It's still hard for me to have a clear mind thinking on it. But it's the truth even if it didn't happen" (Kesey 13). That "truth" is the burning fear and manic roaring of consciousness that makes up the Chief's own narrative, a narrative that has attempted to unveil through McMurphy the hidden identity of the father. But although we can hear the voice, we cannot locate it any more than the Chief can locate his own father. In fact, the underside of the novel seems to suggest that the Chief, like his father, is part of that culture of Vanishing Americans. The Chief, in other words, may have discovered a voice, but he remains invisible, a man without a name other than that of Bromden. The reader is exposed to the "truth" of the consciousness of the Chief, but the problem is that the reader has nothing to measure that consciousness against. In this sense, the Chief is imprisoned by the "truth" that he has created. He has achieved his individuality, but it is an individuality in isolation.

And here again we can see the contradiction in Kesey's own vision. The Chief's isolation suggests that he has achieved the nineteenth century version of the American myth of individualism, a myth that Kesey seems to embrace, but one that helped to destroy the Native American. It is a myth about power and about the inability to trust people unless one has control. Kesey's social vision, as we might call it, is bankrupt in such a context. For despite Kesey's good intentions—and that of the counter-culture in general—we see exposed here that the foundation of that vision is not primarily a celebration of social identity or polymorphous erotic pleasure, but rather a further attempt to legitimate male individual identity and phallocentric control.

Where is the Chief when he is telling the story? Unless he has returned to the Cuckoo's Nest, the Chief seems to be living an invisible life outside of that symbolic order that Kesey has defined through Big Nurse as America and that the Chief thinks of as a matriarchy, an extension of his castrating mother. The hope remains, of course, that the Chief will encounter a different style of life at the Columbian Gorge, perhaps becoming the "father" of an alternative culture, but the underside of the tale hints strongly that the Chief really has no place to go, nor is he sure where he is headed. The Chief remains in fact an indeterminate self much like that bluetick hound to which he compares his narrative. "No tracks on the ground but the ones he's making, and he sniffs in every direction with his cold red-rubber nose and picks up no scent but his own fear, fear burning down into him like steam. It's gonna burn me just that way, finally telling about all this . . ." (Kesey 13).

The combined issues of mixed heritage and gender definitions leave the reader, and I would suggest, Kesey, stumbling for some sort of satisfying resolution. Yet, there are no clear answers offered within the novel. In the tradition of American fiction Kesey chooses to struggle with these issues but at best only illuminates their complexities. William Faulkner, too, examined these issues in his novel, *Light in August*. Faulkner's main character, Joe Christmas, is like the Chief in that he cannot escape the notion that all women are trying to control and exploit him. He, too, lives in a confused world where the anticipated safety of being male, thereby dominant in a patriachy, is denied him because of his mixed heritage and his consequential understanding of social order as a matriachy.

In seeking resolution both authors ignore the primary cause of the conflict: mixed heritage. They neglect to have their characters personally challenge the system of oppression which labels a minority male as beneath a white female, another victim of the oppressive system. Instead, they skirt the issue, each allowing his main character to regain his manhood simply by claiming it with a six-word phrase. Joe Christmas, tired of being a passenger on the roller-coaster of life declares his intention to take control with, "I am going to do something" (Forrey 229–230). While the Chief announces his reentry into manhood with the powerful words, "I been away a long time" (Kesey 311).

Frank Waters' novel *The Man Who Killed The Deer* takes a slightly different track. Like Kesey, Waters develops a main character who feels his manhood is challenged by a matriarchy. Unlike Kesey, Waters chooses to allow Martiniano to recognize and reconcile the source of his conflict: the fact that he has learned the white man's definition of manhood and, later, tries to apply it in matriarchal Indian society. Martiniano relinquishes the fallacy that a man is more powerful than a woman and learns to accept and embrace the strength of the female.

Waters' character grows more than Kesey's. Martiniano does not get sucked into the old patriarchy as does the Chief instead of wandering, he finds a new peace. By integrating his impressions of gender definitions Martiniano is able to achieve relative reconciliation between his heritage and his perception of manhood. Waters' understanding that a minority male's feelings of oppression, seemingly at the hands of a matriachy, could well be the result of a larger male-oriented system, has spared the author some of the harsh criticism dealt to Kesey.

Critics such as Robert Forrey have attacked Kesey claiming that he is sexist. Forrey, for example, places Kesey in the machismo tradition of Hemingway and Steinbeck: "... what we have in Kesey's novel is yet another group of American males trying desperately to unite into a quasi-religious cult or brotherhood which will enable them to sublimate their homosexuality in violent athletic contests, gambling, or other forms of psychopathological horseplay" (229–230). But Forrey's important insight is only half the story.

Kesey has given us the vision of a half-breed, a man of color rooted in a mixed heritage, and he has asked the question—how does such a person, with a dominant white mother, achieve manhood within a heterosexual arrangement? Kesey has begun to explore that question in *Cuckoo's Nest*, but he has failed to understand that such issues of gender and race need to include the insidious structures of patriarchy in their analysis. At the same time, though, the questions that he raises remain important ones, and so reflect the relevance and the uniqueness of Kesey's vision for us today.

WORKS CITED

Cixous, Helen and Catherine Clemont. *The Newly Born Woman*. Trans. Betsy Wing. Minneapolis: Minnesota University Press, 1986.

Falk, Marcia. *Contemporary Literary Criticism*, 64: pp. 221–222.

Faulkner, William. *Light in August*. Canada: Random House, 1959.

Forrey, Robert. *Modern Fiction Studies*, Summer 1975: pp. 229–230.

Hicks, Jack. *In the Singer's Temple*. Chapel Hill: University of North Carolina Press, 1981.

Kesey, Ken. *One Flew Over the Cuckoo's Nest*. New York: Viking, 1962.

Madden, Fred. "Sanity and Responsibility: Big Chief as Narrator and Executioner." *Modern Fiction Studies*, 32.2 (1986): p. 207.

Martin, Terence, *Modern Fiction Studies*, Spring 1973: p. 45

Porter, M. Gilbert. *The Art of Grit*. Columbia and London: University of Missouri Press, 1982.

STEPHEN L. TANNER

The Western American Context of One Flew Over the Cuckoo's Nest

O ccasionally a literary work captives a large audience by vividly embodying the fears and desires that now just beneath the level of articulation. Such
a work evokes a pleasure of recognition; readers are confirmed in a knowledge of their society that they scarcely knew they possessed. Through such
an accomplishment the artist brings into focus social and cultural tendencies
that before had been only partially discerned by the general public. *One Flew
over the Cuckoo's Nest* is such a work. Written between the summer of 1960
and the spring of 1961, the novel preceded the counterculture movement
of the succeeding decade, with its disruption of universities, opposition to
the war in Vietnam, back-to-nature revolt against established authority and
revered technology, and often indecorous rejection of what it viewed as the
affluent complacency of the fifties. Yet the book prophetically contained the
essence of this social-cultural turmoil. More importantly, it dramatically
articulated the nation's queasy suspicion that its valued tradition of self-
reliant individualism was being eroded by institutionalized conformity and
dehumanizing technology.

The novel is further distinguished by having succeeded also as a play
and a film. The play, adapted by Dale Wasserman, was produced in 1963
and revived in 1971. The 1975 film, produced by Michael Douglas and Saul
Zaentz and directed by Miles Forman, won six Academy Awards. More-

Modern Fiction Studies, Volume 19, Number 1 (Spring 1973): pp. 291–320.

over, the novel has frequently been used as a text in a wide variety of disciplines: literature, psychology, sociology, medicine, law, and others. After thirty years, it continues in one printing after another to entertain readers and prompt commentary.

That any novel should have so extensive a literary-cultural impact is unusual. The fact that it was the author's first published novel makes the case even mere remarkable. Did Kesey suspect as he created the story while a creative writing student at Stanford that it would touch such a responsive chord in so many readers? His own answer is no. In a 1983 interview, he said he completed the manuscript, turned it over to Malcolm Cowley, his teacher and also an editor at Viking, and returned to his home in Oregon to proceed directly to writing another novel. "When the reviews came out and as time went by, I realized that I had written a great book. But that didn't occur to me when I was writing it. I had no idea it would be taken like it was." Later in the same interview, when asked what interested him about himself, he said. "It's 'Why me?' What is it about me, my family, my father, this part of the country that caused it to be me who wrote *Cuckoo's Nest?* It is not something I set out to do. It's as though all the angels got together and said, 'Okay, here's the message that America desperately needs. Now, let's pick him to do it.'"[1] Perhaps Kesey would not have accomplished what he did it he had consciously set out to do it. The pressure of such objectives would have been debilitating. He once wrote to his friend Ken Babbs, "The first book one writes is a noisemaker, a play with no pressure, and it may sometimes have that free-swinging song of the cells."[2]

What follows is an attempt to identify some of the elements which generated that "free-swinging song of the cells." I will also try to answer Kesey's own question "Why me?," to explain in some measure what it was about him, his family, his father, and his part of the country that caused him to write *Cuckoo's Nest.*

The Kesey Collection at the University of Oregon contains a 411-page final typescript of the novel and an earlier, typed version of 406 pages with holograph revisions, most of them minor editing changes. In addition there are 37 pages of miscellaneous fragments. The most important of these are three pages of the first draft of the novel's opening scene, which are included in *One Flew over the Cuckoo's Nest: Text and Criticism* edited by John C. Pratt. This edition also includes a two-page sample of the few extant pages of the first draft showing how extensive Kesey's revisions were. More than seven pages of the miscellaneous fragments are stream-of-consciousness pencil scribblings on unlined paper, where Kesey registered the effects of some pills a nurse had brought him during a government-sponsored drug test in which he was a volunteer participant. He recorded his perceptions over a three-hour period, the handwriting becoming larger and more sprawling, the impressions more surrealistic. Such experiments with hallucinogens must have influenced his creation of Bromden's hallucinations. Most of the random manuscript pages, however, are of little use because they are inconsecutive and without recognizable relation to the finished novel.

In an undated letter to his friend Ken Babbs,[3] Kesey says that while be and his family were on a trip to Oregon, a friend who had a grudge against him broke into the small building behind his house in Palo Alto and burned his manuscripts. Some of the *Cuckoo's Nest* material may have been destroyed at that time. In any case, to understand the creation of the novel, we must rely on letters, interviews, related manuscripts and biographical information.

I

One Flew over the Cuckoo's Nest is a product of the American West, specifically of two locations along the Pacific coast: the environs of Eugene, Oregon, and of San Francisco, California. The first was the location of his childhood and formal education; the second was the location where his informal education was catalyzed by other creative minds and by the social-cultural-artistic ferment of that area in the late fifties, particularly the Beat phenomenon.

It is significant that in asking "Why me?" Kesey should mention in particular his family, his father, and his part of the country. These are primary elements in shaping his early development and in turn the products of his imagination. His family along both paternal and maternal lines were farmers and ranchers, the kind of people he described in his second novel, *Sometimes a Great Notion*, as "a stringy-muscled brood of restless and stubborn west-walkers." In the case of Kesey's family the westward migration was from Tennessee and Arkansas to Texas and New Mexico, then to Colorado, where Ken was born, and finally to Oregon. This family line was imbued with traits and values characteristic of the rural West: family ties were strong, physical strength and self-reliance were prized, outdoor activities such as hunting and fishing were an integral part of life, Protestant Christianity informed the rules of behavior, and the pleasures of vernacular talk and storytelling colored daily intercourse.

At family gatherings at his grandfather's farm, Kesey competed with his brother and his cousins in racing, wrestling, boxing, and anything that needed proving. And he absorbed the idiom of vernacular anecdote with its homely but vivid figures of speech. These experiences had lasting effects. The physical competition continued for Kesey in the form of football and wrestling in high school college, and beyond. At the time he was writing *Cuckoo's Nest*, he was trying to quality for the Olympic wrestling team at San Francisco's Olympic Club. Use of the region's vernacular persists in Kesey's talk and writing, in his tendency to communicate in anecdote and trope. The country Protestantism, particularly that of his grandmother Smith, left an indelible impression. In

1972 he said, "I'm a hard shell Baptist, born and raised, and though I thought I had left it I found it in myself at every turn, this basic, orthodox Christianity."[4]

This family background registers clearly in *Cuckoo's Nest*—in the strength, self-reliance, and competitiveness of the hero; in the style of the prose and the language used; in the emphasis on harmony with nature; and in the Christian imagery. Kesey's father was a sort of hero for him, a strong, independent sort of cowboy figure that he likened to John Wayne. Fred Kesey loved the outdoors and brought his sons onto the rivers and into the woods with him from an early age. Ken's hunting and fishing experiences were an important part of his youth, richly nourishing the wellsprings of his imagination. He and his father were strong-willed and their relationship was not without conflict, but Ken retained great admiration for his father, who died in 1969. He said that his father believed a time comes when a son should whip his father. It is an important and delicate matter. "A boy has to *know* he can best his father, and his father has to present him the opportunity." It has to be done in the right way and at the right time. "My father's a wise man and he gave me the chance. Perhaps this is a father's most significant duty."[5]

Father-son relationships—more precisely, the absence of satisfactory father-son relationships—are a crucial matter in *Cuckoo's Nest*. Bromden tells McMurphy, "My Papa was a full Chief and his name was Tee Ah Millatoona. That means The-Pine-That-Stands-Tallest-on-the-Mountain. . . . He was real big when I was a kid."[6] But the Combine (Bromden's term for technologized society) diminished his size, and the loss of strength and self-respect that resulted for his son is a principal reason for Bromden's withdrawal from reality in a mental ward. McMurphy, acting as a surrogate father, incites Bromden to exert his strength, and Bromden eventually bests this symbolic father by lifting the control panel, which McMurphy had failed to budge, and bashing it through the window. Kesey once described his father as "a kind of big, rebellious cowboy who never did fit in."[7] The description, of course, aptly fits McMurphy as well. Obviously, Kesey had reason to single out his father as he questioned himself about the sources of the novel.

The last element mentioned specifically in his "Why me?" question is his part of the country, western Oregon. It is the natural landscape of that region, with its evergreen forests, clear rivers, and seacoast, that forms the norm of health and sanity in the book's central conflict. Bromden is a representative natural man who has been alienated from that environment and whose sanity depends on his reestablishing broken connections. His recovery is marked in stages by a renewed capacity to sense the world of nature. It reaches a climax or epiphany on a fishing boat off the Oregon coast with a cosmic blending of nature and laughter. In readily perceived ways, the novel's regional setting has much to do with its distinctive achievement, and it is likely that recent ecological approaches to literary criticism will further delineate relationships between the book's themes and methods and Kesey's environmentally shaped values and frames of reference. Gilbert Porter perceptively observes that many of the experiences that stimulated Kesey's creativity occurred in California— in creative writing seminars at Stanford, in the interactions of the Perry Lane student community near Stanford, and in his experiences as an aide in the psychiatric wards of the Menlo Park hospital—"but in the transmutation of experience into art, Kesey relocated his world in Oregon, where familiar land- marks provided some stabilizing boundaries for a microcosm psychically out of kilter. Kesey's California experiences suggested a mental ward, but his roots in the Oregon outdoors suggested reality."[8] The history and culture of the Northwest, which constitute a distinctive outlook on American life, permeate the novel just as the region's landscape does.

Another aspect of Kesey's youth in Oregon that helps explain the cre- ation of *Cuckoo's Nest* is his reading and the interests that prompted it and were generated by it. From an early age, he was fascinated by fantasy, by any hint of exciting and mysterious things just beyond the reach of ordinary ex- perience. He read a good deal as a boy, but until high school that reading was mostly comic books, Westerns, and science fiction—comic books such as *Superman, Batman,* and *Captain Marvel;* authors like Zane Grey, Edgar Rice Burroughs, and Jules Verne. This reading was the beginning of a quest, a manifestation of that perennial appetite for transcendent consciousness, a yearning instinctive in most everyone but especially acute in Kesey. He once mentioned this search in an interview. As a boy he had sent for some decals of *Batman* comic-book characters. The package arrived containing a bonus, a small book of magic. This sparked an interest in magic that led him on to ventriloquism and then hypnotism. "And from hypnotism into dope. But it's always been the same trip, the same kind of search."[9] It was this desire that en- ticed him, after he had written two novels, to seek beyond writing—through experiments with electronic media and further experiments with drugs—new forms of consciousness and artistic expression.

He treats the same kind of yearning in an unpublished essay in which he tells of walking as a boy with his dog across the endless rolling prairies near La Junta, Colorado, his birthplace. When he heard a far-off rumbling coming out of the clouds, he thought it was a herd of wild horses one grandpa or the other had told him about—"with teeth like rows of barbwire and eyes like polished steel balls an' breath that'd peel paint." When he told his mother about it, she said, "It's just thunder, honeybun. You was only imagining you saw horses." As a man looking back he asks, "But why, Mama, is it *just* thunder?" And he wonders as he drives across Colorado "What would still roam these prairies if the old creatures had been allowed to breed and prosper, if they hadn't been decimated by that crippler of the imagination: *only.*" He suggests that fact and fiction blend well and both are essential in presenting "the True Happening of the moment." Merely to report as a camera does is just touching the surface, like panning the stream instead of digging for the vein. "The vein lies under the topsoil of external reality: it is not hidden. We've known of it for ages, this vein, but it has been put down so long by *just*, disparaged so long by *only*, that we have neglected its development." He suggests that mining the vein has many advantages. In writing, for example, "it can mean that as much emphasis can be placed on hyperbole, metaphor, simile, or *fantasy* as on actual events." He concludes, "In the vast seas between red and white blood corpuscles Captain Nemo still secretly pilots his Nautilus, this white-haired scourge of Oppression and Warfare. Why not give him his head? Or through the dense growth, of neurons, Lou Wetzel stalks the Zane Grey Indians, silent as moss until he strikes with a chilling war whoop. Why not let him stalk?"[10] Such attitudes are undoubtedly behind the claim by the narrator of *Cuckoo's Nest* that what he tells is "the truth even if it didn't happen" (*CN*, 8).

Comic books. Westerns, and science fiction—these popular genres captured Kesey's fancy and stimulated his imagination in ways he would later take seriously. "A single *Batman* comicbook is more honest than a whole volume of *Time* magazines," he once told an interviewer.[11] He recognized in these popular forms vital American myths that could be employed in serious literature the same way Joyce had made use of classic myths. *Cuckoo's Nest* is informed by the mythology of American popular culture.

II

At the University of Oregon, Kesey was a sort of campus wonder-boy. He involved himself in athletics, theater, and fraternity life. He majored in communications and took courses in creative writing. It was a period of the kind of growth and discovery one would expect when a singularly bright, curious, but relatively uncultured mind is exposed to a university environment, when an emerging charismatic personality is exposed to a wider variety of people and social opportunities, but no matter how stimulating his experiences as an undergraduate may have been, they were not as life-transforming as his experiences as a graduate student at Stanford.

A Woodrow Wilson fellowship enabled him to enter Stanford's creative writing program in 1958. It was a highly regarded program with distinguished writer-teachers such as Wallace Stegner, Richard Scowcroft, Malcolm Cowley, and Frank O'Connor. Perhaps even more important in shaping Kesey's writing skills was the group of students with whom he associated and shared manuscripts and commentary. Among that group were Larry McMurphy, Wendell Berry, Robert Stone, Tillie Olsen, Ed McClanahan, and others whose writing later achieved varying degrees of acclaim. Kesey has likened them to the Green Bay Packers under Vince Lombardi. In addition to the wealth of talent, the seminars were distinguished by a generous spirit of useful critique. Young writers can be hard on each other, quick to give and take offense. However, Kesey's experience with his classmates was positive and resulted in a number of lasting friendships.

An important one of these friendships, and one that clearly illustrates the kind of stimulation they provided, is the one with Ken Babbs. They met in a seminar during Kesey's first semester at Stanford, and during the next few years, while Babbs was in military service, they engaged in a correspondence deliberately intended to provide opportunity for writing practice and mutual evaluation. In a letter to Babbs written while Kesey was working in a mental institution and writing *Cuckoo's Nest,* he suggests that they continue their letters as a way of helping each other,

> because I fog in and forget sometimes that I'm a damn good writer with potential of becoming a great one. Publishing house setbacks slow me down, could stop me and dry me up like a fallen fig. I doubt work that I should know is good. It is more important sometimes to point out the good than it is to distinguish the bad; you're certain of the old standby Bad, no one needs point that out all the time. But you're forever uncertain of the Good.[12]

In the next sentence, he says he is going to send Babbs sections of the *Cuckoo's Nest* manuscript. The quoted passage is interesting in several ways. The fog image brings to mind his narrator's struggle with fog, an intriguing parallel. The publishing house setbacks refer to his attempts to publish "Zoo," his novel about the Beat culture of San Francisco's North Beach, which had won the Saxton Prize at Stanford but was never published. Clearly, at this point in the creation of *Cuckoo's Nest,* Kesey felt a need to firm up his confidence. He wanted a reader's responses and suggestions, but only if they were encouraging. He must have known intuitively the book's strengths and didn't want criticism that whittled them away; he needed reinforcing praise.

He had to send the manuscript to Vietnam, where Babbs was stationed. Babbs annotated it and wrote a long letter of suggestions, including these:

> I don't like the word, the Combine. You're trying to give a name to something that has no name. It's an emotion, a complacency, and a dulling of the senses that we're fighting, and to try and shut all these things into a box and give it a title is taking an easy gambit that isn't there to be had. . . . Throw away the thought that the opponent is real, that it exists. Everyone that reads with any intelligence knows what you're writing about, you don't have to give it a label.

He praised the hero and agreed that individual strength is more important than group action. "All I can say is do him bigger and better and finer, and you'll make everything and everyone else in the book as big and as fine." But again he counseled Kesey not to make the opposing force tangible or specific: "Forget about having the chief name something the Combine, keep it nameless. Don't sum up this total fight into the Big Nurse."[13]

This is reasonable advice and touches upon the principal risk Kesey took in simplifying the forces of good and evil and embodying them in a specific hero and villain. Some critics have shared Babbs's point of view, but the general public has responded positively to the comic-book and Western-showdown simplicity of the book's principal conflicts. In this respect, the novel is a tour de force, an unabashed and skillful use of the appeals characteristic of popular literature and culture.

Kesey was confident enough in his aims that he could resist the advice of a best friend but unsure enough about how he had realized them to be fortified by that friend's praise. Babbs assured him in the same letter that the book had the ingredients of success. "The writing is good, at times rough, but like all your stuff it swings with the wild rhythms of hot life, raw life, good life, and I move out with it, and that's the power of the book for me." He suggested that Kesey might not meet great success for ten or twelve years, but it was coming. The novel appeared in print exactly one year later, and Kesey took satisfaction some months before then in playfully teasing Babbs about his success: "When I got the telegram, direct from Malcolm Cowley, no less, I thought about calling you and rubbing the salt of my fortune into your already smarting literary wounds, but thought better of it when I realized how much more acute the sting would be upon receiving the published book. Unannounced, like an angel of derision swooping down to harass you."[14] But of course he couldn't wait until the book was out before sharing his excitement with Babbs. Perhaps implied in the letter is both Kesey's trust in his own genius and an expression of gratitude for his friend's interest and encouragement.

What Kesey learned from teachers that helped him in creating the novel is difficult to determine with any precision. When asked in 1963 if he had learned anything in his creative writing classes at Stanford, he said he had learned a lot from Malcolm Cowley. What was it he learned? "Well, before Cowley, I studied with James Hall at Oregon. He taught me how *good* writing can be. Cowley taught me how good a writer *I* could be."[15] Cowley had been a visiting teacher during the time Kesey was at work on the novel, 1960-1961, and therefore was the teacher who offered suggestions specifically about *Cuckoo's Nest*. Unfortunately, those annotations and suggestions were not preserved.

Before the seminar with Cowley, Kesey had been taught by Wallace Stegner. His debt to Stegner is problematical. When Gordon Lish asked him what he had learned from Stegner, Kesey replied, "Just never to teach in college," explaining this answer by suggesting that Stegner's writing had been adversely affected by the academic life. "A man becomes *accustomed* to having two hundred people gather every day at one o'clock giving him all of their attention—because he's clever, good-looking, famous, and has a beautiful voice."[16] The sour tone here could have had several sources; maybe it was jealousy or a sense of competition. Stegner was one of the leading writers associated with the West, and Kesey, as westerner, would inevitably be measured against him. But more likely it was a clash of values. Kesey would become a guru of the counterculture or youth-cult movement, a psychedelic impresario in the transition from Beats to Hippies. Stegner was to write critically of that movement. The Bohemianism Kesey was absorbing on Perry Lane and in North Beach probably alienated him from the academic establishment Stegner seemed to represent. Cowley, in contrast, was not an academic—he taught creative writing but was not a full-time professor—and was more sympathetic to the Beat writers Kesey was discovering. Kesey read Kerouac's *On the Road* three times before arriving at Stanford, "hoping to sign on in some way, to join that joyous voyage, like thousands of other volunteers inspired by the same book, and its vision, and, of course, its incomparable hero."[17] Cowley had read the manuscript of *On the Road* while at Viking. He plugged it to his publisher and mentioned it favorably in *The Literary Situation* in 1954, three years before it was published.[18]

One item in the Kesey Collection suggests a certain friction between Kesey and Stegner. It is a chastisement from Stegner that might be related to the clash of perspectives just mentioned. Kesey submitted a paper titled "On Why I Am Not Writing My Last Term Paper." It was one of those things students write when they want to justify failing to complete an assignment by claiming it was not challenging or meaningful enough. Kesey argued that he should be writing a novel instead of doing academic exercises. Stegner would have none of that. His annotation chides Kesey, saying the paper is merely self-expression, which is really self-indulgence. "Now go write that novel, but don't for God's sake let it turn into self-expression."

But regardless of how this reprimand was taken or how Kesey disliked what he viewed as an academic quality in Stegner's writing, there is evidence that he learned from him. According to Kesey's wife, Faye Kesey, both Stegner and Richard Scowcroft played influential roles in Kesey's first year at Stanford. And in letters to Babbs, Kesey acknowledges that Stegner had been right in his emphasis on point of view.[19] Under the stimulus of Stegner, Kesey became preoccupied with point of view, and his first two novels are distinctive in their experimental narrative technique.

Stegner, as far as I know, has not written about his association with Kesey. Malcolm Cowley has. In an essay titled "Kesey at Stanford," he tells of meeting Kesey in his seminar in the fall of 1960. Kesey was not officially enrolled, but as a matter of courtesy, former students were invited to attend. According to Cowley, the class was distinguished and class members developed good relations in discussing each other's work. Cowley's description of the "stolid and self-assured" Kesey resembles Kesey's description of McMurphy: "He had the build of a plunging halfback, with big shoulders and a neck like the stump of a Douglas fir." Kesey read from the manuscript in class and showed the whole thing to Cowley for his critique. Cowley insists that he contributed nothing: "the book is Kesey's from first to last. Probably I pointed out passages that didn't 'work,' that failed to produce a desired effect on the reader. Certainly I asked questions, and some of these may have helped to clarify Kesey's notions of how to go about solving his narrative problems, but the solutions were always his own." John C. Pratt tells us that Cowley discovered rhyme in certain passages, and Kesey made it more explicit in revision. The first drafts seemed to Cowley to have been written rapidly, as evidenced by misspellings and typing errors. Later Kesey would edit with some care. "He had his visions, but he didn't have the fatal notion of some Beat writers, that the first hasty account of a vision was a sacred text not to be tampered with. He revised, he made deletions and additions; he was working with readers in mind."[20] Although Cowley didn't share McMurphy's theory of psychotherapy, he was impressed with the manuscript and was undoubtedly instrumental in its acceptance by Viking. The Cowley connection is one of the elements of chance and good fortune in the concatenation of circumstances resulting in the novel's success.

III

Kesey's life was radically transformed when he moved into Perry Lane and began making excursions to North Beach, just forty miles away. Perry Lane, which no longer exists, was a neighborhood of small cottages housing a rather Bohemian community of students. The story is familiar, told most colorfully by Tom Wolfe in *The Electric Kool-Aid Acid Test*. Kesey grew a beard; began playing the guitar and singing folk songs; read about jazz and drugs; wrote a novel about what was happening in North Beach; volunteered for government-sponsored drug experiments at the Menlo Park Veterans Administration hospital; began, along with friends, conducting drug experiments of his own; took a job as an aide in the psychiatric ward of the hospital; and so on. Repeating as little as possible of the published information about this time in Kesey's life, I wish to provide some new information and to reexamine what is already known as it relates directly to the genesis of *Cuckoo's Nest*.

Kesey has publicly acknowledged his debt to Jack Kerouac a number of times, and he became close friends with Neal Cassady, the model for a main character in *On the Road*. Although the Cassady friendship profoundly influenced Kesey's later activities, it had nothing to do with *Cuckoo's Nest*, which was completed before the two met. It was the spirit of Kerouac's book rather than the literary method that attracted Kesey. He considered Kerouac a reporter rather than a novelist, and he wasn't trying to be a reporter. Kerouac developed a technique of writing "without consciousness" and in "The Essentials of Spontaneous Prose" attacked the idea that revision is important and necessary. He compared the writer to a jazz saxophonist releasing an unrevised flow. Kesey used a similar method in dictating his drug experiences and in freewriting as he planned his novels. But his novels were planned. His working notes for *Sometimes a Great Notion* and "One Lane," an unpublished novel, reveal his self-consciousness about themes and about methods for conveying them. His courses in film and television scriptwriting at the University of Oregon had required him to design his objectives, and he retained the habit. Moreover, his mind has a philosophical quality and is naturally inclined to discover concepts and themes in even commonplace events.

More frequently mentioned in the letters and tapes in the Kesey Collection than *On the Road* is William S. Burroughs's *Naked Lunch*. In lending his copy to Babbs, he called it his "most prized possession." He greatly admired Burroughs's ability to capture the carnal and psychic throb of human experience. Burroughs says near the end of *Naked Lunch*, "There is only one thing a writer can write about; *what is in front of his senses at the moment of writing*. . . . I am a recording instrument. . . . I do not presume to impose 'story' 'plot' 'continuity.'. . . Insofar as I succeed in Direct recording of certain areas of psychic process I may have limited function. . . . I am not an entertainer." As with Kerouac's "spontaneous prose," Kesey adopted the method only in a modified form. Tony Tanner has suggested that Bromden's paranoid fantasies are "a very Burroughs-like vision."[21] And Burroughs's funny, carnival-pitchman style may have contributed something to the creation of McMurphy, who is frequently likened to a carnival pitchman.

There is much in *Cuckoo's Nest* that derived from the Beats, who advocated a return to nature and a revolt against the machine, attitudes that are paramount in the novel. Bromden's Combine is really a tag for the corporate, technical-industrial, suburban values that alienated the Beat generation. Perhaps prompted by or perhaps simply concurrent with critiques by the serious media in the fifties and books like David Riesman's *The Lonely Crowd* (1952), William H. Whyte's *The Organization Man* (1956), and John Kenneth Galbraith's *The Affluent Society* (1958), the Beats viewed America as inhabited by a lonely crowd of gray-flannel-clad organization men, offering its affluence only to those who were willing to pay the price of strict conformity. Kesey accepted these premises but offered an alternative to the Beats' rebellion, which lacked definite shape and direction and was little more than withdrawal from the mainstream. Kesey's is an activist response that adumbrates the counter-culture strategies of the following decade.

The Beat movement was urban; Kesey's roots were rural. This accounts for why he embraced some Beat attitudes and ignored others. His family and regional tradition of self-assertive action prevented his accepting Beat passiv-ity and withdrawal. He told Gordon Lish, "I get weary of people who use pes-simism to avoid being responsible for all the problems in our culture. A man who says, we're on the road to disaster, is seldom trying to wrench the wheel away from the driver." He prefers the troublemaker who tries to make things better. In a letter to Babbs written while he was on duty at the hospital, Ke-sey tells of being called upstairs to listen to a tape about the brainwashing of Korean War prisoners: "It was most enlightening, especially in terms of the book I'm writing. It had a lot to do with the 'Code of Conduct.' Remember it? We used to ridicule it upstairs in the ROTC office at Stanford? Well, I'm be-coming very square or something—but I'm beginning to believe the code has a lot to it, a lot about strength. Strength is the key. We need strong men."[22] McMurphy, of course, meets the need for strong men.

Allen Ginsberg claimed that "the first serious experimentation with al-tered states of consciousness came with the Beats using pot and peyote."[23] He had written *Howl* under the influence of drugs—peyote, amphetamines, Dexedrine. Kesey, who says he wrote parts of *Cuckoo's Nest* under the influ-ence of peyote, was introduced to drugs by the Beat culture. In volunteering for experiments with mind-altering drugs, he was following the lead of the Beats' curiosity about how such substances might affect artistic creation.

In a way, Kesey's attraction to the Beats was an attraction to the Amer-ican tradition of romantic idealism—New England transcendentalism fil-tered through Whitman to writers like Kerouac and Ginsberg. Whitman had added a coarse, fleshy, vulgar element—the glorification of the body and sex. The Beats carried this impulse even further. Kesey was attracted to the idealism and readily embraced the earthiness, which was compat-ible with his western-small-town, locker-room background. *Cuckoo's Nest* is informed by American transcendentalism's preoccupation with nature and self-reliance, but it is couched in earthy, ribald language and action. While Beat writing and behavior affected the curious and impressionable Kesey forcefully, his strong personality shaped by western individualism caused him to gradually filter that influence and retain only what suited his own distinctive purposes. The stages in this process are apparent in his unpublished writing.

The novel "Zoo" is specifically about North Beach. It echoes Kerouac in its descriptions of wine drinking, drug addicts, jazz musicians, stupid and brutal police, interracial marriages, poverty-level Bohemian living, cars scarred by frantic miles on the highway, and talk of nihilism and Zen. It. displays the same adolescent fascination with unconventional behavior as *On the Road*, but it artistically shapes autobiographical experience in the interests of theme in a way that book fails to do. The main character in "Zoo" is torn between his attraction to a new way of life in North Beach and his rural Oregon roots. In Kesey's first two novels, "End of Autumn" and "Zoo"—both unpublished—the Oregon roots prevail. In his life following the writing of those novels, however, the new lifestyle in California prevailed until, after serving six months in prison on a marijuana charge, he returned to a farm in Oregon.

So "Zoo" constitutes one stage in his absorption of the Beat influence. An unpublished short story in the Kesey Collection titled "The Kicking Party" reflects another. The setting is a psychiatric ward. The Five patients wonder why Abel Cramer is an inmate. The paranoids say, "Plotting, the bastard is, plotting to undermine the whole system with his evil laugh and sinful stories!" The head nurse watches him "through her protective glass shield from her sterilized isolation booth." He is talking to "a group of en-raptured patients," telling "one of his heightened, hilarious stories of jazz days or junk days or juice days." Here is the basic situation of *Cuckoo's Nest*, but with interesting differences. Cramer is described as "this fabled hand-some stud-with-goatee." He is a beatnik with a history of drug and jazz obsession. Moreover, he is mentally disturbed and haunted with the fear of madness. At this point on the road to *Cuckoo's Nest*, the charismatic laughter (McMurphy) and the patient on the brink of insanity (Bromden) are com-bined in the same person (Cramer), and that person has been created from a world Kesey had merely visited and read about. The turning point came when he precipitated from this solution two characters, a hero of event and a hero of consciousness, both of whom had their source in the life and culture of his own region. Music remained important, but it too was transformed: from jazz, which Kesey had just discovered, to the country-flavored tunes Kesey had grown up with. In short, Kesey was greatly stimulated by his en-counter with the Beats but had to get most of that influence out of his sys-tem before he achieved the originality *Cuckoo's Nest* and *Sometimes a Great Notion*. What did Kerouac think of *Cuckoo's Nest*? In the Kesey Collection is a letter from Kerouac to Tom Ginsberg at Viking written October 19, 1961. Kerouac, who had read an advance copy of the novel, praises it highly but, perhaps because of his own autobiographical approach to writing, is con-vinced that the author must be the Columbia Gorge Indian himself, who used "Kesey," perhaps his wife's name, to avoid being identified with the "deafmute" hero. He says the author is certainly right about the Combine and praises the way he captures the American lingo. Kerouac even senses the flavor of "real western Indian talk" in the narration. His understanding of narrative personae was no more reliable, it seems, than his knowledge of Native American speech.

IV

Six months after his first volunteer drug experiment, Kesey was working as a psychiatric aide. Both his introduction to mind-altering drugs and his work as an aide were primary experiences in the inception of *Cuckoo's Nest*. As he once put it, "In the antiseptic wilderness of the Menlo Park VA Hospital. I cleared a space and rigged a runway and waited for my muse to take the controls."[24] He expected the hospital work to supply subject matter and hoped the drugs would inspire new awareness and perspective. The first expectation was fully realized. The matter of drug induced inspiration is more complicated.

In his own essay on the origins of the novel, "Who Flew over What?" in *Kesey's Garage Sale*, Kesey says that McMurphy was fictional but "inspired by the tragic longing of the real men I worked with on the ward." He described some of these men in a letter to Babbs. Their resemblance to the patients in the novel is obvious. He cultivated an empathy with these men and tried, through drugs, to glimpse their perspective: "I studied inmates as they daily wove intricate and very accurate schizophrenic commentaries of the disaster of their environment, and had found that merely by ingesting a tiny potion I could toss word salad with the nuttiest of them, had discovered that if I plied my consciousness with enough of the proper chemical it was impossible to preconceive, and when preconception is fenced out, truth is liable to occur."[25] He even persuaded a friend in electronics to rig an apparatus and give him a dose of electric-shock therapy so he could write authoritatively about it.

His sympathetic interest in the plight of patients is revealed in a one-sheet summary in the Kesey Collection headed "Be a good story." He notes that a patient had shown up the night before, having left Brentwood Hospital. "Make it a newer hospital, with better facilities and food," Kesey notes to himself. The man had hopped a freight to Oakland in cold weather and gone three days without food. Arriving at the wrong hospital he had walked to a new one. His feet were blistered and he was hungry and exhausted. Why had he done it? "Because they didn't treat him like a human down there. A man will go through a great deal of physical torment and punishment and cold and hunger—to be afforded at least human dignity."

Also in the collection is a taped conversation in which Kesey and another man who had worked in the same hospital compare their experiences. They agree about the white nurses. They found them hard, tough, trying to prove something. The black nurses were kinder. Kesey tells of working in the geriatrics section and getting in a scuffle with a black aide over the treatment of a patient known as Old Moses. For someone acquainted with the novel, the conversation resonates familiarly.

How realistic is Kesey's portrayal of a psychiatric ward? He worked just as an aide for a relatively short time, and he was not writing as a reporter. His narrator, after all, fades in and out of hallucination, and Kesey was aiming for truths independent of literal accuracy. The question may not even be a fair or useful one to ask. But of course it has been asked, and the answers are varied. John Pratt quotes a British psychiatrist practicing in Canada who provides a list of what he considers the novel's distortions and misrepresentations of psychiatric-hospital care.[26] On the other hand, there are letters in the Kesey Collection from two psychiatrists who find the novel's portrayal of mental care accurate and who wish to quote from it and confer with Kesey on reforms in psychiatric practice. One expresses surprise that Kesey had developed such a remarkable insight in so short a time. "I was in this racket a lot longer than that," he says, "before I realized what was really significant and actually taking place."

A question more relevant to the genesis of the novel and to understanding the process of literary creation is this: what does the novel owe to drug inspiration? Kesey has said on a number of occasions that the inspiration for his Indian narrator came to him while he was under the influence of peyote. One interviewer provides this quote from a December 1971 conversation: "I was flying on peyote, really strung out there, when this Indian came to me. I knew nothing about Indians, had no Indians on my mind, had nothing that an Indian could ever grab onto, yet this Indian came to me. It was the peyote, then, couldn't be anything else. The Indian came straight out from the drug itself."[27] This claim, in one version or another, is the most widely known item of information about the writing of the novel. Kesey also makes the claim in "Who Flew over What?" and insists that it was not simply a matter of peyote being naturally associated with Indians. Bromden was, he insists, an inspiration from outside his experience. This claim merits careful examination for at least two reasons. First, it is linked to the longstanding question of whether artistic creativity can be enhanced by chemical stimulants. And second, it is Kesey's prime example of the creative benefits of mind-altering drugs.

I suggest that this claim should not be taken at face value. To begin with, Kesey is, or once was, temperamentally inclined to a certain credulity in matters of paranormal experience, as is evidenced in the search or quest already mentioned. His imagination has been captured by everything from the *I Ching* to mysteries of a lost pyramid—anything that offers awareness beyond the commonplace. He was very serious about his experiments with drugs and strongly desired to make discoveries. He has likened his volunteering for such experiments to Neil Armstong's volunteering to go to the moon or Lewis and Clark's willingness to explore the West.[28] He used a good deal of the money earned by *Cuckoo's Nest* to finance attempts to find new forms of expression beyond writing through the use of drugs and electronic equipment. "Who Flew over What?" was written during his Merry Prankster era. He needed an example of drug inspiration to justify the Prankster activities and to confirm to himself that he was on the right track. In other words, the assertion that Bromden was the exclusive product of peyote maybe an exaggeration generated by an intense desire that it be true.

In "Who Flew over What?" Kesey says that he wrote the first three pages of *Cuckoo's Nest* after swallowing eight little cactus plants. "These pages," he asserts, "remained almost completely unchanged through the numerous rewrites the book went through, and from this first spring I drew all the passion and perception the narrator spoke with during the ten months' writing that followed." Pratt includes these pages in the background section of his critical edition of the novel, noting that by the final version "Kesey made significant revisions, especially after he had decided upon the novel's point of view."[29] It is true that the germ of the narration is apparent in these first pages, but it is also clear that Kesey has again overstated his case.

There is ample reason why Kesey might have selected an Indian for his narrator. He had, in fact, known Indians—or at least observed them—and reflected upon their victimization. On one of the tapes he talks about having played on a football team with an Indian, and about an Indian employed by his father's dairy company. He describes an Indian with lipstick all over his face, his cowboy shirt splattered with blood. He told Gordon Lish of an Indian in a logging camp who went berserk and attacked with a knife a diesel truck tracing down a highway built on what had been his grandfather's land.[30] He wrote a story at the University of Oregon titled "The Avocados," which tells of two University of Oregon students in Los Angeles. In the company of two Mexican girls, they encounter two Klamath Indians, both World War II veterans. One of them, in a wheelchair, is used once in a while in movies when a classic Indian chief face is needed. The other wrestles occasionally. They make prickly pear wine. Once they were going to save and go back to Oregon. "Now," one of them says, "I hear they screwed all the Klamath Indians." The students drop the girls and drive off to see the city with the Indians. The girls are like avocados: soft on me outside but hard inside. The Indians are like a prickly pear cactus: repellent on the outside but sweet inside.

The most obvious intimation of Bromden in Kesey's early writing is the main character of "Sunset at Celilo," a script he wrote for a radio and television writing course. Jim Smith, a Celilo Indian, returns after five years in the army. "He is from a small tribe of poor hut happy people who have lived on the Columbia for years and fished for salmon at the Celilo Falls for a living." The government has given permission for a dam at the Dalles. The tribe has been paid $28 million, which has been spent recklessly on television sets, expensive furnishings, and Cadillacs. Jim tries to arouse the tribe and threatens to dynamite the dam, but eventually realizes his efforts are hopeless. In a note to Dean Stark, his teacher, Kesey points out that the story is based on fact and the dam will soon be completed.

These examples show that Kesey had considerable experience with Indians from which to draw upon in his creation of his narrator, that Kesey was exaggerating his faith in drug inspiration when he described the sudden, inexplicable appearance of Bromden. On other occasions he has explained more convincingly that drugs do not provide new ideas or information but simply anesthetize inhibitions and preconceptions and thus allow the imagination a certain temporary freedom and fluidity. When asked once whether drugs had anything to do with the lyrical and fantastic descriptions in *Cuckoo's Nest*, he answered, "Yes, but *drugs* didn't create those descriptions any more than Joyce's *eyeglasses* created *Ulysses*. They merely help one to see the paper more clearly."[31]

V

Kesey's stimulating new experiences during his first two years in California clearly had much to do with the genesis of *Cuckoo's Nest*. But the substance of the novel—its principal tone, language, imagery, and comic vision—derives from frontier attitudes and traditions that he inherited from his family and picked up in his region. In demonstrating the indispensability of humor for combating the negative aspects of an increasingly urban and technological society, the novel reasserts the vitality of certain distinctive patterns in American humor, particularly those of nineteenth-century frontier humor. It not only demonstrates these varieties of American humor but also celebrates them. The novel brings patterns of frontier humor to bear on the urban, technological society of mid-twentieth-century America. The humor of *Cuckoo's Nest* is both an example of and a tribute to a distinctive and persistent rural, vernacular tradition in American humor. Part of the reason for the book's popularity is our enduring affection for the unsophisticated, unpretentious, but self-reliant folk humor that evolved along America's shifting western boundaries.

Some confusion about Kesey as a humorist resulted from his role as a counterculture hero and drug guru during California's psychedelic revolution in the early sixties. He was labeled a "black humorist," a term that enjoyed considerable currency in the sixties but has faded from the critical lexicon because it was difficult to define, indiscriminately applied, and eventually mistaken for a racial term. In the late sixties, trying to make sense of black humor as a concept, Hamlin Hill identified its tone as "belligerent, pugnacious, nihilistic." As humor moves into the black zone, he observed, it heads for the irrational and valueless, not seeking the sympathetic alliance of the audience but deliberately insulting and alienating it. He quoted Lennie Bruce as defining the creed: "Everything is rotten—mother is rotten, God is rotten, the flag is rotten."[32]

The year after *Cuckoo's Nest* appeared, Hill had characterized modern American humor as Janus-faced. One face, he wrote, looks upon the native strain rooted in the preceding century, which affirms the values of "common sense, self-reliance, and a kind of predictability in the world." The protagonist of this variety of humor "faces an *external* reality with gusto and exuberance," said Hill. "Even when he launches forth into his version of fantasy, the tall tale, he is based solidly upon the exaggeration of actual reality, not upon nightmare, hysteria, or delusion." Hill labeled the other strain the "dementia praecox school." The antihero of this humor is neurotically concerned with an inner space of nightmare and delusion where unreliability and irrationality abound. Clearly Hill had in mind the trend in modern urban humor to dramatize a sense of inadequacy, impotence, and defeat before the complexities and destructive potential of our century. Its protagonists are repressed, squeamish, and hypersensitive. Their individuality and self-confidence have been compromised by life in a depersonalized mass society. Thus, in Hill's view, modern American humor "releases itself in both the hearty guffaw and the neurotic giggle, it reacts to both the bang and the whimper."[33]

Hill's essays are helpful in clarifying Kesey's relation to the varieties of American humor. Although the principal subject matter of *Cuckoo's Nest* is dementia praecox and its narrator begins his story in a nightmarish state of neurotic fantasy and delusion, the novel is clearly founded upon the values of self-reliance and commonsense harmony with nature. Its victory is that of sanity over insanity, strength over neurotic victimization, and nature over misguided technology. McMurphy's initial exchanges with Harding are confrontations between "the hearty guffaw and the neurotic giggle." McMurphy is the bang, Harding the whimper. Ultimately, of course, McMurphy's earthy, noncerebral humor vanquishes Harding's cynical, intellectual, and timid attempts at wit.

Similarly although Kesey used techniques associated with so-called black comedy, particularly during the period following *Cuckoo's Nest* and *Sometimes a Great Notion,* when he turned from writing to escapades with the Merry Pranksters, he never espoused the attitudes underlying that kind of humor. He gained notoriety within the California counterculture, but his roots were in rural Oregon and a family heritage of western-American values and vernacular stories. He has never strayed far from those roots. His fellow drug guru, Timothy Leary, who had no particular affinity for such roots, noted this a few years ago when he said of Kesey, "I have always seen him as very Protestant and quite moralistic, and quite American in a puritanical way. And basically untrustworthy, since he is always going to end up with a

Bible in his hand, sooner or later." Mark Twain once said, "Humor must not professedly teach, and it must not professedly preach, but it must do both if it would live forever. By forever, I mean thirty years."[34] *Cuckoo's Nest* has met that thirty-year criterion, and its humor is largely Twain's variety in source, method, and purpose.

Recognizing the pitfalls in delineating sources and influences in humor, I want to demonstrate the links between *Cuckoo's Nest* and what, for convenience, I call frontier humor. By this term I mean the indigenous, largely vernacular tradition of humor whose development during the nineteenth century has been described by scholars such are Constance Rourke, Bernard DeVoto, Walter Blair, Hamlin Hill, M. Thomas Inge, James Cox, and Kenneth Lynn. The critical literature generated by the novel has identified some of its similarities with frontier humor, in what follows, I provide a brief but more extensive and specific survey of parallels than has been supplied before and conclude with comments on the function and significance of those parallels.

To begin with, McMurphy is a westerner, a product and an anachronistic afterimage of the frontier. He has lived all around Oregon and in Texas and Oklahoma (*CN*, 186). In the frontier spirit of freedom and movement he has wandered restlessly, "logging, gambling, running carnival wheels, traveling lightfooted and fast, keeping on the move" (*CN*, 84). His hand is like "a road map of his travels up and down the West" (*CN*, 27). As already mentioned, Kesey's family were restless west-walkers, not pioneers or visionaries but just a simple clan looking for new opportunities.

Drawing upon popular culture, Kesey links McMurphy with the most familiar hero of the frontier—the cowboy. He smokes Marlboro cigarettes and is described as "the cowboy out of the TV set walking down the middle of the street to meet a dare" (*CN*, 172). He has a "drawling cowboy actor's voice" (*CN*, 232). Before his first meeting with Harding, he says, "this hospital ain't big enough for the two of us. . . . Tell this Harding that he either meets me man to man or he's a yaller skunk and better be outta town by sunset" (*CN*, 24). He has a "cowboy bluster" and a "TV-cowboy stoicism" (*CN*, 62, 73). He sings cowboy songs in the latrine and has Wild Bill Hickok's "dead-man's hand" tattooed on his shoulder (*CN*, 83, 77). Just before he assaults Big Nurse he hitches up his shorts "like they were horsehide chaps, and pushe[s] his cap with one finger like it was a ten-gallon Stetson" (*CN*, 267). Harding refers to him with an allusion to the Lone Ranger: "I'd like to stand there at the window with a silver bullet in my hand and ask 'who *wawz* that 'er masked man?'" (*CN*, 258). We all effortlessly absorb such cowboy clichés from our culture, but Kesey in addition had read Zane Grey (and named a son Zane) and other writers of Westerns. The widow of Ernest Haycox hired him while he was at the University of Oregon to write plot summaries of her husband's novels. Haycox, a major figure in the genre, appeared in *Collier's* alone an average of thirteen times a year between 1931 and 1949 and did much to shape the nation's conception of the Western hero.

In similar ways, McMurphy is identified with other frontier types such as the logger and gambler. As part of a scriptwriting course, Kesey prepared an outline for a television series to be called "Legends," a treatment of American folk heroes. He was fascinated by such figures as Paul Bunyan, Davy Crockett, Mike Fink, and Pecos Bill. McMurphy is a product of that tradition, with its bragging, exaggeration, and humorous treatment of violence. When Mc-Murphy fights the captain of the rental boat and then the two cheerfully sit down to drink beer together, we are witnessing a familiar pattern in frontier humor. When McMurphy and Harding square off to brag about which is the crazier (frequency of voting for Eisenhower being the principal measure), we are witnessing a fresh twist to the ring-tailed roarer confrontations of old-Southwest humor.

Kesey claims that he didn't see the film version of the novel because he was disgusted with the casting of Jack Nicholson as McMurphy. He referred to him as a "wimp." In Kesey's eyes he was too urban, too lacking in the western vernacular strengths that inspired his conception of McMurphy. Nicholson, I suppose, might have been appropriate for Abel Cramer, the main character in "The Tricking Party," but by the time Kesey wrote *Cuckoo's Nest* he had reverted to the wellspring of his western background. His own pencil drawing of McMurphy suggests rugged physical strength.[35]

Americans have always loved the rustic or apparently simple character who appears naive but is actually bright and clever. One version of this type is the television detective Columbo. The type appeared early in American humor in the form of country hicks outsmarting city slickers. It is part of an anti-intellectual current in American humor. Drawing from a rural, oral tradition represented in his family particularly by his maternal grandmother, Kesey composed "Little Tricker the Squirrel Meets Big Double the Bear," which first appeared in his *Demon Box* and then as a separate children's book.[36] This backwoods animal fable in the vein of Joel Chandler Harris's *Uncle Remus* is a story of the clever little guy who defeats the wielder of unjust power. Arthur Maddox, a musician with roots in rural Missouri, composed music to accompany the narration, and Kesey has performed it with symphony orchestras across the country. It is a tribute to his grandmother and the oral tradition she perpetuated, and it suggests one of the sources for McMurphy.

McMurphy is, to a large degree, a hero from that oral tradition, and the bully he combats is not simply Big Nurse, but also the technological Combine she represents. Harding explicitly identifies this aspect of Mc-Murphy when he acknowledges his intelligence: "an illiterate clod, perhaps, certainly a backwoods braggart with no more sensitivity than a goose, but basically intelligent nevertheless" (*CN*, 56). Elsewhere, he cautions the patients to avoid being misled by McMurphy's "back-woodsy ways; he's a very sharp operator, level-headed as they come" (*CN*, 224). Kesey himself was a diamond-in-the rough when he arrived at Stanford from rural Oregon, but his new friends soon discovered a brilliant mind behind the down-home, college-jock exterior.

Cuckoo's Nest contains other parallels with frontier humor. For example, the novel employs homely but vivid similes, such as "shakin' like a dog shittin' peach pits" (*CN*, 122). McMurphy wrenches language in a way reminiscent of characters in *Huck Finn* and the Southwestern humor that inspired Twain. For instance, when Harding mentions "Freud, Jung, and Maxwell Jones," Mc-Murphy replies, "I'm not talking about Fred Yoong and Maxwell Jones" (*CN*, 56). McMurphy often communicates in anecdotes. Their frontier-humor flavor is illustrated in the one about a rough practical joke that backfires. A man at a rodeo is tricked into riding a bull blindfolded and backwards and nevertheless wins (*CN*, 139). This bears a family resemblance to Twain's anecdote of the genuine Mexican plug in *Roughing It*. Similarly in the tradition of Twain, McMurphy nearly outdoes Huck Finn with his creative lying to the service-station attendants in order to protect his friends. He even receives a discount similar to the way Huck received money with his lie to the slave hunters that saves Jim (*CN*, 200–201). The novel's humor is at times scatological and often earthy and exaggerated, as in the description of Candy reeling in a salmon, "with the crank of the reel fluttering her breast at such a speed the nipple's just a red blur!" (*CN*, 211). Like a good deal of frontier humor, the novel involves masculine resistance to feminine order and control. "We are victims of a matriarchy here," complains Harding (*CN*, 59). Even the novel's narrative method, one of its most important aspects, can be linked with frontier humor. It is an original and rather bizarre adaptation of the frame technique often used in the nineteenth century. Moreover, the use of a hallucinating narrator allows for the elements of tall tale and exaggeration so characteristic of the native variety of American humor.

Another important cultural ingredient in the conception of Mc-Murphy is the kind of character genially pictured in rascals, subversives, and con men so endemic to American humor. Walter Blair and Hamlin Hill observe that "a procession of comic men and women whose life work combined imaginative lying with cynical cheating has been one of the most persistent groups that our humor has portrayed."[37] As new frontiers opened, imaginative scoundrels, in language that raised homely colloquialisms to high art, perpetrated new scams. Everyone is familiar with Twain's king and duke. Several entire books are devoted to the American con man, tracing the type from the Yankee peddler to *The Music Man*. Kesey had a special affinity for this brassy, fast-talking sort of personality. Beginning with his theater activities in college and continuing, through the Merry

Prankster years up to the present, he has availed himself of every opportunity to play this role.

McMurphy's glib pitchman quality is conveyed by auctioneer and particularly carnival images. On first impression he reminds the narrator of "a car salesman or a stock auctioneer—or one of those pitchmen you see on a sideshow stage, out in front of his flapping banners" (*CN, 17*). He is likened to an "auctioneer spinning jokes to loosen up a crowd before the bidding starts" (*CN, 22*). Three other times we are reminded of his "stock auctioneer" manner, his "rollicking auctioneer voice," and his "auctioneer bellow" (*CN*, 72, 199, 268). Bromden refers to him as "a seasoned con" and "a carnival artist" (*CN*, 220). Harding calls him "a good old red, white, and blue hundred-per-cent American con man" (*CN*, 223). McMurphy himself explains that "the secret of being a top-notch con man is being able to know what the mark *wants*, and how to make him think he's getting it. I learned that when I worked a season on a skillo wheel in a carnival" (*CN*, 74). He talks Dr. Spivey into suggesting in a group meeting that the ward have a carnival (*CN*, 97). He draws eyes to him "like a sideshow barker" (*CN*, 233), and as his example begins to have an effect on his fellow patients, they are infected with the same quality: when Bromden returns from a stint in the "Disturbed" ward for resisting the aides, the faces of the other patients light up "as if they were looking into the glare of a sideshow platform," and Harding does an imitation of a sideshow barker (*CN*, 243).

But as one reflects on the carnival motif, it becomes increasingly interesting and complex. In this world of con or be conned, McMurphy is not always in control. Big Nurse is also a sort of technological-age con artist, and when her schemes are in ascendancy, she is described as "a tarot-card reader in a glass arcade case" (*CN*, 171) or "one of those arcade gypsies that scratch out fortunes for a penny" (*CN*, 268). And the patients, including McMurphy, are described as "arcade puppets" or "shooting-gallery target[s]" (*CN*, 33, 49). The carnival motif ranges from the vitally human barker toward the mechanized—toward humanoid machines that manipulate people and forecast the future. Harding, describing shock treatment to McMurphy, compares it to a carnival: "it's as if the jolt sets off a wild carnival wheel of images, emotions, memories. These wheels, you've seen them; the barker takes your bet and pushes a button. *Chang!*" (*CN*, 164). McMurphy, of course, has not only seen those wheels, he has operated them, and therefore Harding's words stun and bewilder him. When he realizes he has been committed and is liable to shock treatment, he is transformed from con man to mark: "Why, those slippery bastards have *conned* me, snowed me into holding their bag. If that don't beat all, conned ol' R. P. McMurphy" (*CN*, 166). Later, when he is wheeled back from a lobotomy, Scanlon refers to him as "that crummy sideshow fake lying there on the Gurney" (*CN*, 270). So during the course of the story, McMurphy (and to some extent the other principal patients) function as con men, marks, and sideshow freaks The novel's poignancy, of course, results from McMurphy's ultimate breaking of the con-or-be-conned cycle by sacrificing himself for others.

Cartoons are another variety of humor that plays a role in the novel. Like the cowboy motif, they are part of popular culture. One of Kesey's characteristic achievements is his use of popular culture (Westerns, horror films, comic books, popular music, etc.) for artistic purposes. And like the cowboy motif, cartoons are related to certain patterns of frontier humor. Bugs Bunny is the quintessential American con man, and Tom and Jerry, Popeye, and others are lively, unsophisticated versions of the little guy versus the bully. America's native forms of humor, with their demotic appeal, naturally provided many themes, characters, and situations for comic strips and animated cartoons.

Cuckoo's Nest makes strategic allusions to the cartoon genre. Harding speaks of their "Walt Disney world" (*CN,* 61). When McMurphy reads, it is "a book of cartoons" (*CN,* 151). As in cartoons, characters swell up large when they are angry or feeling strong and shrink when they are embarrassed or frightened. A hallucinating narrator permits such description; that is part of the brilliance of Kesey's narrative strategy. For example, Pete's hand, as Popeye's might, swells into an iron ball when he resists the orderlies, and when he socks one of them against the wall, the wall cracks in the man's shape (*CN,* 52). This is a cartoon cliché, and much of the novel's violence is of this cartoon variety.

But as with the carnival motif, the cartoon imagery has its dark side. The patients are "like cartoon men" in a negative sense. "Their voices are forced and too quick on the comeback to be real talk—more like cartoon comedy speech." Theirs is "a cartoon world where the figures are flat and outlined in black, jerking through some kind of goofy story that might be real funny if it weren't for the cartoon figures being real guys" (*CN,* 37, 36, 34).

What conclusions can be drawn from Kesey's use of these varieties of humor and particularly the parallels with frontier humor? First of all, he was drawing upon an imagination nurtured in distinctive ways by his family and region. He had to step back from the powerful influences of his California experiences in order to allow that imagination to follow its most natural and vigorous inclinations. Second, he used the patterns of frontier humor not simply for comic effect but also because he wished to assert the values embedded within them against a constricting and depersonalizing urban mass society. There is a nostalgic and celebratory quality in their use, combined with a conviction that such values are not merely relics of a vanished frontier. His second novel, less comic and more ambitious, glorifies these values even more forcefully, a fact that disturbed his radical counterculture friends, whose attitude toward frontier values was ambivalent. Though Kesey went on to immerse himself in the attitudes and behavior of urban radical culture, Norman Mailer was correct in observing in the late eighties that "Kesey has stayed close to his roots and was probably absolutely right to do it."[38] Third, Kesey skillfully used native varieties of American humor in order to accomplish serious purposes. The con man–carnival motif is a principal example. Beneath the humor is a subtle and moving examination of institutionalized victimization and the hardy human strength and unpretentious self-sacrifice that can alleviate it. The cartoon motif is likewise implicated in Kesey's sympathetic treatment of what the novel calls the culls of the Combine. On the whole, the novel demonstrates the enduring vitality and remarkable adaptability of frontier humor.

Kesey was interested in the question "Why me?" The process of literary creation is too complex to allow a complete answer, but the case of *Cuckoo's Nest* is instructive even in its partial demonstration of how an author transmutes life into art. It contributes to our understanding of the effects of chemical stimulants on the creative imagination; and it informs us about the determining influences of family, place, popular reading and viewing, and national literary-cultural traditions.

Notes

1. Quoted in Peter O. Whitmer, "Ken Kesey's Search for the American Frontier," *Saturday Review*, May–June 1983: pp. 26, 27.

2. Quoted in John C. Pratt, ed., *One Flew over the Cuckoo's Nest: Text and Criticism* (New York: Viking, 1973): p. vii.

3. Kesey Collection, University of Oregon, Eugene.

4. Quoted in Linda Gaboriau, "Ken Kesey: Summing up the '60s; Sizing up the '70s," *Crawdaddy*, no. 19 (December 1972): p. 38.

5. Quoted in Gordon Lish, "What the Hell You Looking in Here for, Daisy Mae?" *Genesis West*, 2:5 (1963): p. 27.

6. Ken Kesey, *One Flew Over the Cuckoo's Nest* (New York: New American Library, 1962): p. 186. Hereafter cited parenthetically in the text as *CN*.

7. Ken Kesey, "Excerpts Recorded from an Informal Address by Mr. Kesey to the Parents at Crystal Springs School in Hillsborough, California, Presented under the Auspices of the Chrysalis West Foundation," *Genesis West*, 3:1–2 (1965): p. 40.

8. Gilbert Porter, *One Flew Over the Cuckoo's Nest: Rising to Heroism* (Boston: Twayne, 1989): p. 32.

9. Quoted in Gaboriau, "Ken Kesey: Summing up the 60s," p. 37.

10. Ken Kesey, "A Big Motherfucker," 16–18, Kesey Collection.

11. Lish, "What the Hell You Looking," p. 20.

12. Kesey to Ken Babbs, undated, Kesey Collection.

13. Babbs to Kesey, February 12, 1961, Kesey Collection.

14. Kesey to Babbs, undated, Kesey Collection.

15. Lish, "What the Hell You Looking," p. 25.

16. Ibid., 24–25.

17. Ken Kesey, "The Day after Superman Died," *Esquire*, October 1979: p. 54.

18. Bruce Cook, *The Beat Generation* (New York: Scribner's, 1971): p. 66.

19. Faye Kesey, interview by author, Pleasant Hill, Oregon, June 14, 1980; Pratt, *Cuckoo's Nest: Text and Criticism*, p. 338.

20. Malcolm Cowley, "Kesey at Stanford," in Michael Strelow, ed., *Kesey* (Eugene, Ore.: Northwest Review Books, 1977): pp. 2, 3; Pratt, *Cuckoo's Nest: Text and Criticism*, p. x.

21. William S. Burroughs, *Naked Lunch* (New York: Grove, 1959): p. 221; Tony Tanner, City *of Words: American Fiction, 1950–1970* (London: Jonathan Capps, 1971): p. 376.

22. Lish, "What the Hell You Looking," p. 29; Kesey to Babbs, undated, Kesey Collection.

23. Cook, *Beat Generation*, p. 103.

24. Quoted in Pratt, *Cuckoo's Nest: Tent and Criticism*, p. x.

25. Ken Kesey, "Who Flew over What?" *Kesey's Garage Sale* (New York: Viking, 1973): p. 7; quoted in Pratt, *Cuckoo's Nest: Tent and Criticism*, pp. 340–345, xi.

26. John C. Pratt, "On Editing Kesey: Confessions of a Straight Man," in Strelow, ed., *Kesey*, pp. 10–11.

27. Quoted in E. D. Webber, "Keepin' on the Bounce: A Study of Ken Kesey as a Distinctively American Novelist," p. 144, unpublished thesis, no date or place, Kesey Collection.

28. See Jeff Barnard, "Psychedelic Pioneer Values Family Most of All," *Provo (Utah) Herald*, February 19, 1990, B3, and Whitmer, "Ken Kesey's Search," p. 26.

29. Pratt, *Cuckoo's Nest: Text and Criticism*, p. 333.

30. Lish, "What the Hell You Looking," p. 19.

31. Ibid., p. 24.

32. Hamlin Hill, "Black Humor: Its Causes and Cures," *Colorado Quarterly* 17 (1968): p. 59.

33. Hamlin Hill, "Modern American Humor: The Janus Laugh," *College English*, 25 (1963): pp. 171, 176.

34. Timothy Leary, quoted in Peter O. Whitmer, with Bruce VanWyngarden, *Aquarius Revisited* (New York: Macmillan, 1987): p. 11; Mark Twain, quoted in E. B. and Katherine S. White, *A Subtreasury of American Humor* (New York: Coward-McCann, 1941), p. xxii.

35. Kesey, *Kesey's Garage Sale*, p. 10.

36. Ken Kesey, *Demon Box* (New York: Viking, 1986).

37. Walter Blair and Hamlin Hill, *America's Humor: From Poor Richard to Doonesbury* (New York: Oxford, 1978): p. 43.

38. Quoted in Whitmer and VanWyngarden, *Aquarius Revisited*, p. 63.

Ken Kesey Chronology

1935	Ken Elton Kesey born in La Junta, Colorado, 17 September.
1946	Family moves to Springfield, Oregon.
1956	Marries Faye Haxby.
1957	Graduates from University of Oregon.
1958	Finishes "End of Autumn" (unpublished novel).
1959	Enters creative writing program at Stanford on a Woodrow Wilson Fellowship.
1961	Volunteers government drug experiments and works as a psychiatric aide at Menlo Park VA Hospital. Finishes "Zoo" (unpublished novel).
1962	*One Flew Over the Cuckoo's Nest* is published.
1963	Stage version of *One Flew Over the Cuckoo's Nest* produced.
1964	*Sometimes a Great Notion* is published. Embarks on a cross-country bus trip with the Merry Prankster filming "The Movie."
1965	Arrested in April for possession of marijuana.
1966	Arrested in January for possession of marijuana. Flees to Mexico Returns in late fall and is arrested.
1967	Convicted and spends June to November in the San Mateo County Jail and later at the San Mateo County Sheriff's Honor Camp.
1968	Moves to Pleasant Hill, Oregon. Tom Wolfe's *The Electric Kool-Aid Acid Test* is published.

1969	Lives in London from March to June, doing work for *Apple* (The Beatles music label).
1971	Coedits (with Paul Krassner) *The Last Supplement to the Whole Earth Catalog.*
1973	*Kesey's Garage Sale* is published.
1974	*Spit in the Ocean*, no. 1, including "The Thrice-Thrown Tranny-Man or Orgy at Palo Alto High School" and the first part of *Seven Prayers by Grandma Whittier* is published.
1976	*Spit in the Ocean*, no. 2, including second part of *Seven Prayers* is published. "Abdul and Ebenezer" is published by *Esquire.*
1977	*Spit in the Ocean*, no. 3, including third part of *Seven Prayers* is published.
1978	*Spit in the Ocean*, no. 4, including fourth part of *Seven Prayers* is published.
1979	*Spit in the Ocean*, no. 5, including "Search for the Secret Pyramid" and fifth part of *Seven Prayers* is published.
1980	*The Day After Superman Died* is published.
1981	*Spit in the Ocean*, no. 6, including sixth part of *Seven Prayers* is published. Takes a trip to China to cover the Beijing Marathon.
1986	*Demon Box* is published.
1989	*Caverns*, by O.U. Levon (Kesey and the Thirteen members of his graduate writing seminar at the University of Oregon) is published.
1990	*The Further Inquiry*, a screenplay examining Neal Cassady and the 1964 voyage of the bus *Further*, with 150 color photographs by Ron "Hassler" Bevirt, is published.
1991	*The Sea Lion* (children's book) is published.
1992	*Sailor Song* is published.
1994	*Last Go Round* (with Ken Babbs) is published.
2007	Ken Kesey dies in Eugene, Oregon of complications after surgery for liver cancer.

Contributors

HAROLD BLOOM is Sterling Professor of the Humanities at Yale University. He is the author of 30 books, including *Shelley's Mythmaking* (1959), *The Visionary Company* (1961), *Blake's Apocalypse* (1963), *Yeats* (1970), *A Map of Misreading* (1975), *Kabbalah and Criticism* (1975), *Agon: Toward a Theory of Revisionism* (1982), *The American Religion* (1992), *The Western Canon* (1994), and *Omens of Millennium: The Gnosis of Angels, Dreams, and Resurrection* (1996). *The Anxiety of Influence* (1973) sets forth Professor Bloom's provocative theory of the literary relationships between the great writers and their predecessors. His most recent books include *Shakespeare: The Invention of the Human* (1998), a 1998 National Book Award finalist, *How to Read and Why* (2000), *Genius: A Mosaic of One Hundred Exemplary Creative Minds* (2002), *Hamlet: Poem Unlimited* (2003), *Where Shall Wisdom Be Found?* (2004), and *Jesus and Yahweh: The Names Divine* (2005). In 1999, Professor Bloom received the prestigious American Academy of Arts and Letters Gold Medal for Criticism. He has also received the International Prize of Catalonia, the Alfonso Reyes Prize of Mexico, and the Hans Christian Andersen Bicentennial Prize of Denmark.

TERENCE MARTIN is professor emeritus of English, Indiana University. His books include The Instructured Vision: Scottish Common Sense Philosophy and the Origins of American Fiction.

RUTH SULLIVAN was a professor of English Department at Northeastern University. The Dr. Ruth E. Sullivan Memorial Award was established in 1976 to honor her memory and her academic excellence.

JAMES R. HUFFMAN is professor emeritus of English at State University of New York at Fredonia.

JAMES F. KNAPP is professor of English and Associate Dean for Faculty Affairs -School of Arts and Sciences at the University of Pittsburgh. He is author of *Literary Modernism and the Transformation of Work* (1988) and *Ezra Pound* (1979).

MICHAEL M. BOARDMAN is author of *Narrative Innovation and Incoherence: Ideology in Defoe, Goldsmith, Austen, Eliot, and Hemingway* (1992)

JACK HICKS is author of *In the Singer's Temple: Prose Fictions of Barthelme, Gaines, Brautigan, Piercy, Kesey, and Kosinski* (1981).

WILLIAM C. BAURECHT professor of English, emeritus at University of Wisconsin Oshkosh.

JANET LARSON is associate professor of English at Rutgers University, Newark.

FRED MADDEN is professor of English, emeritus, at Ithaca College, Ithaca, New York.

THOMAS J. SLATER is professor of English and film studies at Indiana University of Pennsylvania. He is the author of *American Silent Film: Discovering Marginalized Voices* (2002) and editor of *Handbook of Soviet and East European Films and Filmmakers* (1992).

THOMAS H. FICK is professor of English at Southeastern Louisiana University

ROBERT P. WAXLER is professor of English at University of Massachusetts, Dartmouth. He is co-editor of *Finding Voices: Changing Lives through Literature* (2005).

STEPHEN L. TANNER is professor of English at Brigham Young University. He is author of *Ken Kesey* (1983)

Bibliography

Allen, Henry. "A '60's Superhero, After the Acid Test," *Washington Post*, June 9, 1974, pp. L1–L3, cols. 4, 1–6.

Alvarado, Sonya Yvette. "Em'ly in the Cuckoo's Nest." *Midwest Quarterly: A Journal of Contemporary Thought*, 38:4 (Summer 1997): pp. 351–362.

Barsness, John A. "Ken Kesey: The Hero in Modern Dress," *Bulletin of the Rocky Mountain Language Association* 23 (1969): pp. 27–33.

Blaisdell, Gus. "SHAZAM and the Neon Renaissance," *Author & Journalist* 48 (June 1963): pp. 7–8.

Blessing, Richard. "The Moving Target: Ken Kesey's Evolving Hero," in *Journal of Popular Culture* 4 (1971): pp. 615–627.

Boardman, Michael M. "*One Flew Over the Cuckoo's Nest:* Rhetoric and Vision." *Journal of Narrative Technique* 9 (1979): pp. 171–183.

Boyers, Robert. "Attitudes Toward Sex in American 'High Culture,'" *Annals of the American Academy of Political and Social Science* 376 (1968): pp. 36–52.

Carnes, Bruce. *Ken Kesey*, Boise State University Western Writers Series, no. 12. Boise, Idaho: Boise State University, 1974.

Falk, Marcia L. "A Hatred and Fear of Women?," *New York Times*, December 5, 1971, p. 5.

Field, Rose. "War Inside the Walls," *New York Herald Tribune*, February 25, 1962, p. 4.

Fielder, Leslie A. "Making It with a Little Shazam," *Book Week*, August 2, 1964, pp. 1, 10–11.

Foster, John Wilson. "Hustling to Some Purpose: Kesey's *One Flew Over the Cuckoo's Nest*," *Western American Literature* 9 (Summer 1974): pp. 115–129.

Gaboriau, Linda. "Ken Kesey: Summing up the '60's; Sizing up the '70's," *Craw-daddy*, no. 19 (December 1972): pp. 31–39.

Gefin, Laszlo K. "The Breasts of Big Nurse: Satire versus Narrative in Kesey's 'One Flew Over the Cuckoo's Nest'." *Modern Language Studies*, 22:1 (Winter 1992): pp. 96–101.

Hague, Theodora-Ann. "Gendered Irony in Ken Kesey's *One Flew Over the Cuckoo's Nest*." *Cithara: Essays in the Judeo-Christian Trdition*, 33:1 (November 1993): pp. 27–34.

Havermann, Carol Sue Pearson. "The Fool as Mentor in Modern American Parables of Entrapment: Ken Kesey's *One Flew Over the Cuckoo's Nest*, Joseph Heller's *Catch-22* and Ralph Ellison's *Invisible Man*." Dissertation, Rice University, 1971.

Hoge, James O. "Psychedelic Stimulation and the Creative Imagination: The Case of Ken Kesey," *Souther Humanities Review* 6 (Fall 1972): pp. 381–391.

Knapp, James O. "Tangled in the Language of the Past: Ken Kesey and Cultural Revolution," *Midwest Quarterly* 19 (1978): pp. 398–412.

Levin, Martin. "A Reader's Report," *New York Times Book Review*, February 4, 1962, p. 32.

———. "Life in a Loony Bin," *Time* 79 (Feb. 16, 1962): p. 90.

Lish, Gordon. "What the Hell You Looking in Here for, Daisy Mae? An Interview with Ken Kesey," *Genesis West* 2, no. 5 (1963): pp. 17–29.

Martin, Terrence. "*One Flew Over the Cuckoo's Nest* and the High Cost of Living," *Modern Fiction Studies* 19 (Spring 1973): pp. 43–55.

Maxwell, Richard. "The Abdication of Masculinity in *One Flew Over the Cuckoo's Nest*," in *Twenty-seven to One: A Potpourri of Humanistic Material*. Ogdensburg, N.Y.: Ryan Press, 1970.

Mills, Nicholaus. "Ken Kesey and the Politics of Laughter," *Centennial Review* 16 (Winter 1972): pp. 82–90.

Napierski-Prancl, Michelle. "Role Traps in Ken Kesey's *One Flew Over the Cuckoo's Nest* (1962)." pp. 227–229. Fisher, Jerilyn (ed. Preface, and introduction); Silber, Ellen S. (ed. Preface and introduction) and Sadker, David (foreword). *Women in Literature: Reading Through the Lens of Gender*. (Westport, CT; Greenwood, 2003): pp. xxxix, 358.

Nastu, Paul. "Kesey's *One Flew Over the Cuckoo's Nest*." *Explicator*, 56:1 (Fall 1997): pp. 48–50.

Olderman, Raymond M. *Beyond the Wasteland: A Study of the American Novel in the Nineteen-Sixties*. (New Haven, CT: Yale University Press, 1972): pp. 35–51.

Peden, William. "Gray Regions of the Mind," *Saturday Review* 45 (April 14, 1962): pp. 49–50.

Pratt, John Clark, ed. *One Flew Over the Cuckoo's Nest: Text and Criticism*, New York: Viking Press, 1973.

Sassoon, R. L. Review of *One Flew Over the Cuckoo's Nest, Northwest Review* 6 (Spring 1963): pp. 116–120.

Schopf, William. "Blindfold and Backwards: Promethean and Bemushroomed Heroism in *One Flew Over the Cuckoo's Nest* and *Catch-22*," *Bulletin of the Rocky Mountain Modern Language Association*, vol. 26, pp. 89–97.

Searles, George J. *A Casebook on Ken Kesey's* One Flew Over the Cuckoo's Nest. Albuquerque: University of New Mexico Press, 1992.

Semino, Elena; Swindlehurst, Kate. "Metaphor and Mind Style in Ken Kesey's *One Flew Over the Cuckoo's Nest.*" *Style*, 30:1 (Spring 1996): pp. 143–166.

Sherman, W.D. "The Novels of Ken Kesey," *Journal of American Studies* 5 (August 1971): pp. 185–196.

Sherwood, Terry G. "*One Flew Over the Cuckoo's Nest* and the Comic Strip," *Critique* 13, no. 1 (1972): pp. 96–109.

Smith, William James. "A Trio of Fine First Novels," *Commonweal* 75 (March 16, 1962): pp. 648–649.

Tanner, Stephen L. "Salvation Through Laughter: Ken Kesey and the Cuckoo's Nest," *Southwest Review* 57 (Spring 1973): pp. 125–137.

———. "Kesey's Cuckoo's Nest and the Varieties of American Humor." *Thalia: Studies in Literary Humor*, 13:1–2 (1993): pp. 3–10.

Tanner, Tony. "Edge City (Ken Kesey)," in *City of Words: American Fiction 1950–1970*. New York: Harper & Row, 1971.

Vitkus, Daniel J. "Madness and Misogyny in Ken Kesey's *One Flew Over the Cuckoo's Nest.*" *Alif: Journal of Comparative Poetics*, 14 (1994): pp. 64–90.

Waldmeir, Joseph J. "Two Novelists of the Absurd: Heller and Kesey," *Wisconsin Studies in Contemporary Literature* 5 (Autumn 1964): pp. 192–204.

Wallis, Bruce E. "Christ in the Cuckoo's Nest: or, the Gospel According to Ken Kesey," *Cithara* 12 (November 1972): pp. 52–58.

Witke, Charles. "Pastoral Convention in Virgil and Kesey," *Pacific Coast Philology* 1 (1966): pp. 20–24.

Wolfe, Tom. *The Electric Kool-Aid Acid Test* (1968). New York: Bantham Books, 1969.

Zaskin, Elliot M. "Political Theorist and Demiurge: The Rise and Fall of Ken Kesey," *Centennial Review* 17 (Spring 1973): pp. 199–213.

Acknowledgments

Terence Martin, "*One Flew Over the Cuckoo's Nest* and the High Cost of Living," *Modern Fiction Studies*, Volume 19, Number 1 (Spring 1973): pp. 43–55. A critical quarterly published by the Purdue University Department of English. © Purdue Research Foundation. Reprinted with permission of the Johns Hopkins University Press.

Ruth Sullivan, "Big Mama, Big Papa, and Little Sons in Ken Kesey's *One Flew Over the Cuckoo's Nest*," *Literature and Psychology*, Volume 25, Number 1 (1975): pp. 34–44.

James R. Huffman, "The Cuckoo Clocks in Kesey's Nest," *Modern Language Studies*, Volume 7, Number 1 (Spring 1977): pp 62–73. © 1977 *Modern Language Studies*. Reprinted by permission of the publisher.

James F. Knapp, "Tangled in the Language of the Past: Ken Kesey and Cultural Revolution," *The Midwest Quarterly*, Volume 19, Number 4 (Summer 1978): pp. 398–413. © 1978 *The Midwest Quarterly*. Reprinted by permission of the publisher.

Michael M. Boardman, "*One Flew Over the Cuckoo's Nest:* Rhetoric and Vision," *The Journal of Narrative Technique*, Volume 9, Number 3 (Fall 1979): pp. 171–183. © 1979 *The Journal of Narrative Technique*. Reprinted by permission of the publisher.

Jack Hicks, "The Truth Even If It Didn't Happen: *One Flew Over the Cuckoo's Nest*," from *In the Singer's Temple: Prose Fiction of Barthelme, Gaines, Brautigan,*

Piercy, Kesey, and Kosinski, (Chapel Hill: University of North Carolina, 1981): pp. 161–176. Copyright © 1981 by the University of North Carolina Press. Used by permission of the publisher.

William C. Baurecht, "Separation, Initiation, and Return: Schizophrenic Episode in *One Flew Over the Cuckoo's Nest,*" *The Midwest Quarterly: A Journal of Contemporary Thought,* Volume 23, Number 3 (Spring 1982): pp. 279–293. © 1982 William C. Baurecht. Reprinted by permission of the author.

Janet Larson, "Stories Sacred and Profane: Narrative in *One Flew Over the Cuckoo's Nest,*" *Religion & Literature,* Volume 16, Number 2 (Summer 1984): pp. 25–42. © 1984 by *Religion & Literature,* University of Notre Dame. Reprinted by permission of the publisher.

Fred Madden, "Sanity and Responsibility: Big Chief as Narrator and Executioner," *Modern Fiction Studies,* Volume 32, Number 2 (Summer 1986): pp.203–217. © Purdue Research Foundation. Reprinted with permission of the Johns Hopkins University Press.

Thomas J. Slater, "*One Flew Over the Cuckoo's Nest*: A Tale of Two Decades," *Film and Literature: A Comparative Approach to Adaptation,* Eds., Wendell Aycock and Michael Schoenecke (Lubbock: Texas Tech University Press, 1988): pp. 45–58. © 1988 Texas Technical University Press. Reprinted by permission of the publisher.

Thomas H. Fick, "The Hipster, the Hero, and the Psychic Frontier in *One Flew Over the Cuckoo's Nest,*" *Rocky Mountain Review of Language and Literature,* Volume 43, Number 1/2. (1989): pp. 19–34. © 1989 *Rocky Mountain Review.* Reprinted by permission of the publisher.

Robert P. Waxler, "The Mixed Heritage of the Chief: Revisiting the Problem of Manhood in *One Flew Over the Cuckoo's Nest,*" *Journal of Popular Culture,* Volume 29 (Winter 1995): pp. 225–235. © 1995 *Journal of Popular Culture.* Reprinted by permission of Blackwell Publishers.

Stephen L. Tanner, "The Western American Context of *One Flew Over the Cuckoo's Nest,*" *Modern Fiction Studies,* Volume 19, Number 1 (Spring 1973): pp. 291–320. Reprinted from *Biographies of Books: The Compositional Histories of Notable American Writings* by James Barbour and Tom Quirk by permission of the University of Missouri Press. Copyright © 1996 by the Curators of the University of Missouri.

Index